Ecological Security

Ecological Security
An Evolutionary Perspective on Globalization

Dennis Clark Pirages

Theresa Manley DeGeest

ROWMAN & LITTLEFIELD PUBLISHERS, INC.
Lanham • Boulder • New York • Toronto • Oxford

ROWMAN & LITTLEFIELD PUBLISHERS, INC.

Published in the United States of America
by Rowman & Littlefield Publishers, Inc.
A Member of the Rowman & Littlefield Publishing Group
4501 Forbes Boulevard, Suite 200, Lanham, Maryland 20706
www.rowmanlittlefield.com

P.O. Box 317, Oxford OX2 9RU, United Kingdom

British Library Cataloguing in Publication Information Available

Library of Congress Cataloging-in-Publication Data

Pirages, Dennis.
    Ecological security: an evolutionary perspective on globalization and
environment / Dennis Clark Pirages, Theresa Manley DeGeest.
        p. cm.
    Includes bibliographical references and index.
    ISBN 0-8476-9500-X (alk. paper) — ISBN 0-8476-9501-8 (pbk.: alk. paper)
    1. Human ecology. 2. Globalization. I. DeGeest, Theresa Manley, 1968– II. Title.
    GF50 .P563 2003
    304.2'8—dc21   2003000431

Printed in the United States of America

♾™ The paper used in this publication meets the minimum requirements of
American National Standard for Information Sciences—Permanence of Paper for
Printed Library Materials, ANSI/NISO Z39.48-1992.

Contents

Tables and Figures

Tables

Figures

Acknowledgments

THIS BOOK has been shaped over the years by discussions with many colleagues and support from numerous sources. We would like to express special appreciation to the University of Maryland's Harrison Program on the Future Global Agenda. We also would like to thank colleagues who have contributed to the book in many ways. We are particularly grateful to Ken Conca, Peter Corning, Ken Cousins, Geoff Dabelko, Heather Dhopolsky, Ted Gurr, Virginia Haufler, Martin Heisler, David Inouye, Melisa Klem, Clark Merrill, Paul Runci, and Sujit Rathod for their valuable insights. We also are grateful to Jennifer Knerr for her persistence and support from beginning to end. Theresa DeGeest would like to thank her husband Paul for his support and encouragement. Finally, we both thank Suellen Pirages for her advice and tireless work with the manuscript throughout the process.

CHAPTER ONE

From International to Global Relations

T HE EARLY YEARS of a new millennium are marked by major discontinuities in the ecological relationships and evolutionary processes that are essential to human well-being. The dynamics of globalization are bringing together peoples and ecosystems that were once comfortably buffered from each other by physical, political, and cultural barriers. A rapidly moving flow of people, animals, plants, products, information, and ideas across borders is producing a planetary mingling of species and cultures with uncertain consequences. An international system composed of sovereign states is being transformed into a global one where national boundaries are becoming much more porous and less important in separating peoples. An acceleration of technological innovation and diffusion is not only helping to hasten these changes, but is broadening access to new kinds of weapons capable of empowering small groups, or even individuals, with tremendous destructive potential.

The origins of many of these contemporary discontinuities and related insecurities are found in the continuing acceleration of technological, demographic, and environmental drivers of change. Innovations in transportation have transformed a world in which steamships once leisurely carried small numbers of people and modest quantities of merchandise across oceans in days or weeks into one in which jumbo jets spirit large numbers of people and substantial cargoes from one continent to another in a matter of hours. Between 1950 and 1998 the number of passenger-kilometers flown internationally grew from 28 billion to 2.6 trillion annually. During the same period international air freight grew from 730 million to 9.9 billion ton-kilometers annually.[1] Advances in telecommunications have transformed a world of telegrams, scratchy transatlantic phone calls, radios, and rudimentary black-and-white television sets into a global city, most of its neighborhoods now linked by fiber-optic cables and telecommunications satellites. Between 1960 and 1998, the number of lines connecting non-cellular phones to the worldwide phone network increased from 89 million to 838 million, and there has recently been an explosion in the number of cell phones. The cost of a three-minute phone call from New York to London plummeted from $245 in 1930 to $3.32 in 1990.[2]

Over the last four decades, the world's population has doubled from three to six billion, and is expected to grow to nearly eight billion over the next quarter century.[3] This increase in population, combined with the resource demands of industrial growth, has placed enormous burdens on the global ecosystem. Also, the Earth's growing population has become much more mobile. The number of people crossing international borders each day is currently in excess of two million, up from 69,000 in 1950.[4]

Over this forty-year period, technologically driven changes have been linked closely to equally dramatic changes in social, political, and economic affairs. The Cold War has dissipated, and many formerly authoritarian states have made strides toward political democracy. Interstate warfare has been largely supplanted by intrastate ethnic conflict. Terrorists and rogue states have been quietly gaining access to more sophisticated and destructive weapons that give them the potential to wreak substantial havoc on increasingly complex societies. With the collapse of socialism in the Soviet Union, capitalist ideas have emerged seemingly triumphant over those of socialism, and global markets quickly have become a reality. Proponents of free trade have won, at least temporarily, a battle with protectionists. Many trade barriers have fallen; international commerce has increased dramatically; and more tightly integrated global equities markets now rise and fall in tandem.

All of these and myriad other related transformations are part of a very rapid and fundamental change now taking place in relations among peoples, and between them and nature. These dynamics are integrating previously isolated societies, and the ecosystems that have shaped them, into an emerging global system. The lure of economic efficiencies, worldwide markets, and related profits gives momentum to this globalization process. But there are ecological risks, increasing social costs, and growing personal insecurities associated with it, as this large-scale and seemingly uncontrolled transformation destabilizes established relations among peoples, and between them and the natural systems that sustain them.

The quest to gain a better understanding of the likely impacts of these dynamics on the future well-being of human societies begins with the humbling observation that *Homo sapiens* is but one of millions of species coevolving in an interlocking web of mutual dependence. Like most other animals, *Homo sapiens* has spent much of its evolutionary history living in small and isolated units akin to biological populations. Environmental pressures, as well as encounters with other organisms, have shaped the evolutionary courses of these historically small, relatively isolated, human groups. But the dynamics of globalization are now dramatically changing the environments in which these groups are living.

While large-scale military engagements in the contemporary world have been diminishing, concerns growing out of technological, environmental, cultural, and economic change are growing. More widespread global travel and commerce brings with it increasing biological risks to human beings and ecosystems as the number of pathogens and other potentially disruptive organisms hitchhiking with people and cargos increases apace. As a nascent global society becomes more highly integrated, there are growing threats of socioeconomic maladies, such as economic recession or inflation, developing in and spreading from the system's most vulnerable units. In this emerging global economy, jobs gained in low-income countries often represent jobs lost elsewhere. A related penetration of a secular global culture, a so-called McWorld, into traditional settings is often a psychologically wrenching experience for the people who are impacted.[5]

An Eco-Evolutionary Perspective

This period of acceleration, growing complexity, and "future shock" is also characterized by a dearth of theories useful in anticipating these large-scale changes and emerging insecurities.[6] A related lack of foresight has led to frequent recriminations in academic and policy circles over "why we missed" forecasting critical upheavals and discontinuities such as the revolution in Iran, the collapse of the Soviet Union, the two energy crises, the surprising intensity of ethnic conflict in the former Yugoslavia and many other parts of the world, the emergence of a significant group of "failed states," an extremely deadly worldwide AIDS epidemic, and the growing destructive power of terrorist networks.[7] While a spate of recent books dealing with topics ranging from the end of history to the collision of tectonic plates of human culture has stimulated thinking about some of these larger questions, they fail to capture systematically the causes and consequences of massive sociopolitical shifts now attending the birth of global relations.[8]

One of the reasons for these failures is that more traditional theories of international relations attribute causality to states and sovereigns engaged in a never-ending quest for power and privilege. Yet, these theories ignore dramatic changes in the ecological, technological, sociocultural, economic, and philosophical contexts within which these supposedly perpetual great power rivalries take place.[9] These more traditional perspectives ignore the impact of vital ecological relationships and evolutionary processes on human fortunes. An attempt is made in this book to develop a dynamic eco-evolutionary theoretical perspective to analyze and anticipate the many synergies, issues, problems, and conflicts that are likely to arise in an emerging era of globalization. Technological innovation, demographic shifts, and environmental change are identified as driving forces altering ecological equilibria and creating discontinuities in evolutionary processes. Thus, challenges to human well-being and security are not seen to originate mainly in sovereigns and their motives, but increasingly from the interaction of these techno-ecological forces of change with existing societies, institutions, and value systems.

Contemporary globalization, its synergies and its discontents, is being driven, enabled, and shaped by this interrelated cluster of techno-ecological pressures. The development and diffusion of new technologies is the primary factor transforming the world's socioeconomic landscape and enabling global markets to develop, but it is also generating a growing agenda of problems, the solutions to which increasingly lie beyond the reach of individual sovereigns and states. Only a few decades ago, transoceanic aviation was a novelty, and international phone calls were rare, expensive, and difficult. Fifty years ago, the first prototype jet passenger plane, the Comet, rolled onto a runway. And the first transatlantic cable, which opened up affordable telephone communication between the United States and Europe, was laid only in 1956. Today, innovations in aviation, satellites, telecommunications, and computers are bringing people into personal and mediated contact in unprecedented numbers. Satellite television, the Internet, cell phones, and fax machines are generating an explosion in the flow of information and images that promises to create a new global culture.

As a consequence of these developments, the time and distance barriers that once afforded political leaders and corporate executives the luxury to reflect and deliberate on emerging issues and challenges are rapidly disappearing.[10] The diplomatic "cable" is now obsolete as news leaps from remote parts of the world almost instantaneously via CNN and other worldwide news services. Images of what used to be distant and obscure events, such as a massacre in East Timor, ethnic cleansing in Kosovo, or bombing runs in Afghanistan, flash quickly around the world, and provide material for the evening news. Few places are any longer truly remote; even the government of distant Bhutan ushered in the new millennium by beginning to offer two hours of television daily, at least partially as a response to a growing number of satellite dishes and brisk sales of video-tapes in that country.

While the tidal wave of technological innovations currently diffusing around the world is the most obvious and potent source of changes and discontinuities, various kinds of demographic shifts are also having a significant impact on an emerging global system. The industrialized countries have experienced a demographic transition, and many of them have reached, or even moved through, zero population growth. But the total number of people making a claim upon the planet's resources continues to increase. A tide of population growth that began to swell in the 1950s has yet to ebb in many parts of the world. In densely populated countries, often there is little available land or economic opportunity for rapidly growing numbers of restive young people, and a significant portion of them, intent on finding employment, is migrating to industrialized countries. By contrast, in those industrialized countries where population growth has tapered off to near zero, there is a quite different agenda of emerging policy issues and potential conflicts associated with aging popula tions, shrinking workforces, and underfunded pension systems.

The last of the three forces shaping the future of an emerging global system, ecological change and increasing environmental vulnerability, is currently creating major problems and forcing significant socioeconomic adjustments in many parts of the world. Water is in dangerously short supply in many areas; the ability of the atmosphere and hydrosphere to provide essential environmental services is being severely taxed. A buildup of greenhouse gases is creating significant climate change. A large number of species is being exterminated annually by human activities. And new and resurgent diseases threaten humanity with epidemics.

Because of the rapidity and scope of these changes and challenges, there is a clear and growing need to use an eco-evolutionary perspective, foresight, and anticipatory thinking in making both domestic and foreign policy. But policy-makers don't usually take a long-term view of the ecological consequences of their actions (or inactions) and often are caught unprepared to deal with emerging systemic problems.[11] Developing an understanding of the trajectory that the rapidly changing global system is now following is essential in order to avoid the harsh consequences of failing to recognize emerging problems and issues that could generate tragedies in the long run. Intelligent management of change in the tumultuous evolving global system requires a futures perspective, as decisions taken now will have their most significant impacts on a very different future world.

This current venture in eco-evolutionary theorizing neither makes neo-Malthusian assumptions about inevitable global decline, nor relies on cornucopian assumptions about the benevolence of new technologies. Rather, technological innovation, demographic shifts, and environmental change are seen as forces that both open up new possibilities and raise new challenges for evolving human societies becoming increasingly integrated into a global system. A better understanding of these forces of change and their likely future impacts on crucial evolutionary processes can both sharpen perceptions of the trajectory that the future global system is likely to follow, and enhance our collective abilities to deal with an emerging agenda of global problems.

Globalization and Insecurity

The ongoing globalization process represents an unprecedented change in the way that people think about the world and connect with each other. It frees people and organizations to interact more directly with counterparts in other parts of the world without the state acting as a barrier, buffer, or intermediary. It also means much enhanced contact of many kinds among previously isolated societies. Boundaries of all kinds are being eroded as people and products are moving more rapidly and freely from place to place.

The economic core of globalization is largely consensual. It is spurred by the free market ideas of political economists such as Adam Smith, David Ricardo, and their more contemporary counterparts. It is supported by the policies of international financial and trade institutions such as the World Bank, International Monetary Fund, and the World Trade Organization. It is essential to the continued momentum and viability of mature industries that have largely saturated domestic markets, and must find new markets abroad.

This revolution in human affairs brings obvious benefits, but also exacts considerable costs. On the positive side, a more refined global division of labor, a worldwide flow of capital, and elimination of trade barriers theoretically could optimize total world production of goods and services. An associated flow of people, images, ideas, and information could create greater understanding and even synergies among people in the many different neighborhoods of an emerging global community. But globalization is a double-edged sword. This broad transformation is also making borders much more porous to various kinds of migrants ranging from destabilizing ideas to pathogenic microorganisms. In many ways, the dynamics of globalization weaken the powers of existing governments simultaneous with a growing need for wiser and better governance in the face of a broad array of new challenges.

The globalization process feeds on deeper economic integration, a process spurred by promises of greater wealth to be derived from a worldwide flow of capital and division of labor. The logic of economic globalization lies in economies of scale and a more optimal use of human and natural resources resulting from reduced trade barriers. Indeed, reduction of trade barriers since World War II has been a significant factor in spurring global commerce. Merchandise trade amounted to 27 percent of global gross domestic product (GDP) in 1980 and grew to 37 percent by 1998.[12] Developments in transportation, computers, and telecommunications are expanding the reach of global commerce. Currencies move more freely across borders, and a global equities market is now a reality. Even worldwide retail shopping, courtesy of e-commerce, is a growing area of commercial activity for an increasing number of people with Internet access.

But economic integration also can bring with it increasing uncertainty and insecurity due to the new four horsemen of a globalized economy: contagion, destabilization, exploitation, and dislocation. More closely linked economies can become victims of contagious economic viruses moving from weaker to stronger ones, as did the Asian flu of the late 1990s. Thus, there is persisting fear that inflation, recession, or other forms of economic weakness, originating in countries such as Russia, Turkey, Thailand, Argentina, or Brazil, could undermine the health of the global economy. In a freer world market, weaker economies, in turn, are vulnerable to hit-and-run destabilization tactics that can destroy the value of their currencies. Witness the destabilization of the Malaysian *ringgit* or the Indonesian *rupiah*, also in the late 1990s. Economic integration can bring with it the twin problems of exploitation and dislocation: exploitation of cheap labor and natural resources in less industrialized countries, the so-called race to the bottom, and a related loss of jobs in industrialized countries as global corporations move production from one country to another in search of lower costs.[13] There also is a growing threat from global corporations that have wealth and power greater than that of many countries. These companies often operate beyond the reach of national authorities, but are not yet subject to any significant global governance.

Economic globalization is closely tied to ecological globalization. The growth of worldwide commodity markets facilitates ecological imperialism, pollution, and destruction of ecosystems in poor countries in order to maintain high consumption levels in rich ones. Furthermore, large numbers of people and significant quantities of agricultural commodities and raw materials are increasingly in motion around the world, facilitating the unintended spread of plants, pests, and microorganisms into new ecosystems. Various kinds of potentially destructive hitchhikers, ranging from gypsy moths and zebra mussels to pathogenic microorganisms, are moving with these people and cargoes, often doing extensive damage to the ecosystems in which they relocate.[14] From the time of plagues associated with the expansion of the Roman Empire to the influenza that moved around the world during World War I, periods of increased contact among previously separated peoples and ecosystems often have been accompanied by significant ecological changes and even epidemics.[15]

Globalization also brings with it the potential for better cultural understanding, facilitated by more frequent and extensive contact among peoples. Telecommunications growth in an increasingly connected world is accelerating enormously the worldwide flow of ideas, images, and information.[16] Such additional personal and mediated contacts could increase mutual understanding and expand cultural horizons. Communications satellites, the Internet, enhanced telephone communication, and access to global television make it increasingly difficult for authoritarian regimes to censor incoming or outgoing information. This was vividly demonstrated by live reporting of student demonstrations from Tiananmen Square in China in 1989, and reinforced by the rapid media-aided transformation of political systems once behind the so-called Iron Curtain.

But this aspect of globalization also has the potential to increase insecurity and anxiety by destroying the social fabric of traditional societies. To this point, the globalization of culture has been very much dominated by the significant "soft power" of the United States in particular, and the industrialized countries in general, embodied in control of the worldwide flow of ideas and images.[17] This onslaught of cultural power threatens, over time, to transform a world of diverse societies into a monoculture. Just as ecosystems are much more likely to flourish if they have a diversity of species capable of adapting to changing conditions, preserving a similar diversity of cultures may well be crucial to future sociocultural adaptation.[18] This cultural simplification could be a long-term threat to the nourishing of much-needed human ingenuity.[19]

Paradoxically, globalization can be a modernizing force while also strengthening the hand of tradition. In the face of increasing cultural uncertainty, the basis for identity and political action frequently moves downward to more fundamental levels of social organization; there is, thus, a contrary tendency to seek personal safety by reinforcing ties to traditional ethnic groups. Should the source of insecurity be attributed to a rival group, communal warfare or ethnic conflict is a likely result.

There is considerable controversy about the depth and durability of contemporary globalization. Skeptics argue that this phenomenon is hardly new. They point out that trade as a percentage of GDP is no higher now than it was in the 1920s. Other critics see an emerging world that soon will be made up of three large trade blocs—the European Union, Asia, and the Americas.[20] But a larger group of scholars takes a contrary view. For them deeper globalization is now inevitable, and it is driving a profound transformation in the nature of world politics and economics. Some go so far as to suggest that domestic political and economic systems are now being substantially transformed by external pressures, and that the current trajectory is leading to a global civilization.[21]

An attempt has been made by the journal *Foreign Policy* to measure empirically changes in globalization over time by constructing a globalization index. This globalization index contains four components. *Economic Integration* measures the most obvious indicators such as trade, capital flows, and foreign direct investment. *Political Engagement* reflects the extent to which countries belong to international organizations and host foreign embassies. *Personal Contact* measures international travel, telephone traffic, and cross-border transfers. Finally, *Technology* measures the number of Internet users, Internet hosts, and secure servers. When these indicators are combined, the index shows substantial increases in globalization over time. For example, foreign direct investment stood at $1.27 trillion in 2000, compared to only $203 billion in 1990. International travelers made nearly 700 million international trips in 2000, compared to 457 million a decade earlier.[22] It is as yet unclear, however, what the long-term impacts, if any, of more recent terrorist events will be on future globalization.

The position taken here is that the scope, pervasiveness, and acceleration of cross-border activity really do represent an unprecedented revolutionary leap in contact among peoples. While the percentage of GDP now entering world trade may not now be much higher than during some previous historic peaks, the total quantity is much larger than in the past and is still growing. Furthermore, a much greater portion of domestic economic activity is now counted in the formal GDP statistics than was the case in previous eras of trade expansion. The pace of globalization has been rapidly accelerating. But more important is that the impact of contemporary globalization is now felt directly by the individual. Trade no longer is exclusively handled by governments or large trading companies, but rather now penetrates to the individual consumer using the Internet to buy directly from foreign sources. People can buy foreign goods, stocks, or currencies with the click of a mouse. And this round of globalization is about much more than trade. It is about an enhanced worldwide flow of everything, ranging from people, products, and animals to philosophies. A firmly entrenched telecommunications infrastructure and the emergence of a nascent global culture make it extremely difficult to reverse the globalization process.

While the power of the state to control its economic fortunes, the fate of its currency, the flow of images and information across its borders, and the interaction of its citizens and organizations with those in other countries is likely to continue to erode, it is not obvious that the future course of globalization will necessarily be a smooth one. Obviously not all state boundaries will wither away quickly in the face of globalization, nor will nationalism disappear overnight. A worldwide economic depression, large-scale sabotage by terrorist organizations, or the rapid spread of communicable diseases could lead to a hasty retreat. The emergence of "mad cow" disease and the spread of hoof and mouth infections in the European Union in the 1990s, for example, quickly reinforced some old national divisions and mistrust.[23] The terrorist attack on the World Trade Center followed by much heightened border security in the industrialized countries also gave a major jolt to the forward progress of globalization.

Journalist Thomas Friedman has offered a colorful description of individuals who could stir up a backlash against globalization. He divides them into three categories: turtles, wounded gazelles, and fundamentalists.[24] The turtles represent those with no technical skills, people such as blue collar workers who don't possess the knowledge to adjust to a computerized world, and thus are left behind by the brisk march of new technologies. The wounded gazelles are those who sprint forward to adjust to a new world, and for one reason or another subsequently fail; people such as Malaysian Prime Minister Mahathir, who embraced the idea of a technotronic civilization only to have his vision collapse along with the Asian economies. But there also remains a hard core of fundamentalists who simply are unwilling to give up the psychological comfort of traditional beliefs, or even positions of power buttressed by tradition, in order to embrace a "modern" identity. As was the case during the early phases of the Industrial Revolution, those who profit most from socioeconomic change will be the globalization revolution's staunchest supporters. But worldwide economic growth is the cement that supports continued globalization. Should the engines of economic growth sputter, a backlash could quickly spread among those who perceive themselves to have little stake in the process.[25]

Globalization is thus a multifaceted, complex, and rapidly moving process: the product of liberal economic theories nourished by market economies. It is driven, enabled, and shaped by the forces of technological innovation. Within it lies the potential for social progress or regress. Economic and cultural globalization bring the promise of prosperity, openness, and increased tolerance and understanding, as well as the threat of economic dislocation and a resurgence of fundamentalism. Ecological globalization holds some promise of more economically rational use of the Earth's resources, but also carries the risk of significant environmental deterioration, particularly in the commodity-exporting countries, as well as the potential for the much more rapid worldwide spread of pathogens. But sadly, in the face of a growing need for better and more visionary governance in order to manage complex emerging challenges, there is now a growing power and creativity vacuum.

Just as contemporary globalization represents a revolutionary leap in organization and complexity, there is a parallel need for a revolution in ways of thinking theoretically about new synergies, tensions, and insecurities in the emerging global system. The current frenetic pace of change, and associated emergence of global problems, could be more effectively managed through better theoretical understanding and anticipation of them. But a dearth of theories capable of dealing with the causes and consequences of globalization, as well as the future of the nascent global system, is a major handicap in dealing with these new realities.[26] The rest of this chapter is devoted to laying out the elements of an eco-evolutionary theoretical framework useful in thinking about the causes and consequences of increased globalization.

Human Populations—The Fundamental Unit

Homo sapiens, like most other primates, has spent much of its history evolving within small, self-contained groups or biological populations. These genetically similar human extended families, clans, tribes, or ethnic groups historically have been a fundamental source of identity, loyalty, and governance. Theories that attempt to anticipate the course and consequences of globalization are best grounded in ecological and evolutionary principles that recognize the persisting significance of this basic biological and cultural unit. A biological population can be defined as "a dynamic system of interacting individuals. A population consists of all those within a species that are potentially capable of interbreeding with each other."[27] For most of history the fortunes of these dispersed populations of *Homo sapiens* were determined by the local availability of food and other resources, as well as by life and death struggles with other species, groups, and microorganisms.

More recently, however, there has been an accelerated mingling of human societies through conquest, trade, and migration. In spite of decades of attempts to erode these loyalties through "nation building" in much of the less industrialized world, however, a vast number of people still identify with, marry within, and are willing to fight for the perceived interests of these fundamental biological and sociocultural units. The globalization process is steadily removing barriers that separate peoples, and now it is at least technically possible for any human male and female in the world to marry. The United States, in particular, has been a cosmopolitan melting pot with a record of racial and ethnic barriers falling more rapidly than in many other parts of the world. But in much of the rest of the world, cultural traditions have eroded more slowly and, particularly in rural areas, the vast majority of people still marries its "own kind." In many parts of the world marriages between members of different ethnic groups are still unusual. Hausas rarely marry Yorubas, Serbs rarely marry Albanians, and Koreans rarely marry Japanese.

Membership in biological populations is indicated by genetic similarities created over hundreds of generations of reproducing within the confines of these basic groups. These often visible biological traits provide cues that serve both to unify peoples internally as well as to distinguish them from others. But social scientists interested in determining the boundaries of these groups need not go into the field to take blood samples. Since biological populations are normally coterminous with societies, they also can be identified by their common cultures, reflected in shared systems of cognition, norms, values, and institutions. An obvious indicator of group membership is the use of a common language or dialect. "Peoples are marked off from each other by communications barriers, by 'marked gaps' in the efficiency of communication."[28] If all of the current face-to-face and telecommunications contacts among human beings could be analytically mapped, obvious clusters of people that interact much more frequently with each other than with others would emerge. While close examination of these communication patterns would reveal some sharp drop-offs coincident with the borders of states, there would be significant clusters within and across them, representing societies that are not integrated into or limited by the boundaries of countries.

Persisting human populations or societies thus can be identified either by their shared gene pools or cultures. While the forces of globalization increasingly give rise to transnational groupings or communities, human societies remain potent actors in the globalization process because they represent psychological communities knit together by covariance, the belief that the well-being of the individual is tied to that of the community. These communities are the basic units upon which people have depended for security over the generations. They are held together by primordial ties and give people something to fall back on in times of crisis.[29] But they are also the units that are increasingly penetrated by the forces of globalization. These human societies, or ethnic groups, thus are a much neglected basic unit in building theories of global relations, and offer an important starting point in understanding the origins of many contemporary issues and insecurities. But because of the historical period in which the international relations discipline emerged, an era dominated by a concern with nationalism and nation building, this theoretical legacy contains a heavy emphasis on the sovereign, the state, or the nature of the state system.[30]

Most large existing states contain two or more significant ethnic groups. These groups also often straddle national borders. Thus, state politics in most countries, or even interstate rivalries, have been and still are to a significant extent driven by various ethnic interests. Many of the nations of the world are actually predominant ethnic groups that have come to dominate the relevant state politics and economics. These groups often use their power to advance their own agendas and enhance control over resources. Ethnic conflict can erupt as resistance to the hegemonic claims and acts of another ethnic group, or a coalition of ethnic groups, that controls the state. Despite concerted attempts at nation building in the postcolonial world, it is still various forms of ethnic identity, buttressed by shared religious beliefs, that command the basic loyalties of billions of human beings around the world.

The origins of human societies are still somewhat shrouded in the mists of history. Careful genetic detective work, however, has pieced together a mosaic that begins with modern humans (*Homo sapiens sapiens*) in Africa and the Middle East more than 100,000 years ago.[31] Within sixty to seventy thousand years, small groups of this curious and industrious species had ventured outward to reach distant parts of the planet.[32] By the beginning of the first century C.E., much of the habitable world was loosely occupied by thousands of human populations, for the most part evolving genetically and culturally in relative isolation from each other. Over all, human societies have spent at least nine times as many years becoming differentiated from each other as they have in coming together.[33]

Beginning very slowly thousands of years ago, and gaining momentum more recently, there has been increasing contact and integration among societies. The actual number of distinct human societies remaining in the contemporary ethnically complex world, and their relative resistance to assimilation, is a subject for further research. But the number of languages still spoken is a good surrogate measure of persisting societies. There are currently about six thousand languages spoken around the world, although linguists think that at least half will be dead or dying within fifty years.[34] Most of the world's remaining languages are spoken in seventeen tropical countries where the great majority of the world's nonassimilated peoples live. The most significant of these countries are Papua New Guinea with 860 spoken languages, Indonesia with 670, Nigeria with 427, India with 380, and Cameroon with 270. When Brazil, Australia, and Mexico are added to the seventeen tropical countries, 70 percent of all contemporary languages are accounted for. Europe, by contrast, is very homogenized, being home to only 3 percent of the world's spoken languages.[35]

From a more political perspective, geographer Bernard Nietschmann has estimated that there are between three thousand and five thousand nations in the world, defined as communities whose shared identity is based on common ancestry, institutions, beliefs, language, and territory.[36] Two political scientists, Gunnar Nielsson and Ralph Jones, have used more stringent criteria to identify 575 existing ethnic groups as active or potential nations.[37] Focusing very specifically on the potential for ethnic conflict, political scientist Ted Gurr has identified 275 "politicized communal groups" that have either been discriminated against economically or politically or have taken political action in support of collective interests since World War II.[38]

It would be difficult and not overly rewarding to take a precise census of the number of distinct populations or ethnic groups active in the contemporary world, particularly since that process would now be complicated by the dynamics of globalization. The key point is that there are thousands of such identifiable peoples, the vast majority of them in the Global South, that have remained reasonably biologically and culturally distinct. In fact, much of the literature on nation building in the 1960s and 1970s focused on the need to integrate such diverse ethnic groups into the mainstream in emerging nations, a process that has been far from successful.[39]

In some countries, such as contemporary Iceland or Japan, there is now one clearly dominant ethnic group occupying and controlling the state, and thus very little potential for ethnic conflict. Far more frequently, however, two or more populations coexist within the boundaries of the same state. In countries like Somalia, Indonesia, Sierra Leone, Sri Lanka, Angola, Burundi, or Russia, turf disputes based on local identities have sparked nasty conflicts. There are many other countries, like Nigeria, where cauldrons of multitribal conflict continue to simmer. Finally, there are also "diaspora" populations with common identities, sprawled across several countries, such as the Kurds in the Middle East, peoples of North African origin in Europe, or those of Chinese origin in many parts of the world. These groups often play an important role in regional politics and economics.[40]

This is not to claim that there are no other sources of identity or primordial loyalties. Religion and nationalism remain potent forces that often serve to channel the loyalties of ethnic groups. Nor is this to claim that ethnic groups are by nature destined to fight each other. Much of the time they peacefully coexist.

Rather, the critical point is that there are a variety of vital and relevant units below (and above) the level of the state that provide building blocks for an eco-evolutionary perspective on globalization.

The extent to, and the conditions under which, sub-national groups are assimilated by a state or brought directly into the globalization process is a complex and important question. Understanding the activities, interests, and cohesion of sub-national groups should be a priority concern in theorizing about the emerging global systems. But one of the implicit assumptions that have dominated recent scholarship, as well as U.S. foreign policy, is that ethnic groups, given time, will assimilate peacefully into state structures, and eventually a nascent global community. But evidence from many parts of the world indicates that such assimilation may be a slow, difficult, and troublesome process.[41]

Coevolutionary Processes

Human groups, populations, or societies have been shaped over time by biological and sociocultural evolution, two parallel and linked processes. These processes have facilitated the survival and success of *Homo sapiens* over countless centuries by adapting both bodies and behavior to changing environmental constraints. Since the early movement outward from Africa and the Middle East, myriad relatively isolated human populations have been aided in their struggles to persist by the passing of survival-relevant genetic and cultural information from one generation to the next through these two linked evolutionary processes.

The genomes (genetic templates) that define current human populations biologically are products that have been shaped by both tens of thousands of years of reproducing within the group, and by the group's interaction with changing environments, other peoples and species, and microorganisms. The human bodies that have resulted from this often slow process of natural selection represent a treasury of information about past adaptations to the changing constraints of diverse ecosystems. Those populations that have collectively been able to better adjust biologically to environmental circumstances have been able to reproduce and flourish while those less well adapted have been evolutionary casualties. Biological evolution has thus been a harsh learning process from which survival-relevant traits or characteristics have continually been selected and passed on to successor generations.

Recent research on the human genome indicates that people share more than 99.9 percent of all genes in common. Yet, the shared evolutionary experience of thousands of relatively isolated human populations in vastly different environments has produced very visible differences among them.[42] For example,

peoples living in tropical climates have evolved to appear quite different physi-
cally from those who have adapted to conditions of bitter cold and little sunlight
in Arctic environments.[43] Resulting physical features such as height, pigmenta-
tion, hair color, or facial characteristics provide cues used by group members to
identify their ethnic kin. Persisting human societies have maintained both biological and cultural identities by mating almost solely within the group, and, for
the most part, they have been hesitant to admit outsiders.[44] This behavior is not
uncommon among other species; even bees seemingly are capable of discern-
ing very subtle physical differences that serve as the basis for excluding "alien"
bees from their hives.[45]

The fate of *Homo sapiens*, however, is not only shaped by genetic factors.
The species is quite distinct from others by virtue of profiting from a parallel
process, sociocultural evolution, operating through spoken, written, and other
forms of communication.[46] Human cultures are the ideational counterpart of the
biological genome and consist of packages of behavior, perceptions, values,
norms, beliefs, ideas, and institutions. These cultural templates also are shaped
by experience, but are passed on through socialization processes. Although
some groups are more successful at learning and educating successor generations than others, all persisting human societies have profited to a great extent
from this second evolutionary mechanism.

Sociocultural evolution and the resulting "sociocultural genomes" are in
many ways similar to their biological equivalents.[47] Both evolutionary processes
yield products that serve to differentiate peoples. Both processes produce information that is crucial to group survival. Both operate on principles of natural
selection. Those biological phenotypes that are better adjusted to environmental changes survive and reproduce in greater numbers and thus shape future
populations. Likewise, societies made up of people who are creative, cooperative, flexible, and capable of learning are likely to innovate, be synergistic, and
survive challenging periods of transition.[48] By contrast, noncreative societies
incapable of adjusting to changing circumstances often decline or collapse, and
thus contribute little to the collective knowledge base of the human race.[49]

While there are many similarities in these two processes, there are also
some basic differences. Biological evolution lends itself more readily to quanti-
tative analysis because individual genes can be identified as carriers of specific
pieces of information (traits) across generations. But there is no readily identifiable similar unit of information in sociocultural evolution. Whole packages of
interrelated ideas, concepts, and beliefs are transferred from one generation to
the next, and the search for a basic informational unit equivalent to the gene,
such as a "meme," has been less than successful.[50]

There are also some important differences in how this survival-relevant information is acquired and communicated. Genetic information depends upon mutation as a source of variation, is refined through reproductive success, and can only pass vertically from parent to offspring. Sociocultural information, by contrast, originates in thinking and observation, can pass both across and within generations, and can be modified through learning experiences in a relatively short period of time. The sociocultural flow of information can be more flexible than its biological counterpart, as it is being constantly revised within each generation through research and learning, and is passed on continuously through socialization processes.

Finally, biological natural selection provides little help in anticipating future conditions, as it is a product of experience in past environments. Sociocultural evolution, by contrast, can be anticipatory, because future environments and potential problems can be envisioned. At least in theory, policies can be devised and put in place to avert future dangers. For example, a biological adjustment to a substantial increase in global temperature could not be anticipatory, and could only take place gradually across many generations. People possessing genetic characteristics permitting them to flourish in warmer conditions would produce offspring, and thus contribute to the future gene pool, while others not capable of coping with heat theoretically would fail to live to a reproductive age in a much hotter and more humid world. Socioculturally, however, researchers have already identified the greenhouse effect as a significant future threat to well-being, and fledgling cooperative efforts are under way to begin to change patterns of human behavior that result in a build-up of greenhouse gases.

There are also close coevolutionary relationships between the two processes.[51] Biological natural selection has influenced the evolution of cultures through the differential survival of individuals, and thus the beliefs and values that they carry and transmit. In reverse, sociocultural factors have had a very direct impact on the differential survival of people and their biological traits. For example, during the plagues that periodically decimated medieval Europe, people with more plague-resistant immune systems survived, reproduced, and passed on these genetic characteristics to their children. And along with these genes, they passed on sociocultural characteristics: their values, beliefs, and patterns of behavior. Similarly, individuals who were socially less gregarious, or even recluses, were more likely to survive plagues because of their relative lack of contact with diseased human beings. Along with these rather unenviable social characteristics, they passed on their genes and thus helped to shape biologically succeeding generations.[52]

None of this is to suggest that genetic traits are the more significant determinants of how human populations or ethnic groups interact with each other or respond to environmental challenges. Nor is this to suggest that ethnic identities are anchored in genetics and thus fixed and immutable. There is a great deal of controversy over the origins, durability, and meaning of ethnicity. Some claim that ethnic identity remains primordial, and cannot be easily erased, while others stress that it is a social construct that can be manipulated.[53] The simpler argument here is that, whatever the dynamics that created them, distinct human societies (ethnic groups) have long existed, and provide a logical starting point in building eco-evolutionary theory.[54]

There is growing evidence of the importance of genes in shaping people's lives, but *Homo sapiens* is still distinguished as the thinking animal.[55] The biological nature of human beings provides a genetic template, a foundation that, to a greater or lesser extent, is modified by learning experiences. Genetic characteristics surely provide a strong basis for the evolution of culture. But socialization processes play a critical role in modifying many of the behavioral tendencies carried by genes. Because ethnicity must be socially constructed, it can be modified over time. It can be manipulated, demolished, or reconstructed.[56] The ongoing process of ethnic identity construction or destruction is fluid, and involves an ongoing dynamic interaction between the biological and sociocultural genomes and the physical and social environments in which people are located.[57]

Thus, contemporary human populations/societies can be seen as the products of these two kinds of interrelated evolutionary processes. But techno-ecological change drivers are combining to alter rapidly the contexts within which these evolutionary processes operate. Technological innovation is transforming a world once composed of thousands of different societies into one global system. Demographic shifts are creating pressures for increasing human migration and the related mingling of peoples. Plant and animal species are also on the move; invasive species often are displacing indigenous ones. Pathogenic microorganisms are moving rapidly into unexploited territories. And the evolutionary wisdom that has been shaped over time within thousands of diverse cultures is now being absorbed into a growing global monoculture. But some peoples are much more resistant to assimilation than others, and continuing pressures to integrate human populations into larger units will remain a source of tension and potential conflict well into the new millennium.

Ecological Security

Safeguarding the integrity of these evolutionary processes, and learning from the totality of ecological and sociocultural experience, is crucial to future human well-being in a rapidly changing world. And preserving the stability of the ecosystems within which evolutionary processes are taking place is also essential. But technological innovation and associated globalization are now causing significant discontinuities in evolutionary processes, and ecosystems are being dramatically transformed. This amounts to unraveling the work of thousands of years of biological and sociocultural learning, and is filled with potential perils.

Throughout recent history security policies have evolved mainly to protect societies and states from predatory neighbors. Conflicts over power and privilege, within and among societies, have been all too common, and have resulted in more than two hundred million deaths. Traditional security policies thus have focused heavily on defending peoples and their economic interests by military means. "At its most fundamental level, the term security has meant the effort to protect a population and territory against organized force while advancing state interest through competitive behavior. The state has been the prevailing entity for guaranteeing security, and state-centered theories have dominated discussions of international relations, particularly since World War II."[58] Given the destruction that has been associated with violent conflicts over wealth and power since ancient times, limiting security concerns to mainly military matters is understandable, if not entirely logical. Peoples, nations, and empires have been making war on each other since before the dawn of civilization. Foreign armies massed on borders have presented vivid threats of devastation, mayhem, and death.

A parallel source of insecurity, however, has been the varied ravages of nature that, over time, have been responsible for killing and injuring much larger numbers of people. Ecosystemic challenges such as plagues, pestilence, pollution, blizzards, floods, and droughts, often aided and abetted by intemperate human behavior, have taken countless human lives. But unlike military conflicts, the causes of these kinds of suffering have been poorly understood, and people have known of no effective remedies for dealing with them. Thus, the security paradigm that has evolved over time has emphasized the use of military force to protect power and privilege while mostly ignoring these less well understood, but often more serious, ecological threats to human well-being. They have been seen as matters better addressed through prayer than defense spending.

In the three decades since the 1972 Stockholm Conference on the Human Environment, considerable attention has been paid to the need to rethink the changing nature of security threats. There has been a spirited debate in academic and policy circles over the wisdom of extending security concerns and activities to encompass environmental threats to well-being.[59] More recently this debate has expanded to encompass threats from infectious disease.[60] The argument for an eco-evolutionary approach to security policy, which is developed here, suggests moving beyond these rather stale debates over small and incremental changes in security perspectives, and moving to a totally new security paradigm. It suggests starting from scratch and rethinking the ways that security policies are formulated and spending priorities determined. This approach begins with the not unreasonable observation that promoting human security in an era of globalization means moving beyond the rather moribund post–Cold War agenda that was originally shaped by fear of communism, and addressing a much broader array of nonconventional security challenges. It also suggests that a more robust assessment of the causes of and potential cures for widespread human misery and premature human deaths should initially inform the discussion.

While the military adventures of neighbors have certainly been a major cause of death and destruction in the past, other threats to well-being, such as famines and plagues, have exacted much greater numbers of casualties. But since such events historically have been considered to be the work of God or gods, there has been little perceived utility in using the public treasury to deal with them. Thus, the "Black Death" (bubonic plague) carried by *Rattus rattus* in the fourteenth century certainly sparked a great deal of fear, given that 30 to 40 percent of those exposed to the disease perished. But the basic "defense" strategies that were perceived to be efficacious at that time were prayers, pogroms, and self-flagellation.[61]

In the twentieth century, as over much of history, casualties from military combat paled in comparison with deaths and suffering due to disease and famine. While the eyes of the world were focused on the military horrors of World War I, for example, an influenza virus spread worldwide and caused more than 20 million human fatalities, many times the total of battlefield deaths.[62] It is estimated that all of the wars of the last century resulted in the deaths of 111 million combatants and civilians, an average of 1.1 million per year. This figure is roughly comparable to the toll of the twentieth-century famines, which accounted for 75 million deaths, an average of 750,000 per year. But infectious diseases are currently killing nearly 14 million people yearly![63]

The world is still a militarily dangerous place, but there now are signs of the beginnings of a subtle shift in security thinking. In the industrialized countries, preparation for large-scale cross-border warfare has of necessity given way to dealing with asymmetrical challenges: rogue states, terrorism, and intranational quarrels in ethnically divided and sometimes failing states. And there is at least a discussion of security being related to economic well-being and environmental integrity.[64] As a result, U.S. military forces in recent years have been involved in protracted actions against terrorists as well as humanitarian operations as diverse as mediating disputes among clans in Somalia, providing relief to victims

of conflict in Bosnia, halting ethnic cleansing in Kosovo, restoring some semblance of order to ecologically and politically ravaged Haiti, and providing disaster relief to flood victims in Bangladesh.[65]

Thinking about security within this suggested new framework means moving well beyond these small efforts to add some humanitarian and environmental concerns to the security agenda. It means moving ecological wisdom and
evolutionary processes to the core of strategic thinking in order to provide a
more relevant definition of security for an emerging global society. It also entails
taking concrete steps to develop defenses against the deadly scourges that now
ravage the bulk of the human race. For example, it is estimated that if spending
on health care in the world's sixty poorest countries would be increased from the
present $13 per capita to $38 per capita by 2015, about eight million lives could
be saved each year. This would mean a total contribution from the industrialized
countries in the vicinity of $38 billion, a small fraction of current military spend-
ing.[66] Advances in a number of sciences now are yielding a much better understanding of the causes of and remedies for plagues, famines, and other disasters,
thus opening up new opportunities to attack and contain these nonmilitary
threats to human security.

Figure 1.1 depicts the elements of this suggested approach to thinking
about security. As the diagram indicates, biophysical and sociocultural evolution
are parallel and linked processes moving forward over time. Technological innovation is a semi-autonomous force having an impact on both kinds of evolution.[67] Ecological security rests on the preservation of four dynamic equilibria
or balances: between human demands and nature's ability to provide resources
and services; between the size and demands of human populations and those of
other animals; between medical technologies and health policies and the changing number and nature of pathogenic microorganisms; and between the growing
resource demands of populations and the ability to manage potential conflicts
over them.[68] Challenges to ecological security can come from changes either in
nature or in societies. For example, a sociocultural change such as rapid human
population growth could cause the collapse of environmental systems or the
extinction of other species. Similarly, biophysical changes, such as the onset of a
period of drought, the growth or decline of animal populations, or changes in
the virulence of pathogenic microorganisms, could create disequilibria and significant human casualties. Ecological security can be strengthened by enhancing the capabilities of societies to anticipate and manage challenges to the
integrity of these coevolutionary relationships.

This definition of ecological security as dynamic coevolutionary equilibrium raises questions about the place of human beings in these evolutionary

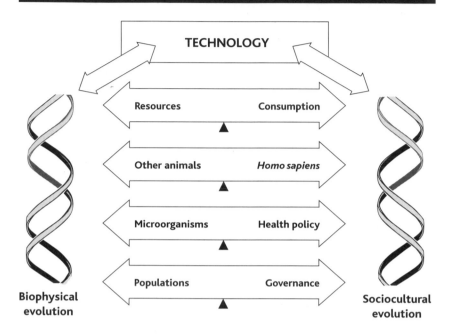

FIGURE 1.1. Ecological Security

TECHNOLOGY

Resources   Consumption

Other animals   *Homo sapiens*

Microorganisms   Health policy

Populations   Governance

Biophysical   Sociocultural
evolution   evolution

processes, and their future survival strategies. For example, wouldn't the security of the human race be better served by "technoforming" nature, an alternative involving use of chemical and other types of weapons against competitor species and potentially destructive microorganisms? While following this path might seem attractive in the short run, in an increasingly complex and interdependent global ecosystem such a "scorched earth" policy might well rebound to the detriment of human beings. Beneficial microorganisms could be wiped out along with those that are pathogenic. And, while eliminating pests and weeds might seem desirable, collateral damage, particularly to "keystone" species, could have unforeseen ramifications for the delicate ecosystems that sustain all forms of life.[69]

Ecological security is, therefore, strengthened to the extent that needs for resources and environmental services can be met without damaging sustaining natural systems. Human populations, like those of other species, tend to grow until they approach the carrying capacity of the territory that they occupy. But carrying capacity changes over time. These Malthusian dramas in which populations grow until they are checked harshly by the shifting limitations of physical environments have been frequently repeated throughout history. Now, from regional droughts and famines to global warming, there are abundant signs of growing imbalances between the spiraling demands of people and the sustaining capabilities of ecosystems. In spite of the sometimes benevolent impact of new technologies, in many parts of the world growing numbers of people live very close to the margin. For them, living space is at a premium, fresh water and sanitation are minimal, and food and fuel supplies are problematic. While the world's population as a whole has now seemingly passed through the peak period of growth, a continuing population explosion in the less industrialized countries and pressures on environmental systems associated with industrialization there are causing severe environmental degradation, increased vulnerability to disease, and even violent conflict.[70]

The well-being of human populations also has been, and still is, influenced by interactions with other animal species. *Homo sapiens* doesn't possess many of the physical attributes, such as sharp claws and long legs, essential to compete successfully in the wild. Over much of history, animal predators have represented a considerable threat to human survival, and animal pests have threatened food supplies. People still share habitats with various kinds of dangerous animals in many parts of the world, and are frequently in direct conflicts with them. Periodic rampages of elephants and tigers in "humanized" parts of India, or the nuisance activities of bears, deer, and raccoons in suburban areas of United States, are obvious, if not usually deadly, examples of continuing skirmishes between man and beast. But locusts, grasshoppers, aphids, and other insects still flourish and periodically attack crops, thus upsetting equilibria and creating food insecurity. From biblical times to the present, these and similar insects have been persistent threats to human welfare.[71]

Technological innovations, ranging from rifles to insecticides, have tipped this balance in favor of people in most parts of the world, and it is now *Homo sapiens* that threatens the survival of other animals. This growing disequilibrium between human beings and other species is now increasing because of the size and economic activities of people. Not only are people now a direct threat to wildlife, but this extinction is also an indirect threat to future human well-being because of loss of biodiversity, particularly of vital keystone species that perform critical tasks within ecosystems.

Perhaps the most serious current and future threat to ecological security is destabilization of the historically tenuous relationship between *Homo sapiens* and pathogenic microorganisms. Threats from a host of pathogens with which people have coevolved are certainly not new. History is littered with the corpses of people who have succumbed to various diseases. But there is now considerable evidence that sociocultural transformations, demographic shifts, environmental deterioration, increasing globalization, and even terrorism are making *Homo sapiens* much more vulnerable to new and resurgent diseases.[72] "At the root of the resurgence of old infectious diseases is an evolutionary paradox: the more vigorously we have assailed the world of microorganisms, the more varied the repertoire of bacterial and viral strains thrown up against us."[73]

Homo sapiens and a wide variety of microorganisms have coevolved over centuries, and for much of this time the relationship has been marked by peaceful coexistence. This stability has been facilitated by the evolution of the human immune system, honed by repeated encounters with pathogens. Periodically, however, this delicate truce has been disturbed when human populations, for one reason or another, have come into contact with novel pathogens. For example, rats and their flea passengers traveling with caravans from China to Europe were a vector for the bubonic plague that struck previously unexposed Europeans during the Middle Ages. Similarly, the discovery of the Americas by Europeans opened up a two-way flow of microorganisms that wreaked havoc in both places.[74] Many aspects of contemporary globalization bring people more frequently into contact with pathogenic microorganisms to which their immune systems have never been exposed. And now *Homo sapiens* potentially is creating more dangerous pathogenic microbes for use in its own internecine quarrels. The next few decades could well see an outbreak of rapidly moving plagues brought about by various kinds of changes in man–microbe relationships.[75]

Finally, the last dimension of ecological security, preserving dynamic equilibrium among human societies, has much in common with traditional ways of thinking about security. It involves identifying the ecological roots of friction among societies, and taking steps to prevent this discord from escalating into conflict. But rather than beginning with sovereigns, motives, states, and interests as causes of conflict, the focus shifts to more basic eco-evolutionary causes of disequilibrium. Beneath the surface, conflicts among peoples frequently originate in technological and ecological imbalances.[76] Security can be strengthened by developing institutions to address the relevant demographic, environmental, and technological sources of disequilibrium among societies before potential quarrels get transformed into protracted social conflicts.

This perspective, stressing eco-evolutionary sources of conflict among human societies, can shed new light on the origins of historical and more contemporary conflicts. For example, it has been suggested that lateral pressure, caused by population growth, competition for resources, and growing technological capabilities, was a key ingredient in shaping World War I.[77] In the Middle

East, clashes between Iraq and Iran, Iraq and Kuwait, and Israel and Palestinians have been clearly related to the rapid population growth rates in the region, and the desire to control critical resources such as water and oil. The tragedies in Kosovo were at least partly triggered by Serb perceptions that the ethnic Albanian birthrate was much higher than its own, and related fears of losing political and cultural dominance. And various regional conflicts, such as those involving Kurds in the Middle East or different tribes in Africa, certainly are catalyzed by differential population growth and related struggles over resources.

Governance and Ecological Security

Governments have emerged from evolutionary processes as a way of promoting collective welfare.[78] The nature and functions of governments have changed over time in response to growing complexity.[79] Governments can protect evolutionary processes through an authoritative allocation of values. They can create and legitimize institutions, and pass laws regulating citizen behavior.

The equilibria defining ecological security are now recognized to be of such importance to collective well-being that they are usually defined as public goods. Public goods are provided by governments because of their essential nature and because it is difficult for the private sector to do so. Public goods are denoted by the fact that one person's consumption of them doesn't come at the expense of others, and when they are provided, no one can be excluded from using them. Thus, protection from aggression, freedom from disease, and prevention of environmental deterioration are usually classed as public goods. But as globalization increasingly infringes on state capabilities, the ability to provide these and other public goods effectively may lie increasingly beyond established governments.

Because governments are responsible for providing public goods for citizens, they play a crucial role in providing the underpinnings of ecological security. Thus, keeping disease in check is usually the responsibility of national public health services. Most industrialized democracies provide basic health services to citizens as a matter of course. Containing epidemics is public business, and for the most part isn't considered a source of profits for the private sector. National environmental protection agencies are charged with protecting vanishing species and remedying assaults on nature, often the result of private interests seeking to maximize profits. Protecting biological diversity or the environment are not matters safely left to market forces.

Defense of a country against foreign aggression has generally been considered to be a critical public good. Providing other aspects of ecological security is now similarly coming to be seen as a collective responsibility. Even the World

Bank lists ecological security concerns alongside other pure public goods that ideally are to be provided by states. Public health is considered to be as important as property rights. But, according to the bank, some form of governance beyond the state is now also needed in an emerging global society to promote positive externalities from economic development, such as education, and to deal with negative ones, such as environmental pollution.[80] Given the rapid pace of globalization, strengthening ecological security now means moving some of these essential governance functions beyond the state level, and creating global public goods.[81]

While ongoing globalization processes are increasingly infringing on the ability of the state to govern, little growth in legitimate authority beyond the state is yet evident. Over the last three centuries the state has provided people a buffer in their interactions with the outside world. It has also provided the many public goods required for social progress. But for many reasons, the power of markets is growing and that of states is weakening.[82] Managing the fallout from globalization requires either strengthening the authority of the state or building some new form of governance.

The list of challenges to human well-being now best handled beyond the state is lengthening. The spread of the Industrial Revolution to heavily populated countries has created a legacy of worldwide pollution problems, including global warming, that must be addressed beyond the state level. And a nascent postindustrial revolution is creating new challenges to evolutionary processes that cannot be easily handled by individual states. Advances in biotechnology are opening up the possibility of a wholesale redesign of nature, creating new forms of life and potentially undermining the wisdom of millions of years of natural selection. A global telecommunications revolution is having a dramatic impact on sociocultural evolution, making societies permeable to a variety of often unwanted electronic intrusions from outside sources. Activities that may be illegal when carried out within states (such as gambling or pornography) are now within easy electronic reach of potential customers courtesy of the Internet or satellite television.[83] And the growing economic and political clout of the largest global corporations now matches or exceeds that of a significant number of countries. If annual corporate incomes are compared with gross national products (GNP), of the one hundred largest economic units in the world, fifty-two are corporations and forty-eight are countries. General Motors compares favorably with Thailand, and the Wal-Mart economy is about the size of that of Poland.[84]

In summary, the challenges of globalization to existing governments are growing enormously. Events are accelerating and there is a growing need for anticipatory thinking. But new forms of governance beyond the state are only emerging slowly, generally only in response to, rather than in anticipation of, these growing challenges.

A Strategy for Inquiry

The ability of most governments to anticipate future consequences of the current frenetic pace of globalization unfortunately is limited. The bulk of human experience has been with extended stretches of relative stability that have required little unusual initiative in governance, and not with periods of wholesale transformation, such as the present. Contemporary ways of thinking about governance and processing issues are themselves an evolutionary legacy of these long stretches of stability. Existing political institutions are thus best suited to processing mundane issues in a stable and predictable world. They are not designed for foresight, anticipating and dealing with the consequences of revolutionary change.

Because of the pressures of mutually reinforcing technological, demographic, and environmental currents of change, the context within which relations among states and peoples now take place is being radically altered. Existing worldviews, values, ethical systems, norms, and institutions, the persisting products of sociocultural evolution, are under assault, and these hereditary sources of wisdom are now often seen to be giving poor guidance in dealing with the rapidly changing physical and social worlds. Developing and implementing an anticipatory framework for thinking and governing is now imperative in attempting to cope. Thus, the strategy pursued in the following chapters is to analyze past, present, and likely future trajectories of techno-ecological drivers of change, and to anticipate their impact on evolutionary processes and ecological security.

This approach doesn't assume a mechanistic causal relationship between these change drivers and human societies. These currents of change will continue to create challenges to established ways of doing things, but creative and flexible societies will have the capability of dealing effectively with them. Human beings are capable of anticipatory thinking, research, and creative problem solving. The knowledge, motives, and aspirations of people count; otherwise there would be little reason to write this book. But in the past, public debate and policymaking have normally taken place *in response to* rather than *in anticipation of* serious issues. Thus, concern with world population growth crystallized only after a worldwide explosion was well under way, worries about the environment developed only after pollution became pervasive, a significant attempt to deal with HIV / AIDS only developed after millions of people had perished, and concerted action against terrorists only began after thousands of people had been killed by them in a televised slaying. The hope is that the theoretical perspective and research strategy suggested in this book will help to transform passive citizens and governments into anticipatory ones, using ecological and evolutionary wisdom to shape policies needed to preserve and enhance future ecological security.

The next five chapters focus on the impact of demographic and ecosystemic changes on ecological security. The challenges to the equilibria defining ecological security inherent in shifts in the size, age distributions, growth rates, and migration patterns of human populations are explored in chapter two. Chapter three assesses the capabilities of the hydrosphere and atmosphere to deal with the challenges of growing numbers of people living at higher levels of industrialization. Chapters four and five focus specifically on the ecology, economy, and politics of two of the most crucial resources needed for human wellbeing: energy and food. Chapter six completes this exploration of challenges to equilibria by examining the shifting relationships among human beings, other species, and pathogenic microorganisms.

The last three chapters of the book focus on the human element: sociocultural evolution and ecological security. The impact of technological innovation and diffusion on ecological security, and the related agenda of interstate economic and sociocultural harmonization issues raised by globalization, are explored in chapter seven. Chapter eight takes up some of the difficult questions associated with the growing gap between rich and poor countries and the potential for creating an ecologically secure model of socioeconomic development for a future world of eight to nine billion people. The last chapter reflects on the very difficult, but crucial, problem of finding ways to build global governance in order to provide essential public goods in the face of the diminishing powers of states to do so.

CHAPTER TWO

Demographic Change and Ecological Insecurity

THE QUEST to understand emerging challenges to ecological security begins by focusing on demographic changes. Substantial shifts in population growth rates, age structures, and consumption patterns can disrupt any of the four equilibria that define ecological security. The last fifty years have been dominated by concern over the destabilizing effects of rapid population growth. While such population growth persists in many parts of the less industrialized world, other kinds of demographic shifts, such as reduced birthrates and lengthening life spans, present new kinds of challenges in other parts of the world. There are four kinds of significant demographic changes taking place in the contemporary world that, either individually or in combination, have the potential to disrupt ecological security: rapid population growth, differential growth, large-scale migration, and aging.

Rapid population growth has been the most notable recent challenge to the evolutionary equilibria that define ecological security. For much of history populations of *Homo sapiens* grew slowly, their size limited by resource availability, predators, and disease. While the impacts of individual tribes or clans on local ecosystems might have been significant, the global impact of early population growth was very small. The slow worldwide spread of the Agricultural

Revolution led to very modest population increases, but it has been the more recent spread of the Industrial Revolution that has fostered a tremendous increase in the world's population and its environmental impact. In 1650, there were only about five hundred million human beings distributed across the Earth's surface. This number doubled to one billion by 1850. By 1927, the world's population had doubled once again to two billion. The next doubling, to four billion, occurred by 1974, taking only forty-seven years. At the turn of the millennium, the world population growth rate had slowed somewhat from historic highs, but there were still more than six billion people living on an ever more densely populated planet.[1] Nearly 6 percent of the people who have ever lived are on the Earth at the present time.[2] And the world's population is expected to grow to nine billion within five decades.[3]

Differential population growth is a closely related and potentially destabilizing phenomenon. When neighboring societies are growing at very different rates, the one growing more slowly can become fearful of being dominated or even absorbed by the one growing more quickly, and thus take preemptive measures. These fears often may be justified because history shows that societies growing in numbers and capabilities often develop "lateral pressure" to move against their neighbors to gain additional resources.[4]

A third kind of demographic change, large-scale migration, whether from rural to urban areas within a country or from one country to another, can create various kinds of tension in the areas to which people move. Over the last two decades, for example, large numbers of migrants and refugees have swept into Germany from Central and Eastern Europe, into France from North Africa, into Zaire from Rwanda, and into the United States from Mexico, the Caribbean, and South America. These migrants have frequently met with various kinds of hostility ranging from demands for their return to countries of origin to murder.

Paradoxically, even a significant slowing of population growth can present political, economic, military, and social challenges. Japan, most European countries, and to some extent the United States have all recently experienced declining birthrates that, in combination with the increased use of life-prolonging medical techniques, are shaping "graying" societies. This birth dearth, combined with declining mortality, eventually could lead to intergenerational conflicts between young people, who will be forced to pay higher taxes in the future to support retirement and medical care programs, and their aging beneficiaries. A dwindling future workforce could well be faced with paying rapidly growing costs of generous entitlement programs that were created when labor forces were growing and economies were booming.

Demographic changes also will have a major impact on the future characteristics of the emerging global system. At the beginning of the twenty-first century, nearly 20 percent of the world's population lived in relative affluence in the countries of the Global North. The remaining 80 percent lived in the less industrialized Global South, often in precarious circumstances. Over the next quarter century differential population growth will lead to a noticeable change in the composition and fortunes of the world's citizens. By 2025, an additional 1.6 billion people likely will be added to the 5 billion already in the Global South. These 6.6 billion people will account for nearly 84 percent of the world's population at that time.[5] This continued rapid population growth is expected to create more challenging living conditions there, and drive increasing numbers to migrate to the Global North. Simultaneously, governments in the Global North are likely to confront a much different agenda of issues brought about by declining fertility, aging, and dwindling labor pools.

A Demographically Divided World

There is now a sizable difference between population growth rates in the less industrialized countries on the South side of the demographic divide and those of the industrialized North (see tables 2.1 and 2.2). If comparable data for the thousands of societies on the sub-state level were readily available, there would be even larger disparities. The world's industrialized countries have passed through a period of demographic transition in which beliefs and values governing reproduction have changed, and birthrates have fallen in response to rising affluence. In this demographically more mature part of the world several countries are even experiencing population decline. In the less industrialized portion of the planet, however, young and restive populations continue to grow. The result is a deepening demographic fault line separating the two.

On the southern side of this demographic divide, it is a large and growing number of young people in search of limited opportunities that poses a variety of threats to stability, while on the northern side, it is the increasing number of older and retired persons that presents a different kind of challenge. These demographic differences can be expected to create quite different sets of policy challenges over the next three decades. On the less affluent side of the demographic divide, rapid population growth and spiraling resource demands will continue to overwhelm the sustaining capabilities of the physical environment. But on the more affluent side of the divide, increasingly gray populations will face problems of aging, such as chronic diseases, increasing medical care costs, and crises in entitlement programs.

TABLE 2.1. Population Growth Rates—Slowest Growing Countries

Global North	Populationa	Rate of Increaseb	Projected Populationa 2025	Projected Populationa 2050
Russia	144.4	- 0.7	136.9	127.7
Germany	82.0	- 0.1	80.0	70.3
Italy	57.8	0.0	55.0	46.0
Spain	39.8	0.0	36.7	30.8
Greece	10.9	0.0	10.4	9.7
Sweden	8.9	0.0	9.4	9.5
Austria	8.1	0.0	8.3	8.2
United Kingdom	60.0	+0.1	64.1	64.2
Belgium	10.3	+0.1	10.3	10.0
Portugal	10.0	+0.1	9.3	8.2

Source: PRB, 2001 World Population Datasheet.
Notes: Countries with populations over four million; data for 2001.
aPopulation in millions.
bRate of Increase is the birth rate minus the death rate.

TABLE 2.2. Population Growth Rates—Fastest Growing Countries

Global South	Populationa	Rate of Increaseb	Projected Populationa 2025	Projected Populationa 2050
Yemen	18.0	+ 3.7	39.6	71.1
Chad	8.7	+ 3.3	18.2	33.3
Congo, Zaire	53.6	+ 3.1	106.0	181.9
Madagascar	16.4	+ 3.0	30.8	47.0
Burkina Faso	12.2	+ 3.0	21.6	34.3
Mali	11.0	+ 3.0	21.6	34.3
Somalia	7.5	+ 3.0	14.9	25.5
Benin	6.6	+ 3.0	11.7	18.1
Nicaragua	5.2	+ 3.0	8.6	13.3
Eritrea	4.3	+ 3.0	8.3	13.3

Source: PRB, 2001 World Population Datasheet.
Notes: Countries with populations over four million; data for 2001.
aPopulation in millions.
bRate of Increase is the birth rate minus the death rate.

These demographic differences can be traced to the impact of industrialization. As the Industrial Revolution took firm hold in the countries of the Global North, greater affluence, better diets, and innovations in medical care decreased infant mortality and increased life expectancy. In turn, these changes contributed to a steady evolutionary shift away from pro-natalist norms. With each newborn child having a much higher likelihood of surviving to adulthood, there was less perceived need to have large numbers of children. It is this transition from a pro-natalist mentality to more stable reproductive norms that now lags behind the diffusion of medical technology and related declining infant mortality in the Global South. In these countries, decisions about family size are still heavily influenced by prescriptions based on the experience of past generations; wisdom that lags behind new demographic realities and that still cautions couples to have large numbers of children in order to make certain that some will survive to carry on the family name.

These differences in growth patterns are illuminated by the theory of the demographic transition, which is derived from the historical experience of the industrialized countries.[6] According to this theory, there are three demographic stages, and possibly a fourth, through which societies sequentially pass (table 2.3). The first stage is characteristic of pre-industrial societies where high death rates offset high birthrates, resulting in fairly stable populations. In the second stage, characteristic of industrializing countries, death rates drop due to,

TABLE 2.3. Four Stages of the Demographic Transition				
Development Stage	Period of History	Birth Rates	Death Rates	Growth Rates
Stage One	Pre-Agrarian and Agrarian	High	High	Slow growth
Stage Two	Industrializing	High	Declining	Rapid growth
Stage Three	Fully Industrialized	Low	Low	Zero growth
Stage Four	Postindustrial/ Postmodern	Lower	Low	Decline

among other things, better medical care and nutrition, which cause declining infant mortality and longer life spans. At the same time, birthrates remain high, resulting in significant population growth. In the third stage of transition, as beliefs and norms governing reproduction change, birthrates drop to match the lower death rates, and population equilibrium is reestablished. Some demographers claim that there is an enduring fourth stage of transition, where birthrates continue to drop and stay below death rates, resulting in a long-term net population loss.[7]

The United States has now passed through three stages of the demographic transition, but has not yet moved into a fourth. Figure 2.1 illustrates the distribution of the U.S. population at four points in time. In 1900, the United States resembled the contemporary industrializing countries moving through the second stage of the transition. This is indicated by the large portion of the population at the base of this population pyramid. Over time, the United States has been moving toward a population rectangle, with a fairly even distribution of numbers across all age groups as the birthrate has diminished and the number of elderly has continued to grow.

There are very few societies in the world that have been untouched by industrialization. But in them, pro-natalist norms and values govern behavior, having evolved from generations of experience with high infant mortality. Couples adhering to traditional values feel that morally and socially they are doing the "right thing" by having large numbers of children. Many countries on the less industrialized side of the demographic divide have moved well into the second stage of the demographic transition. Having received the benefits of a surge of life-saving medical technology transfer, these countries have experienced a substantial drop in infant mortality and an increase in life expectancy. But birthrates remain high because it takes time to "unlearn" the norms and behavior that have slowly evolved from historical experience. Thus, in countries as diverse as Libya and Haiti, birthrates still remain well above death rates, particularly in rural areas, because of this evolutionary discontinuity. Couples continue to behave reproductively as if mortality rates and life expectancies are the same as those once faced by their grandparents, but the long-term survival prospects of their children have markedly improved.

Countries in this second stage of the demographic transition face an additional problem called demographic momentum. This problem results from a "youth bulge" in these rapidly growing populations. In many African countries, for example, nearly one-half of the population is under the age of fifteen years, and only about 3 percent is over sixty-five years. If, by some demographic miracle, couples in these countries were to cut back to two-child families immediately, there still would be considerable future population growth. The momentum inherent in such age distributions, with so many people yet to pass through their reproductive years, would reverberate as surges of population growth for many decades.

In stark contrast, on the North side of the demographic divide most of the industrialized countries have already moved well into the third phase of the demographic transition. In this phase, the social dynamics associated with industrial modernization produce a shift toward much smaller families. For example, in Denmark in 1950 the statistically average woman produced 2.6 children during her lifetime, much more than the 2.1 required for zero population growth. By 1985, this had dropped to 1.5, although by the beginning of the new millennium there had been a slight rebound to 1.7.[8] In West Germany the 1950 figure was 2.1, but by 1985 it had dropped to 1.3, where it remained at the end of the century for all of Germany.[9]

A fourth stage of the demographic transition seems to be emerging in a number of European countries. In Germany and Italy, for example, couples now choose to have only one child or even no children at all, resulting in below replacement birthrates and a population decline. In other countries, such as Belarus, Latvia, and Russia, difficult economic times associated with a period of political and economic transition have led to similar reproduction choices.

For the industrialized world as a whole, there is now an average of eleven births and ten deaths per one thousand people, yielding a minuscule population growth rate of 0.1 percent annually. But on the less industrial side of the divide, there are still twenty-five births and only eight deaths per one thousand, yielding a population growth rate of 1.6 percent.[10] A smooth progression by the presently less industrialized countries into the third stage of the transition, similar to that experienced by the early industrializers, cannot be assumed. It is unclear whether many of the less industrialized countries can avoid a "demographic trap," created by a surge in the number of young job seekers in the face of little economic opportunity, and thus become affluent enough to move into the third stage. These countries appear now to be economically bogged down and unable to muster the resources required to modernize rapidly enough to avoid severe environmental and economic deterioration brought about by persisting high birthrates.

Complicating the chances for economic growth and a related demographic transition in much of the Global South is the devastating impact of HIV/AIDS. Of the estimated 42 million people now living with HIV/AIDS, approximately 95 percent are living in the Global South, where the impact of

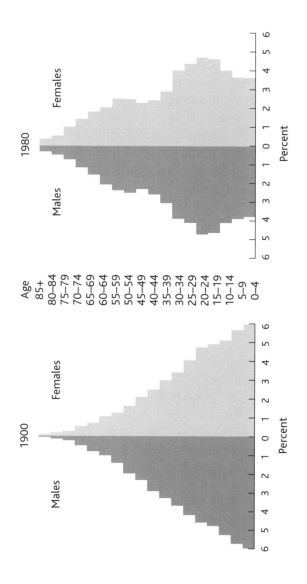

FIGURE 2.1. U.S. Population by Age and Sex, 1900, 1980, 2000, and Projections for 2020

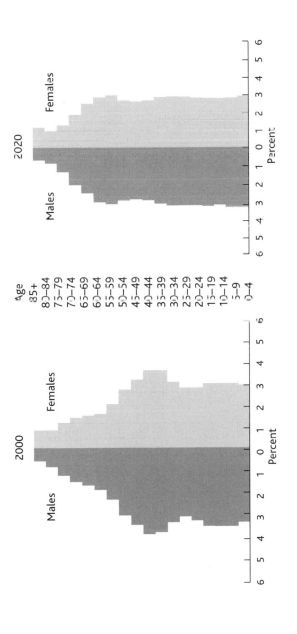

Source: Martha Farnsworth Riche, "America's Diversity and Growth: Signposts for the 21st Century," *Population Bulletin* (June 2000).

the pandemic has been devastating.[11] Particularly in sub-Saharan Africa, life expectancy has been cut dramatically by AIDS. By 2010, the estimated drop in life expectancy at birth will be twenty-four years in Kenya, twenty-six years in Nigeria, forty years in Zimbabwe, and forty-four years in Botswana.[12] It is unclear whether this tragedy will spark a resurgence of fertility as an evolutionary response to increasing death rates, or whether hopelessness and despair will increase to the point that they cause a decline in the birthrate.

Exploding Populations

The growing ecological insecurity of the last fifty years has been driven by a population explosion taking place primarily in the Global South. Paradoxically, this population growth, which has been a persisting problem over these decades, has been essential to past species survival. Evolutionary logic suggests that those species that reproduce more prolifically are more likely to prevail in competition with those that do not. Thus, in the contemporary world solitary animals such as pandas and orangutans, and other animals that mate infrequently, are in danger of extinction, while rabbits proliferate.[13] Similarly, one of the reasons that *Homo sapiens* has persisted as a species is a strong drive to reproduce. Most of human history has been a struggle for survival in the face of predators and disease. Thus, a strong sex drive combined with pro-natalist values has represented both biological and sociocultural evolutionary wisdom that has facilitated human success. But currently predators are less threatening, and advances in medicine have, over time, reduced deaths from disease. Yet, in many parts of the world people still reproduce at rates much more suited to the conditions experienced by past generations.

Rapid population growth can destabilize all four equilibria that define ecological security. This growth places stress on natural systems. For example, in the densely populated Global South burgeoning populations are experiencing increasing numbers of so-called natural disasters as people press into marginal areas—river basins, coastal lowlands, areas prone to earthquakes—that can be occupied only at great risk.[14] It has been estimated that 60 percent of the less industrialized world's poorest people live in ecologically vulnerable areas.[15] Trees that can be used for firewood are rapidly disappearing before axes wielded by growing populations, and the related deforestation is increasing soil erosion and flooding. Arable land is also a scarce resource in the Global South. As competition from industry and urbanization grows, the per capita availability of cropland has decreased throughout the world. In the Global South per capita availability decreased from 0.21 hectares per capita in 1984 to 0.18 hectares per capita in 1994.[16]

Water shortages are another source of insecurity in many areas of the world. Rapidly growing populations in the Middle East, for example, are competing for very limited supplies. Relations between Israelis and Palestinians have been worsened by arguments over control of water; Jordan and Syria have repeatedly accused each other of stealing water from the small river running between the two countries. Similarly, Syria, Turkey, and Iraq periodically feud over the use of water from the Tigris and Euphrates Rivers.[17] Israel and Lebanon are quarreling over the right of the Lebanese to withdraw water from the Wazzani River, upstream from Israeli territory.[18]

Population pressures on land and water are linked to malnutrition and even starvation. While on a global scale growth in food production has slightly exceeded population growth over the last decade, this has not been the case in many individual countries. When data for the period 1989–1991 is compared with that for 1996–1998, food production per person actually declined in ninety-one countries.[19] Rapid population growth also destabilizes relationships with other species and microorganisms. As populations grow and search for additional resources, they often take them at the expense of other species. Population growth has resulted in clear-cutting forests, developing coastal areas, dredging rivers, and filling in wetlands, which have all in turn contributed to the destruction of critical habitats for thousands of species around the world.

While the twentieth century has been characterized by remarkable progress in the struggle against the many diseases that afflict human beings, there are now indications that the rapid growth in human numbers, the increasing density of human populations, poverty, and ecological changes are making human populations much more vulnerable to various kinds of pathogens.[20] The World Health Organization estimates that one-quarter of the world's population, mostly in poorer countries, is subject to chronic intestinal parasitic infections. Of the approximately 18 million annual deaths due to communicable diseases and nutritional deficiencies, HIV / AIDS now kills about 3 million people, tuberculosis about 1.7 million people, and malaria about 1 million. In addition, millions of others die prematurely from a host of other diseases.[21]

Many of the bacteria and viruses that pose these threats are not new. They have coexisted with *Homo sapiens* in various parts of the world for long periods of time. It is changes in human behavior, population growth, patterns of residence, poverty, and rapidity of transport that have altered the people–microbe balance.[22] In the words of Nobel Laureate Joshua Lederberg, "[S]ome people think that I am being hysterical, but there are catastrophes ahead. We live in evolutionary competition with microbes—bacteria and viruses. There is no guarantee that we will be the survivors."[23] Thus, the greatest future threat to human security may not come from thermonuclear explosions, but from disrupting the equilibrium with microorganisms too small to be seen by the human eye.

Rapid population growth can also lead to violence. The end of colonialism resulted in a number of newly independent states in many parts of the Global South, most notably in Africa. More often than not, these states were delineated out of political expediency, with little recognition of ethnic differences. This resulted in cases where ethnic groups were divided among states (for example, the Kurds straddling four countries in the Middle East) and where competing ethnic groups were subsumed within single states (such as Rwanda, home to both Tutsis and Hutus). Population growth and unequal resource distributions are considered to be factors contributing to environmental scarcity. Population dislocations, economic turmoil, and compounding stress on the state have followed cases of documented environmental scarcity in places such as Rwanda, Pakistan, and South Africa.[24]

Rapid population growth is at least partially responsible for a widening economic gap between North and South. Between 1985 and 1995, for example, there was a decline in real per capita gross domestic product (GDP) in forty-seven countries on the southern side of the demographic divide, a situation that has persisted into the new century.[25] This decline is mirrored in large differences in consumption of goods and services: the richest 20 percent of the world's population now consumes 86 percent of all goods and services, while the poorest 20 percent consumes only 1.3 percent.[26] Economic stagnation or decline is often related, in turn, to political turmoil and insecurity. There is a close tie among rapid population growth, poverty, environmental deterioration, social violence, political instability, and authoritarian forms of government. When politics must deal with an authoritative allocation of deprivations instead of benefits it is difficult for democratic regimes to survive. In Haiti, for example, the very high birthrate has led to environmental deterioration, socioeconomic decline, and repeated violence associated with authoritarian regimes.[27] These maladies led the United States to intervene militarily in Haiti on humanitarian grounds in the late 1990s, but the troops eventually departed, leaving Haiti in much the same precarious economic and political shape.

The future course of world population growth and its consequences are difficult to predict with precision. But it is likely that the worldwide growth rate will continue to diminish slowly over the next few decades. However, in the short term in poverty pockets of the Global South pro-natalist norms will continue to produce substantial population growth and related Malthusian outcomes. This, in turn, will lead to more disease, retard economic growth, increase radicalism and terrorism, and create pressures for migration to other countries.

Growth among Neighbors

Whether within or among states, differential growth has the potential to create tension and conflict. In countries as diverse as Rwanda, Somalia, and Canada, friction among ethnic groups sharing the same political jurisdiction and growing at different rates has led to political instability and social conflict. Societies or countries with low population growth rates often perceive themselves to be potential victims of rapidly growing neighbors. Israel, with an annual rate of natural population increase of 1.6 percent, feels threatened by Arab neighbors with populations that are now growing at between 1.7 and 3.7 percent.[28] Israel compensates for this perceived imbalance by encouraging large-scale Jewish immigration, particularly from countries undergoing hard times. This, in turn, has increased the number of Israeli settlements and tension with Palestinians in the West Bank and Gaza areas who fear that the migrant influx will continue to increase pressure on their lands. As former Israeli Prime Minister Shamir once put it succinctly, "A big immigration needs a big Israel."[29]

In general, the rapid growth of Islamic populations compared to their non-Islamic neighbors has been a persisting source of friction. Given the recent surge in terrorist acts, neighbors of Islamic countries understandably are somewhat insecure in the face of these burgeoning populations. There is now a demographic fault line stretching the length of the Mediterranean. Rapidly growing Islamic populations to the south of the line appear threatening to the demographically more stable countries to the north. On the European side of this fault line, almost all countries have reached or are approaching zero population growth; the Islamic countries of Northern Africa, by contrast, are growing at about 2.1 percent annually. The current population of North Africa, 177 million, is expected to grow to 251 million by 2025, while the European countries, with a population of 727 million, are expected to decline to 717 million over the same period. In France and Italy, the total fertility rate, defined as the average number of children a woman has during childbearing years, is 1.9 and 1.3, well below replacement rate. In North Africa, by contrast, large families are still the rule. In Algeria, the total fertility rate is 3.1, and in Libya, it is 3.9.[30]

Given its historical ties to North Africa, France has been most directly affected by migration pressures from neighbors. Migrants have been a big issue in French politics, and the National Front—the right-wing political party of Jean-Marie Le Pen—has been able to garner a significant portion of the national and regional vote while demanding that all immigrants be returned to their countries of origin. Germany has also been affected by these migration pressures from the South and the East. Discontent with immigration laws

and an influx of immigrants has been manifest in sporadic violence against foreigners. But immigration is a major issue for the entire European Union, as
freedom of internal movement now means that migrants can move from one
European Union country to another, once they manage to gain entry into any
member country.

The unstable situation in the territory of the former Soviet Union offers
a vivid example of the pressures of differential population growth. During the
1980s, the population of the Russian Republic was growing at only 0.7 percent
annually while the populations of the Turkmen, Uzbek, Kyrghish, and Tajik
Republics were growing at between 2 and 3 percent. Furthermore, 17 percent
of the population of the former Soviet Union was Islamic, and this portion
was growing at four times the rate of the Russian population.[31] The sporadic
violence that continues to occur in this part of the world, including persisting tensions in Chechnya, is at least partially a reflection of the legacy of differential growth rates among the ethnic populations of this now politically
volatile region.

Even within the United States, where actual violence based on ethnicity
is rare, the differential growth of various minorities is reshaping the contours
of politics. The non-Hispanic, white portion of the population, which has traditionally controlled the two major political parties, is nearing zero growth,
while various minorities, reinforced by immigration, are growing much more
rapidly. The United States Census Bureau projects that the U.S. population will
grow from 275 million to 404 million over the next fifty years. But the white,
non-Hispanic portion of the population will drop from nearly three-quarters
of the total to just over one-half.[32] The differential growth of populations
within the United States will be especially prominent in certain states where
immigration has had the largest impact. By 2025, California, Hawaii, New
Mexico, and Texas will all be minority-majority states, where the collective
minorities will make up over half of the population.[33] California became the
first state to reach this condition in 1999. Between 1990 and 1999, the Asian
population of California increased by 36 percent and the Latino population by
35 percent, while the white population actually declined by 3 percent.[34] Of the
270 electoral votes needed to win the presidency, 95 are now allocated to these
minority-majority states, suggesting that the impact of differential growth will
be significant on national as well as state and local politics.[35] By 2050, it is estimated that Hispanics will comprise 24 percent of the U.S. population, African
Americans 14 percent, Asian Americans 8 percent, and Native Americans 1
percent. And shortly after 2050, no single racial group will account for a
majority of Americans.[36]

People in Motion

Rapid population growth also spawns urbanization and migration. The pressures of rural population growth in less industrialized countries, combined with perceived (and often illusory) economic opportunities in urban areas, are driving and luring large numbers of young people into already teeming cities. But others, driven by demographic pressures, declining economic opportunity, and political instability, are moving, legally and illegally, across the international demographic divide. Between 1990 and 2000, the number of people living outside their countries of birth or citizenship grew from an estimated 120 million to 200 million. If all of these migrants located in one place they would form the world's sixth largest country.[37] Remittances sent home by workers living abroad rose from $30 billion in 1988 to $65 billion in 1999, having a significant impact on the economies and well-being of their home countries as well as their countries of employment.[38] Recent projections suggest that by 2020, as many as eight million Mexicans will migrate to the United States, unless Mexico is able to create the one million jobs per year needed to keep pace with population growth.[39]

People are motivated to migrate for a variety of reasons. Historically, the largest number has moved in search of better economic conditions. But contemporary migration is also being fueled by refugees from military conflicts, ethnic violence, natural disasters, and state failures. And contemporary migrants now differ from their predecessors in that they frequently travel back and forth between country of origin and country of residence, often having no intention of being assimilated.[40]

It is difficult to define and measure the numbers and types of migrants and refugees in the world today. A large share of migrants and refugees remains in the countries of origin as internally displaced persons. A slightly larger portion crosses boundaries only within the less industrialized world, and an even smaller share crosses the demographic divide into the industrialized countries. Millions of migrants cross borders quite legally each year, and there are several million contract laborers living abroad at any given point in time. But it is illegal migrants, asylum-seekers, and refugees that create political issues.

The most troublesome political and moral dilemmas are associated with refugees. Unlike most migrants, refugees relocate solely as a result of "push" factors that force them from their homes. Often they are intended or unintended victims of military conflicts or ethnic cleansing, and it is difficult to refuse their requests for asylum. But other cases are not always clear and become political. In the United States, for example, refugees from Castro's Cuba have generally fared much better than those from Haiti. Immigration officials in many industrialized countries have recently seen a large increase in numbers of people seeking political asylum based on a wide variety of claims, some valid and others concocted. In most countries, the wheels of immigration justice often turn very slowly, permitting those seeking asylum to stay for long periods or to slip quietly out of sight.[41]

Disasters also contribute to the world's flow of refugees. After Hurricane Mitch struck Central America in the Fall of 1998, thousands of refugees began traveling north through Mexico to the United States. They were in search of jobs in order to send money back to relatives to help rebuild homes and communities destroyed by the hurricane. The influx of refugees caused the United States to allow Honduran and Nicaraguan refugees who were already living in the United States illegally to apply for "temporary protected status." Under this status, these refugees could legally stay and work in the United States for up to eighteen months. In practice, however, even those refugees that arrived later were not often deported. Instead the new migrants found jobs in the underground workforce, estimated at more than fifteen million people.[42]

Precise data on migrants and refugees are difficult to obtain because of the ever-changing nature of population movements, and the fact that many migrants do not like to be found and counted. The United Nations High Commission for Refugees estimates that in the late 1990s there were about 12 million refugees living in foreign countries, another 6.3 million were internally displaced, and another 1.4 million were either asylum-seekers or returnees. Thus, protracted conflicts, civil wars, ethnic cleansing, and a variety of similar human tragedies have created a large population of semipermanent refugees, many of whom live dreary and hopeless lives under primitive conditions in refugee camps. Afghanistan tops the list of countries that have created refugees, with 3,809,600 Afghans registered as refugees abroad, although many have returned since the defeat of the Taliban. Iraq and Burundi follow with 631,000 and 554,000 respectively. The pieces of the former Yugoslavia have collectively created numbers of refugees similar to those of Iraq, as have Somalia, Angola, and Sudan.[43] In addition, tens of millions of refugees remain unofficially displaced within countries and represent the fastest growing group of displaced persons. It is estimated that there are ten million internally displaced people in Africa and five million each in Europe and Asia.[44]

Rapid urbanization is the legitimate and unforced movement of people within countries. But it also can create political, economic, and social problems. Worldwide in 1965, 36 percent of the population lived in cities. Currently, the portion living in cities is nearly 50 percent.[45] In the low income countries, however, the number of people living in cities is exploding. In Asia, the number of people in cities will grow from the present 1.5 billion to 2.6 billion by 2030. And in Africa, the number will grow from the present 297 million to 766 million.[46]

The portion of people living in urban areas worldwide is expected to grow to 58 percent by 2025. About 90 percent of this urban growth will take place in the less industrialized countries.[47] Many migrants to urban areas will become squatters, having little chance to own land or a home of their own. At the beginning of the millennium, half of the world's absolute poor lived in urban areas. This was especially true in Latin America where the number of urban poor nearly tripled between 1970 and 1990. Although the figures for Asia had been improving in the mid-1990s, the downturn in many Asian economies changed that trend. In Africa, the rural poor still outnumber the urban poor, though the gap is narrowing. And, in Central and Eastern Europe the transition toward a market economy has resulted in high levels of urban industrial unemployment.[48]

Cities in the less industrialized countries are giant resource sinks, creating a large "ecological footprint" over the surrounding countryside.[49] Large quantities of food must be imported to sustain ever-increasing numbers of urbanites. But growing cities also need increasing amounts of water for drinking and sewage treatment, water that is often not available. In Dhaka, Bangladesh, for example, only one-fifth of the population is served by a sewer system. In Bangkok, Thailand, rising demand is depleting the groundwater in much of the city so fast that parts of it are sinking at a rate of 5 to 10 centimeters per year. In Mexico City it is estimated that the center of the city has dropped about eight meters over the last fifty years due to groundwater extraction. In addition, urban sprawl often destroys much of the fertile agricultural land surrounding cities. It is estimated that 476,000 hectares of arable land is being transformed to urban uses annually in the less industrialized countries.[50]

Rapid urbanization is giving rise to a large number of sprawling and polluted "megacities," cities with populations over ten million. Projecting urbanization trends forward to the year 2015, current growth rates suggest there will be twenty-three megacities, nineteen of which will be in the Global South.[51] Providing adequate housing, sanitation, transportation, jobs, security, and other amenities for rapidly growing numbers of urbanites will be a staggering undertaking. So will be the task of maintaining order and preventing epidemics among the restless army of unemployed in these crowded and polluted megacities.[52]

Mexico City is expected to be the largest of the world's cities in the middle of this century and is experiencing many of the destructive environmental problems associated with rapid urbanization. Today's seventeen million people already challenge urban planners. Located in a basin at an altitude of 7,300 feet, Mexico City lacks sufficient fresh air to meet the competing needs of people, automobiles, and industry. Ozone readings reached such high levels in 1992 that the government expanded a one-weekday-per-week ban on each urban automobile to two weekdays per week, thus theoretically keeping 40 percent of the region's automobiles off the streets on any given weekday.

But the growing megacities may not be the most important part of the problem. Estimates suggest that by 2015, there will be 516 cities with populations between one and ten million that face more mundane urban sprawl problems.[53] Secondary cities, like El Alto in Bolivia, experiencing a growth rate of 9 percent per year, are now the fastest growing cities. Unlike Sao Paulo, Mexico City, and other megacities, these secondary cities usually are left to cope with rapid urbanization with little assistance from international agencies.[54]

Even cities in the industrialized North face some of these same problems. New York City has a major task in disposing of the 26,000 tons of trash the city generates each day.[55] This aspect of New York's "reverse ecological footprint" has resulted in trash being exported to the state of Virginia, where citizens, politicians, and even the governor have been reconsidering the wisdom of providing more landfill space in light of the associated environmental impacts.[56]

Population Implosions and Social Insecurity

Although not as obvious or well studied as other dimensions of demographic change, moving rapidly toward zero population growth, or even into population decline, can also have significant socioeconomic and political consequences.[57] The aging or graying of societies results from a combination of declining birthrates and longer life spans. The state of Florida offers a contemporary snapshot. Despite the presence of Disney World, Mickey Mouse, and scores of young visitors, Florida has become such an enclave for the aged that it has given rise to the term "Floridization." The concentration of senior citizens in Florida, comprising 19 percent of the state's total population, offers a window on the future of many industrial countries. Italy is expected to reach the graying levels of Florida in 2003, followed by Japan in 2005, and Germany in 2006. The United States as a whole is projected to do so in 2021.[58]

Many industrialized countries are now approaching a possible fourth stage of the demographic transition, and have reached or even dropped through zero population growth. Zero population growth occurs in countries with a well-balanced age structure when their fertility rate is equal to approximately 2.1. This rate allows theoretically for the replacement of each married partner. Eventually, this results in the portion of the population under fifteen years of age shrinking and that beyond retirement age—benefiting from longer life expectancy—continuing to grow. In the industrial countries as a whole, 14 percent of the population is now over age sixty-five and only 19 percent is under age fifteen. In Germany and Bulgaria, the portion under fifteen and over sixty-five is equal, while in Italy and Spain, the portion over sixty-five is slightly larger.[59] There are now eighty-three countries and territories that have below replacement fertility rates.[60]

The many socioeconomic implications of graying have not yet been adequately explored and publicized, both because the greatest impact of this demographic shift still lies ahead, and because of the politically explosive nature of associated distributional issues. As Michael Boskin, a former chairman of the U.S. Council of Economic Advisers, forewarned many years ago, "A confrontation between workers and retirees will arise that will create the greatest polarization along economic lines in our society since the Civil War."[61] Aging in the most impacted countries could lead to a variety of intergenerational skirmishes as the unfunded liabilities growing out of entitlement programs created during a period of rapid growth must be paid for at a time when there will be much smaller labor forces to contribute to them. Growing elderly populations understandably feel entitled to receive promised pension and medical benefits, but they are presently unfunded or woefully underfunded.

Over the past 25 years, the number of people of pensionable age in Organization for Economic Cooperation and Development (OECD) countries, excluding Mexico and Turkey, rose by 45 million, while the population of working age rose by 120 million. Over the next 25 years, the number of people of pensionable age is projected to grow by another 70 million, while the working age population will rise by only 5 million. The share of the total population employed will drop from 47 percent in 2005 to 39 percent in 2030.[62] It has been estimated that by the year 2030, 27 percent of the population of Switzerland and 26 percent of the population of Germany will be over age 65. In the United States and Japan, 20 percent will be over age 65.[63]

This graying will alter dramatically the future aged (or old-age) dependency ratios in the industrial countries. An aged dependency ratio is calculated by dividing the number of people over 65 years of age in a country by the number of those of working age (15–65). In the United States, this ratio is expected to be about 0.21 in 2010, meaning that theoretically one elderly person could be supported by taxes raised from about five people in the labor force. But, of course, not all people aged 15–65 will be employed. By the year 2030, this dependency ratio rapidly increases to 0.35, meaning that each person over 65 could theoretically be supported by only three active workers. In France, this ratio rises from 0.28 to 0.44 during this same period and in Germany from 0.32 to 0.45.[64] In both of these countries in the year 2030, there will be only slightly more than two potentially active workers for each potential retiree. These figures conjure up visions of a new proletariat toiling long hours in order to pay the taxes necessary to keep politically organized retirees in the style to which they've become accustomed. Because most of these future obligations are presently significantly underfunded, the two or three workers supporting each retiree will likely have to provide the bulk of entitlement funding, clearly a politically explosive situation.

While the United States is not yet severely impacted, many European countries and Japan—much further along the road to Floridization—are already confronted with the need for action. The consequences of aging are even more dire in these countries because their populations "are aging even faster, birthrates are lower, the influx of young immigrants from developing countries is smaller, public pension benefits are more generous, and private pension systems are weaker."[65] In addition, people are retiring earlier. In a study that included 14 industrial countries, the labor force participation rate of men aged 55–64 in 1970 was between 59 percent and 91 percent. By the mid-1990s, the rate had fallen to between 42 percent and 85 percent. The rate had fallen from 81 percent to 42 percent in the Netherlands, from 71 percent to 43 percent in France, and from 91 percent to 64 percent in England. In labor-starved Japan, however, the rate dropped only from 90 percent to 85 percent, and in the United States, it dropped modestly from 81 percent to 68 percent.[66] Average retirement ages in industrial countries have dropped accordingly. In France, the average retirement age for men was 64.5 in 1960. It had dropped to 59.2 by 1995. In the United States, it only dropped from 66.5 in 1960 to 63.6 in 1995, while in Japan there was little change, a drop from 67.2 to 66.5.[67]

The insecurities associated with aging are not limited to the industrially advanced nations. In China, a vigorous family planning policy stressing one-child families, which was begun in 1978, has led to more rapid graying than is taking place in many other countries. The dilemma facing Chinese leaders is that the one child per family policy, a measure made necessary in order to preserve some semblance of equilibrium between China's huge population and the physical environment, has resulted in an aging population long before enough economic growth has taken place to create the financial reserves or economic capacity necessary to support extensive social programs. Similar long-term problems can be anticipated in the former socialist countries of Central Europe where a demographic transition has been completed without a preceding period of rapid economic growth.

Adding together the future retirement and medical burdens associated with graying in all of these countries, it is very likely that the generous systems of social protection that evolved in an era of expansion and exuberance are going to increasingly be the cause of social insecurity and subject to controversy. Unfunded and underfunded pension systems and growing medical care costs will place heavy demands on smaller workforces. In fact, the controversial Bush decision to seek import curbs on foreign steel in 2001 were at least partially driven by pension obligations in the domestic steel industry, where the biggest U.S. steel makers have up to six retirees for every active worker.[68] Very rapid economic growth based on increased productivity could help meet obligations such as these for a while, but such growth will be problematic, particularly given a shrinking labor supply.

Within the United States, the problems associated with an aging population raise difficult political issues. The AARP, which used to be known as the American Association of Retired Persons, is now one of the largest and most politically active membership organizations. Composed of members who have reached at least 50 years of age, the AARP is active in all aspects of politics. Conversely, younger people are less politically active and tend to vote less frequently. Recent estimates indicate, for example, that in 2002, 23 percent of those voting were over 65, while only 10 percent of those voting were under 30. Because of continuing demographic shifts and differential participation in politics, by 2022, 33 percent of those voting will be over 65 and 8 percent will be under 30.[69] Because future generations cannot now vote, and are not well represented in politics, one of the first casualties in the political bargaining for future government funding may well be education and other programs for the dwindling number of young people.[70] Already in the United States, per capita federal spending on the elderly is ten times higher than per capita federal spending on children under 18. This will likely get much worse over the next thirty years.[71]

Aside from pension obligations, another serious problem associated with graying in the United States is medical care for a growing aged population. General health care costs are predicted to rise from 13.4 percent of GDP in 1997 to 16.6 percent in 2007.[72] This will create funding problems for both public and private sectors.[73] Within the next twenty years, it is expected that the costs of medical care for the aged in the United States will surpass the costs of social security benefits. The increasing costs of medical care in the United States, the higher costs associated with caring for those over sixty-five (estimated between three and five times the cost of caring for people under sixty-five), the very high cost of prescription drugs, and the increasing number eligible for the government-sponsored and funded Medicare program will compound the long-term economic challenges of an aging population.[74] While other industrial countries will have similar medical care problems, most of them provide prescription drugs to seniors through national health services, and they have been able to keep down drug costs by negotiating bulk purchases from pharmaceutical companies. Thus, they are in a somewhat better position to manage future costs than is the United States.

Concern over the impact of graying in the United States is just now surfacing, and politicians try to avoid openly discussing the tough budgetary choices that must be made in the near future. Instead, they rely on phantom projections of perpetual rapid economic growth that will increase tax revenues, or on myths that privatizing social security will make these problems disappear. And notions that these discontinuities can be addressed effectively by rapidly bolstering population size through tax incentives for having more children or by opening the immigration floodgates can be dismissed as both misleading and environmentally insensitive. In the United States, as well as in the rest of the graying societies, a continuing dialogue about the relative burdens to be shouldered by future young people living in graying societies is clearly needed as are new ways of thinking about retirement.[75]

Summing Up: Building Demographic Security

Ecological insecurity can be greatly reduced through population policies designed to restore equilibria among human societies, and between them, nature and other organisms. Continuing to slow population growth in the Global South is one obvious requirement for building a more secure world. But attempts to confront population growth issues are politically difficult because many politicians are unwilling to challenge the pro-natalist norms that were shaped during the long period when the future well-being of *Homo sapiens* was insured through vigorous reproduction. As John Weeks has so deftly put it, "all nations that have survived to the present day did so by overcoming high levels of mortality."[76] Unfortunately, U.S. population policies have vacillated from one administration to the next, as have those of governments in many of the less industrialized countries.

One of the barriers to dealing effectively with population growth is a contemporary explosion of interest in human rights at the expense of concern for human responsibilities. Instead of tackling tough sociocultural issues of value and behavior change required to restore global population equilibrium, the demands of various special interests have come to dominate population forums. At the 1994 UN International Conference on Population and Development in Cairo, for example, the deliberations were hijacked by various interests pressing their causes at the expense of resolute action on family planning. As Lindsey

Grant put it, nowhere does the resulting UN "Programme state that population growth should stop. Nowhere are growing countries urged to give high priority to stopping (or even slowing) population growth."[77]

The Cairo Conference indeed represented a paradigm shift in thinking about demographic change. Unlike the preceding UN conferences, the Cairo Conference program no longer emphasized or even contained population targets. In their well-intentioned concern to prioritize the enhancement of women's status, and their rights to family planning, education, reproductive, and other basic health needs—much of which is instrumental in changing pro-natalist behavior—the delegates to the Cairo Conference seemed to neglect the ultimate goal of containing population growth. Thus, the Cairo Conference closely paralleled and anticipated the work of the 1995 Fourth World Conference on Women in Beijing.[78]

In 1999, the United Nations five-year review and assessment of the Cairo Conference found a lack of funds needed to implement the agreement to be the biggest problem. At the Cairo Conference, participating countries had agreed to increase annual spending on family planning to a total of $17 billion by 2000 and $22 billion by 2015. The industrialized countries committed to funding one-third and the developing countries committed to funding two-thirds of the total. Currently the industrialized countries have reached less than one-third of their goal, while less affluent countries are paying about 70 percent of their share.[79]

Even so, success stories resulting from changes endorsed and implemented under the Cairo Action Plan have begun to emerge. Declining fertility in all regions of the world seems to indicate that economic prosperity is not the essential precursor to population stabilization. Increased education of women and awareness of family planning options, along with increases in use of contraception, also seem central to the success stories. For example, Tunisia's fertility rate dropped from 5.1 children per woman in 1983 to 2.8 children in 1998. At the same time, the prevalence of birth control increased from 41 percent among women in 1983, to 60 percent in 1998. Similar significant decreases in fertility rates have accompanied increases in contraceptive use in Morocco, Sri Lanka, Iran, and Brazil.[80] And even Iran reached replacement-level fertility in 2000, a huge drop from 5 children per woman in 1989.[81]

But there are still many roadblocks to the implementation of effective family planning. Among them are persistent quibbling over the depth and causes of these problems, among those claiming to be population scholars. While there is a preponderance of scholarly opinion that the world's population has grown much too large, many academic hairs have been split over its optimum level.[82] Pro-natalists have only muddied the waters by declaring that the human population is the ultimate resource and that population growth, along with the lengthening of human life, is a moral and material triumph.[83] These naive optimists, for the most part living in comfort in the affluent countries, have ignored the suffering of the large numbers of starving and malnourished in the less affluent neighborhoods on the disadvantaged side of the demographic divide. But their arguments are readily embraced by politicians who would rather ignore these controversial issues.

The contentious nature of the domestic and international politics of family planning hinders efforts to shape long-term coherent policies to deal with population growth. On the international level, a split between countries of the Global North and South on these issues first became apparent in 1974 at the World Population Conference in Bucharest, Romania. The industrial countries, led by the United States, sought the adoption of a World Population Plan of Action that would have made family planning a central part of economic development efforts. But many leaders from less industrialized countries portrayed this as an intrusion into their internal affairs and argued that economic development must take priority over family planning as it is the "best contraceptive." This split persisted over the next decade, and surfaced again at the 1984 International Population Conference in Mexico City. At the Earth Summit of 1992 and the subsequent 1994 Cairo conference, the core issue of rapid population growth was downplayed because of pressures from religious and women's groups pressing their own agendas, and from politicians representing poor countries who blamed the bulk of the world's environmental ills on the industrial world.

Discontinuities in U.S. policy also have been an important part of the problem. The United States has historically been at the forefront of aid for family planning activity. Throughout the 1940s and 1950s, noted demographers such as Dudley Kirk, Frank Notestein, and Kingsley Davis called attention to the likely impact of colonialism and subsequent independence on population growth. These insights influenced U.S. policy, and every secretary of state from Dean Rusk to George Schultz took worldwide population growth to be a serious problem. The United States began to encourage family planning as part of development policy during the Kennedy administration, and this emphasis persisted through the Carter administration.[84] Since the mid-1980s, however, support has been wavering, held hostage to increasingly bizarre domestic politics. In 1984, United States family planning advocates were astonished when former Secretary of State James Baker, addressing the World Population Conference in Mexico City, broke with tradition and declared population growth to be a "natural phenomenon" that neither advanced nor hindered economic growth.[85]

The United States once funded about 20 percent of the United Nations Population Fund budget. With programs in 130 countries, this is the largest multilateral agency providing family planning services. Although it has policies that preclude the funding of programs associated with abortion, in 1985 it gave a $10 million grant to China—a country that approves of abortion as a method of family planning—to support maternal and health care as well as contraceptive research. The Reagan administration, seeking to placate domestic anti-abortion forces, turned this modest grant to China into an abortion issue and began withholding the U.S. contribution.

When former President George Bush was elected to office in 1989, there was hope that the U.S. contribution to the UN organization would be restored. Bush had been an outspoken advocate of family planning in the 1960s and 1970s, and even advocated making contraceptives available worldwide on a "massive scale."[86] But family planning assistance under Bush was again held hostage by anti-abortion fundamentalists, and the funds were not restored.

The Clinton administration took a more vigorous position on population growth issues and provided $540 million for international family planning in 1995, the largest total ever. In the following years, funding was provided, but in smaller amounts, until 1999 when a Republican-led Congress succeeded in blocking all U.S. government funding of the UN group, and continued to limit administrative flexibility in support of it.[87] The selection of another Bush as president in 2000 led to further setbacks based on religious ideology, as the new president issued an executive order in February 2001 blocking all government funding for family planning groups that in any way advocate or promote abortion. Bush later followed this by refusing to contribute the $34 million dollars that Congress had allocated for the UN Population Fund.[88]

Managing future migration within and among countries will also be difficult, but reducing population growth could prevent many of the conflicts that produce bumper crops of migrants and refugees. Stemming the influx of people into the cities of less industrialized countries requires local action and, for the most part, hasn't been a high priority. This situation could also be somewhat ameliorated by successful family planning efforts. Future sustainable development, however, requires creating alternatives to the migration leading to growth of megacities. This could include educational efforts to keep people from migrating to already dangerous, overcrowded, and polluted cities. Other alternatives might include redirecting development funding to smaller cities and rural areas, as well as increasing economic incentives to farmers in order to keep more people in agricultural occupations.

Coping with the future uncertainties of graying requires anticipatory thinking and action on a large scale. Unfortunately, little present political gain is seen in addressing future deficits by increasing current taxes. And, as politicians in graying countries on the northern side of the worldwide demographic divide slowly begin to grapple with their own extensive retirement and medical care obligations, they will be less likely to provide the amounts of family planning and economic assistance necessary to help the less industrial countries spring out of their demographic traps.

Finally, carrying out a successful global population strategy requires that countries of the Global North live up to their aid commitments, and make significant new ones to leaders of countries who are willing to grapple with population growth problems. But such actions need not be justified solely on the basis of altruism. It is much more cost effective to spend money to promote economic development, good government, and family planning in potentially unstable countries than it is to engage in expensive military actions to restore order later. It is clearly in the self-interest of the wealthy countries to stem the rising tide of political instability, ethnic conflict, illegal immigration, and terrorism by dramatically reducing the large economic disparities between the countries of the Global North and South

CHAPTER THREE

An Assault on the Global Commons

A DYNAMIC EQUILIBRIUM between the requirements of human populations and the servicing capabilities of the ecosystems in which they live is a crucial component of ecological security. Environmental conditions have played an important role in shaping the nature of societies. In general, environments of plenty, with temperate climates, abundant food supplies, and mineral wealth, have offered opportunities for civilizations to flourish. Environments of scarcity, by contrast, have often shaped "Spartan" societies, characterized by more authoritarian political rule and frequent conflict with neighbors.[1] Similarly, sociocultural evolution has had a significant impact on physical environments. How societies have chosen to define progress and to develop economically obviously has had a significant impact on nature.

Societies are often in competition with each other and other organisms for various kinds of resources. In a technical sense "a resource is anything needed by an organism, population, or ecosystem, which, by its increasing availability up to an optimal or sufficient level, allows an increasing rate of energy conversion."[2] Put more simply, ecosystems contain a variety of resources, such as water, minerals, food, and fuels, that are essential to the growth and well-being of societies. Some resources, such as solar energy, are renewable (income) sources and are not depleted when used. Others, such as fossil fuels, are nonrenewable (fund) sources and can only be consumed once. The rapid growth of various human populations and the resource requirements of higher levels of living are now severely taxing supplies of many kinds of natural resources.

This conventional way of thinking about resources, as materials to be consumed, neglects another important role played by the environment in insuring well-being. *Homo sapiens*, and other creatures, rely heavily on the environmental services provided by "common property" resources (commons) such as the atmosphere and hydrosphere.[3] These systems not only provide the fresh air and water that are required to sustain life, but they perform other essential functions. The constantly moving hydrosphere supplies water for agricultural and industrial uses, as well as waste dispersal capacity for the sewage and other pollutants associated with urban settlements and an industrial way of life. The atmosphere provides similar services such as dispersing noxious urban gases, protecting life on Earth from penetrating ultraviolet solar radiation, and insulating the surface of the Earth from the extremely cold temperatures of outer space.

Human populations, like those of other animals, tend to expand until they approach growth limits set by resource availability. Animal populations tend to overshoot these limits because resources available to them are relatively fixed; in most cases they can only increase their numbers substantially through migration. *Homo sapiens*, however, uses technological innovation to more efficiently utilize resources. Our species also has learned from experience, and now has begun to limit reproduction to levels that can be sustained. Still, many contemporary societies persistently press close to resource limits, and population size is often harshly curtailed by sudden fluctuations in resource availability, particularly food and water. Brushing up against limits is often visible in the form of famines, disease, and other human tragedies that are commonly written off as "natural" disasters.[4]

In the contemporary world, it would seem obvious that people living in densely populated less industrialized countries, such as Haiti or Bangladesh, are pressing much closer to nature's limits than are those living in many industrialized ones. But this is not entirely true. These poorer countries lack the technology to enhance the productivity of their own resources and the capital to import resources from abroad. They cannot use strategies that have been pursued by many industrial countries. The Netherlands, for example, one of the world's most densely populated countries, supports its population by casting a large ecological footprint over the rest of the world, obtaining many required resources from abroad, thereby substantially augmenting its own resource base.[5]

As the world's population has grown dramatically, and an energy-intensive industrial revolution has spread across the face of the Earth, maintaining access to adequate supplies of natural resources has become a critical concern for many countries. Some industrialized countries have grown economically by using mostly indigenous resources, while others have acquired them from abroad, either through trade or use of force. Many European countries supported their early industrialization with ample domestic coal reserves, but now must import substantial quantities of petroleum and natural gas. The United States originally was endowed with generous quantities of petroleum, but decades of consumption have depleted reserves, and now more than half of petroleum consumed comes from abroad. The Japanese have never had large reserves of petroleum and natural gas, and have geared their foreign policy to ensure supplies from other countries. Thus, large quantities of petroleum and other resources are now traded in increasingly global markets in order to meet deficiencies in countries that don't have resources adequate to meet domestic needs. But given the size of the world's growing population, and the industrialization aspirations of populous countries such as China, India, and Indonesia, there is legitimate concern about both the future adequacy of the world's natural resource base and the integrity of the global systems that provide essential environmental services.

During the late 1960s and early 1970s, a period of rapid worldwide population and economic growth, concern developed over the ability to meet the projected resource requirements of a future, more densely populated and industrialized world. In March 1972, a group of scientists and politicians attending a meeting at the Smithsonian Institution was shocked by a presentation based on computer projections that indicated "if the present growth trends in world population, industrialization, pollution, food production, and resource depletion continue unchanged, the limits to growth on this planet will be reached sometime within the next one hundred years."[6] With sales undoubtedly spurred by the first energy crisis in 1973–1974, and the related panic over gasoline, the book previewed at the Smithsonian meeting, The Limits to Growth, raised consciousness of a "global problematique," a baffling and seemingly intractable tangle of future growth-related planetary environmental and resource difficulties.

The concern over limits was picked up by the Carter administration, which commissioned a large interagency study of future population, environmental, and resource problems. The group that coordinated this Global 2000 Report concluded its evaluation of population and resource trends with a letter to the president with this warning:

Environmental, resource, and population stresses are intensifying and will increasingly determine the quality of human life on our planet. These stresses are already severe enough to deny many millions of people basic needs for food, shelter, health, and jobs, or any hope of betterment. At the same time, the Earth's carrying capacity—the ability of biological systems to provide resources for human needs—is eroding. The trends reflected in the *Global 2000* suggest strongly a progressive degradation and impoverishment of the earth's natural resource base.[7]

While the subsequent Reagan–Bush years in the United States were a period of nonbenign neglect of global environmental issues, international organizations stepped forward and raised new questions related to the long-term sustainability of growth in resource consumption. In 1987, the World Commission on Environment and Development, which focused on problems of long-term sustainable development in a world in which "the results of the present profligacy are rapidly closing the options for future generations," presented their report to the General Assembly of the United Nations, thus legitimizing concern over future sustainable development.[8] Since that time, a number of conferences, including the Rio Conference on the Environment and Development in 1992, and a sustained effort to assess the impact of global warming, have taken place under the auspices of the United Nations Environmental Program (UNEP) and the Intergovernmental Panel on Climate Change (IPCC).[9] In the United States, the election of the Clinton–Gore team in 1992 and the publication of the then–vice president's book *Earth in the Balance* brought many of these issues once again to public attention.[10]

The extent to which environmental and resource problems may stymie future industrial growth and/or lead to conflict remains a topic for much more research. Some argue that most required resources are abundant, environmental conditions are improving, and looming problems will be solved by a combination of human ingenuity and new technologies.[11] People in this camp generally recognize no resource limits to growth, and anchor their arguments in extrapolations from past performance. On the other hand, numerous others foresee the approach of limits on a global scale, and a future of linked population problems and resource dilemmas. While a decline in the prices of many basic commodities over time seems to buttress somewhat the case of the former, events of the last three decades—two major and two lesser oil crises; sporadic localized food shortages and famines; a decline in per capita fresh water quality and availability in many parts of the world; a deterioration in the health of the world's oceans and fisheries; a diminishing supply of stratospheric ozone;

substantial evidence of global greenhouse warming; and an increased incidence of infectious diseases—all tend to support a somewhat less bullish position.

Sorting out the future impacts of natural resource and environmental limitations on ecological security is a challenging task. The pessimistic forecasts made in the 1970s assumed that rapid growth in population and resource consumption associated with the global spread of industrialization would continue indefinitely. But slowing rates of population growth (possibly a reaction to the pessimistic forecasts themselves), lengthy periods of lackluster economic growth in many parts of the world, an economic structural transformation taking place in advanced industrial economies, and technological innovations leading to new efficiencies in mineral extraction and use have combined to keep down demand for and prices of many basic commodities. On the other hand, if the future industrialization and consumption aspirations of China, India, Indonesia, and other poor countries with large populations are to be met, this would put tremendous pressure on the world's resource base and severely tax the natural systems that provide critical environmental services.

Resources differ in both their abundance and importance. Without oxygen, water, or food, human beings would quickly perish. But if all of the bauxite in the world were to disappear over the next ten years, life would still go on. With only a few exceptions, nonfuel minerals are still relatively abundant and widely distributed over the surface of the Earth. A huge increase in consumption would be required to deplete them. But the future supplies of fossil fuels and water are much more problematic, as is maintaining the integrity of the Earth's atmosphere and hydrosphere in the face of continuing industrialization.

Energy is the most critical of needed resources because it can be used to create or transform others. Adequate fresh water supplies are a problem in many areas of the world. Abundant and cheap energy, were it available, would make desalinization a feasible solution in many places. Future increases in world food production are unlikely to come from bringing much new land under cultivation, but mainly through increased mechanization of farms and the use of more irrigation and fertilizer. And if there were abundant and cheap energy, marginal deposits of many nonfuel minerals would become economically viable, thus increasing world reserves considerably.

Assessing the adequacy of the world's natural resource base and environmental systems to support future growth in human populations and material consumption is a complicated, but urgent, matter. The rapid growth of the world's population combined with a surge of industrialization is severely stressing the physical environment. The extent to which resource-intensive industrialization and mechanization of farming take place in countries like India, China,

and Indonesia, which together account for nearly 40 percent of the world's population, will largely determine the fate of the atmosphere, energy reserves, and
many other species that share the planet. The remainder of this chapter
addresses crucial questions concerning the ability of the hydrosphere and atmosphere to continue to provide the resources and environmental services that are
critical to future ecological security.

Water: Not a Drop to Drink

When seen from space, Earth appears to be a planet with a superabundance of
water. Unfortunately, 97 percent of this water is saline and found in the world's
oceans and seas. Much of the remainder is locked in glaciers and permanent
snowcover. Less than 1 percent of the total water supply is readily available as
fresh water for human use.[12] Even so, the total amount of fresh water presently
available is more than enough to meet needs on a global scale, if it were distributed more evenly. But this is not the case.

The world's rivers, streams, lakes, and aquifers provide the fresh water
essential for life on the planet. On a global scale, agriculture is by far the biggest
consumer of fresh water, accounting for 69 percent of all available water withdrawn. Industrial uses account for 23 percent of withdrawals, and the remaining 8 percent is accounted for by domestic uses.[13] But the hydrosphere also
provides other important services. The world's surface water is the habitat for
thousands of marine and freshwater species. It also serves as a system for dis-
persion of human wastes and the effluents from industrial processes. And,
though the precise ways in which the hydrosphere shapes the world's climate is
unclear, an essential role for the oceans in moderating it is undisputed.

In addition to these services, the world's waters are a source of many
resources on which people have come to rely. The most obvious include the fisheries that provide an increasing share of the world's protein and calories.
Worldwide, more people get their protein from fish than any other source;
between 15 and 20 percent of all consumed animal protein comes from aquatic
animals.[14] In addition to serving as an essential food source, fisheries support an
estimated thirty million jobs around the world, of which 95 percent are in the
Global South.[15] Fisheries also help countries in the Global South earn foreign
exchange. Approximately half of the world's fishery export trade originates in
the South, and 85 percent of this trade is exported to countries in the North.
And, as a result of fish farming, these figures are growing.[16]

In addition to these more traditional resources, other marine resources are
just beginning to be explored and understood. The wealth of biodiversity exist-

ing in marine ecosystems around the world is of increasing potential importance in an era of biotechnology. For example, coral reefs are commonly considered the aquatic equivalent of terrestrial rainforests, with a rich diversity of plant, mammal, and fish species. But there currently is a growing tide of human threats to the world's oceans, lakes, and rivers, putting the services and resources upon which human societies have come to depend at increasing risk.

There are currently about 6,918 cubic meters (m^3) of surface freshwater runoff available annually for each of the Earth's inhabitants. About 8 percent of this supply is withdrawn for use each year. Availability varies greatly among regions. In South America, 28,702 m^3 of water are available per person, while water availability in Asia is less than 15 percent of that figure. Europe is also relatively short of fresh water with only 8,547 m^3 available per person. In both Asia and Europe, 15 percent of all available runoff is withdrawn each year, while in South America only one percent is withdrawn.[17]

These variations in water distribution and availability become more stark when countries are compared. In Brazil, 31,424 m^3 are available per person annually, while in the United States, the figure is only 8,983 m^3. Nearly 20 percent of available water is withdrawn annually in the United States. In the world's more arid countries, however, water is much less available. In Egypt, there are

TABLE 3.1.	Renewable Water Resources (RWR) and Estimated Year 2000 Per Capita Withdrawals (PCW)—Selected Countries	
Country	Annual RWR (km³/yr)	Estimated PCW (m³/yr)
Brazil	6,950	216
Canada	2,901	1,431
China	2,830	412
Congo, Democratic Republic	1,019	7
Czech Republic	58	269
France	198	591
India	1,907	497
New Zealand	397	532
Nigeria	280	100
Russia	4,498	527

Source: Gleick, *The World's Water 2000–2001*, tables 1 and 2.

TABLE 3.2. Shared International River Basins		
Basin	Area of Basin (km²)	No. Sharing Basin
Danube	779,500	17
Nile	3,038,100	12
Niger	2,117,700	11
Congo/Zaire	3,699,100	11
Rhine	195,000	9
Zambezi	1,388,200	9
Amazon	5,866,100	8
G-B-Mª	1,675,700	8
Tarim	950,200	7
Jordan (Dead Sea)	42,800	7

Source: Gleick, *The World's Water 2000–2001*, table 7.
ªGanges–Brahmaputra–Meghna

only 43 m³ of water available per person, and theoretically all of it is now being withdrawn from streams at least once. Similarly, in Israel there are only 289 m³ per person, and withdrawals represent 109 percent of the water available.[18] China, with its huge population, has 2,231 m³ available per person, with annual per capita withdrawals averaging 461 m³, or about one fifth of the available surface water supply. In China, as in many other countries, there are large discrepancies in local availability, and the uneven distribution of water supplies has left people in some regions woefully deficient.[19]

Access to water is a source of tension and potential conflict in many regions, since nearly half of the world's land area is in water basins shared by two or more countries.[20] Nineteen of the world's largest rivers have five or more countries sharing the river basin. The Danube River has seventeen countries sharing its basin. The Congo and Niger Rivers each have eleven countries sharing their basin.[21]

The arid Middle East is the region experiencing the most obvious water-related tension.[22] Turkey maintains control of the flow of the Euphrates River into Syria and Iraq, and periodically has restricted the river's flow in order to fill a huge reservoir behind the Ataturk Dam. Israel is chronically short of water, and water politics has worsened tensions with Israel's neighbors as well as with

Palestinians. Egypt relies almost totally on the Nile River for irrigation water, and is dependent on upstream countries, Ethiopia, Uganda, and Sudan, to maintain a steady flow. But these upstream countries have their own rapidly growing populations, and a need for more Nile River water for new irrigation projects.[23]

Other regions have similar potential water rivalries. In South America, thirty-eight rivers flow through more than one country. Brazil is in a dominant upstream position on several rivers, and this has sparked tensions with Argentina over new dam construction. South Asia has several tense situations related to river systems shared by India, Pakistan, Nepal, and Bangladesh.[24] And tensions between the United States and Mexico, as well as among western states, persist over use of Colorado River water that flows south from the United States into Mexico.

The condition of this global fresh water supply also is a cause for concern in many parts of the world. Nearly 1.2 billion people lack access to clean drinking water, and 1.7 billion have no access to a sanitary sewer system.[25] In both industrial and industrializing countries, water quality has been compromised by wastes, pesticides, and fertilizers. In the less industrialized areas of the world, human sewage is still a major cause of water pollution. In these areas only about one-third of rural residents and two-thirds of urban residents have access to sanitation facilities; untreated human sewage is frequently dumped directly into rivers.[26] Most of the wastewater generated in the industrial countries now receives some form of treatment before being returned to streams, however, much of that generated in the less industrialized countries is returned to streams without the benefit of treatment.

The situation in India is typical of that in many less industrialized countries. The Ganges River is considered sacred by Hindus, and nearly one million people take a "holy dip" in its polluted waters every day alongside raw sewage and cattle corpses. In the 1990s, more than 400 million gallons of untreated municipal sewage, industrial waste, agricultural runoff, and other pollutants were being discharged into the river every day. Floating cattle carcasses were so common that a special breed of snapping turtle was introduced into the Ganges to reduce the amount of decaying debris.[27] Between 40 and 45 percent of the people who now take a regular dip in the river have skin or stomach ailments, but these people deny that the "holy water" could be responsible.[28] Only about 30 percent of India's one billion people have bathrooms in their homes or easy access to public toilets, and no more than 250 of the country's 4,000 cities and towns have sewer systems. Contaminated water causes about 80 percent of all disease in India, and each year 500,000 children die from diarrhea.[29]

It is estimated that by 2025, one-third of the world's population "will struggle just to find water to drink and bathe in, much less grow food."[30] This threatens the ability of future generations in many areas to meet their water needs. Looming water shortages have occasioned two different kinds of responses. On the one hand is an increasing privatization of water supplies. On the other is a greater emphasis on guaranteeing access to water as a basic human right. The North American Free Trade Agreement (NAFTA) defines ordinary water of all kinds (other than sea water) as a tradable commodity subject to free trade provisions.[31] Thus, Canadians now fear that U.S. companies will get involved with exporting Canadian water to arid portions of the United States. British Columbia banned the bulk export of water in 1998, but an American company filed suit against the Canadian national government, seeking compensation for profits lost because of the province's actions.[32]

A second, and quite different, response to growing water insecurity is to press for public access to an adequate supply of fresh water as a basic right. Peter Gleick has argued that a basic right to water has implicitly existed in human rights declarations since the Universal Declaration of Human Rights in 1948, and that explicit references have been made at various international environmental and water conferences since the 1970s.[33] Although estimates vary for what should constitute a basic water requirement (BWR), they tend to fall between 20 and 40 liters per person per day for drinking water and sanitation services. An additional 15 liters is required if water for basic food preparation and bathing is also included. Gleick recommends that a BWR of 50 liters per person per day be set to meet these four core needs.[34]

Protecting the Oceanic Commons

Oceans are a fragile commons that holds a treasury of resources that are of growing importance to human welfare. But as human populations have continued to grow and technological advances in fishing have improved efficiency in the industry, the rate at which the world's fisheries are being depleted has increased rapidly. Estimates suggest that over two-thirds of the world's main fish stocks are either fully exploited (44 percent), overfished (16 percent), depleted (6 percent), or slowly recovering (3 percent).[35] The need to protect the long-term sustainability of these common property resources has led to concerted efforts to make short-term sacrifices in order to allow the fisheries to recover and replenish. There is now a notable shift away from resource allocation in fisheries toward resource conservation and longer-term stewardship. A large number of local, regional, and migratory fisheries treaties aim at ensuring the long-term sustainability of species.

Fish are not the only living marine resources in need of protection. Many other marine species, including marine mammals, avians, amphibians, and invertebrates, have been overhunted or overfished, leading to severe population declines, or even extinction. Other factors contributing to the decline include pollution, disease, and loss of habitat. As a result, the number of marine species listed as either threatened or endangered under the U.S. Endangered Species Act increased from twenty to sixty-one between 1975 and 1999. Another forty-two marine species are considered candidates or have been proposed for listing.[36]

Protecting living marine resources (LMRs) requires more than simply limiting hunting and fishing activities. Preserving LMRs requires protection of ocean and coastal habitats so that marine species have a healthy place in which to live. Ocean and coastal habitats in the United States support some of the most valuable and diverse biological resources known, including 66 percent of all U.S. commercial and recreational fish and shellfish, 45 percent of all protected species, 50 percent of nongame migratory birds, 30 percent of migratory waterfowl, and thousands of other species. Preserving habitat integrity requires the protection of areas along the coastal zone, including estuaries, wetlands, and marshes. Even areas far removed from the coast, such as a river's watershed, can impact marine health. As the transition areas between land and sea, coastal zones play a critical role in linking land-based human activities with marine ecosystems.

Threats to fisheries and marine species habitats come in several forms including the damming of rivers, coastal zone development, and point and nonpoint sources of pollution. Historically, rivers have been dammed, seawalls have been built, and other types of alterations have been made in order to make nature conform to the perceived needs of society. Although well intentioned, these structural alterations often have resulted in sedimentation problems in rivers and streams, beach erosion, and the near elimination of fisheries spawning in some areas. For example, the extensive damming of the Columbia and Snake Rivers in the northwestern United States has resulted in the severe decline of several species of salmon. Fortunately, one of the trends that has recently emerged has been a shift in thinking about the value of dams. The average number of new large reservoirs built per year declined in all regions of the world from 1980 to 1998, even though the cumulative total continued to grow.[37]

Other threats to LMRs come from both point and nonpoint sources of pollution. Point sources include pollution from ships, factories, and coastal development. Nonpoint sources are more difficult to identify because they can be either spatially or temporally distant from the resulting pollution. Typical nonpoint sources of marine pollution include lawn fertilizers and agricultural runoff. The resulting nutrient overenrichment has created areas with seasonally depleted oxygen levels (hypoxia). This, in turn, has resulted in places devoid of marine life, known as dead zones. There has been a persisting dead zone in the

Gulf of Mexico at the mouth of the Mississippi River. The Mississippi River flood of 1993 caused a doubling of the area affected by hypoxia in the Gulf, and the dead zone expanded to over 18,000 square kilometers, remaining about that size for several years thereafter.[38] Other evidence of marine pollution is manifest in the form of red and brown tides, areas of explosive and overwhelming algal growth, and the emergence of microbial predators, for example, pfeisteria, which attack species of fish and, in turn, threaten human health.

Given the serious nature of these challenges, some progress has been made in many issue-specific areas that can be addressed by regional and international agreements. Progress also has been made in scientific assessment and monitoring in order to ensure the sustainable health of the oceans and their living resources. Improved understanding has led to the establishment of marine sanctuaries and protected areas around the world. Improved data gathering has led to better understanding of complex interactions between people and the oceans, and resulted in integrated coastal zone management plans.

At the same time that technology has been aiding in the fight against marine ecosystem degradation, reinvigorated efforts at international cooperation, supported by the umbrella agreement of the United Nations Convention on the Law of the Sea (UNCLOS), have been evolving. In addition to the UNCLOS treaty, marine habitat and species protection is framed in more than thirty-five agreements dealing with specific use and access issues under the auspices of the International Maritime Organization (IMO). Complementing these international efforts are numerous bilateral and multilateral agreements that specifically address local and regional issues. In addition to fisheries-specific agreements, there are other agreements to address the overharvesting of specific marine species such as whales or sea turtles and agreements to address marine mammals in general, including the Convention on the Conservation of Antarctic Marine Living Resources and the Convention on the International Trafficking in Endangered Species.[39] These continuing efforts provide a sense of optimism for the future. Although the United States is not yet one of the 133 parties to the third UNCLOS treaty, much of the treaty has become customary international law, and therefore prevails on the world's oceans and waterways.[40]

Taken as a whole, the framework of the third UNCLOS treaty mirrored closely the theoretical arguments articulated by Garrett Hardin in the late 1960s. Hardin argued that commons could only be protected from overutilization and eventual ruin in one of two ways: either by the establishment of mechanisms for coercion mutually agreed upon by the majority of the people affected, or by privatizing common pool resources into individual and exclusive territorial claims. In negotiating the UNCLOS treaty, the countries of the Global South, for the most part, pursued the first path toward sustainable usage by arguing that the resources of the oceans are the common heritage of mankind, and therefore should be managed and utilized to the benefit of all states and peoples. Conversely, the industrialized countries of the Global North pursued the second path. They worked to privatize the oceans by arguing for larger territorial seas, claimed exclusive access to the resources of the outer continental shelves of coastal states, demanded new and larger Exclusive Economic Zones (EEZs) of 200 miles, and suggested proprietary rights to newly discovered manganese nodule fields on the deep seabed. By the end of the negotiations in 1982, the third UNCLOS treaty was responsive to almost all U.S. interests with the single exception of deep seabed mining provisions. And all countries are currently seeking to expand their EEZs by virtue of a provision that allows them to move beyond 200 miles if they can prove that a "natural prolongation" of their land mass goes further. This could ultimately result in 5 percent more of the ocean floor being claimed as EEZ.[41]

In the late 1960s, discovery of polymetallic "manganese" nodules on the floor of the ocean stimulated interest in harvesting these resources. These nodules contained, among other minerals, small amounts of cobalt and manganese, both of which were considered strategic metals. This discovery, of potential strategic and commercial value, inflated the perceived importance of deep seabed mining. As originally negotiated, the United States and other countries of the Global North objected to the deep seabed provisions on economic and institutional grounds. The economic objections were based on the envisioned mandatory technology transfers to a mining arm of an International Seabed Authority (ISBA) known as the Enterprise; competitive advantages granted to the Enterprise such as guaranteed loans, direct subsidized funding, a ten-year exemption from royalty payments to the ISBA; and a requirement that mining consortia relinquish to the Enterprise one-half of each claimed mine-site.[42] Objections of an institutional nature included opposition to a 25 percent U.S. funding requirement without guarantees of U.S. representation on the ISBA Council, lack of a U.S. veto over binding decisions of the ISBA, and the ability of the ISBA to impose production limitations on all seabed mining. Taken together, these economic and institutional requirements were unacceptable to the United States and some other industrial countries. As a result, the United States and most other industrialized countries chose not to either sign or ratify the UNCLOS treaty, and instead began to establish bilateral agreements among themselves to recognize private claims to deep seabed mining sites and the mineral resources located within.[43]

In 1990, the United States, working with the United Nations, initiated and led new negotiations that revised the deep seabed part of the UNCLOS treaty.

The agreement completely eliminated technology transfer requirements, restricted subsidies for seabed mining, and eliminated the ability of the ISBA to establish production limits for protecting land-based producers. The agreement established a finance committee comprised of the five biggest contributors to the budget, including the United States, and guaranteed the United States a seat on the ISBA council. This guaranteed seat would allow the United States, acting in concert with only two other industrialized countries, to effectively veto decisions in the council.[44] The agreement was opened for signature in July 1994. Shortly after, President Clinton signed both the UNCLOS treaty and the agreement, and sent them forward to the U.S. Senate for ratification. To date, the Senate has not taken action on either the Law of the Sea Treaty or the Agreement on Deep Seabed Mining, and it is doubtful that it will in the near future.

Atmospheric Turbulence

The most important service provided by the atmosphere is to supply people with an adequate quantity of fresh air. In much of the world, particularly in rural areas, an abundant supply of clean air is available. Most of the industrialized countries have made steady progress in reducing stationary point-source air pollution, but, particularly in the United States, urban air pollution from an ever-increasing number of automobile, truck, van, and sport utility vehicle emissions is a growing problem. The most serious threats from air pollution, however, are found in the rapidly growing cities in industrializing countries. Although the damage from such pollution is very difficult to measure, it is evident that hundreds of thousands of people in the Global South die annually from diseases related to air pollution, and hundreds of millions of lives now are being shortened because of foul air.

Mexico City and Cairo are typical of these large, industrializing, and highly polluted cities. With nearly seventeen million inhabitants, Mexico City is the second largest city in the world. Located at an altitude of nearly 7,300 feet, pollution of its relatively thin air is a serious problem. A tremendous amount of smog is generated by small factories and the more than three million automobiles on urban streets. Air quality readings rise to dangerous levels on about one-third of all days each year.[45] In Cairo, more than twelve million people are regularly exposed to "black fog," a product of vehicle exhaust, lead fumes, and other gases and particulates held in place by atmospheric inversions. The city has some of the worst air on Earth. It is estimated to cause between ten thousand and twenty-five thousand deaths per year.[46]

Although polluted air remains a serious local or even regional problem in many areas of the world, industrialization continues to generate much more serious long-term threats to atmospheric integrity. The atmosphere performs other vitally important services, including protecting life on Earth from penetrating ultraviolet radiation from the sun and acting as a blanket to keep the planet warm. Without the presence of essential atmospheric trace gases, all life forms would be continually bombarded by lethal ultraviolet radiation, and temperatures at the surface of the Earth would be about $33°$ C colder, similar to those found on the surface of Mars.

Life on the Earth's surface is protected from deadly ultraviolet solar radiation (UV-B) by stratospheric ozone. Ozone found near the Earth's surface, often above cities, is considered to be a pollutant. But ozone in the stratosphere, where about 90 percent of it is located, is essential to human survival. Although often mentioned as a "layer," this protective ozone is actually found in small quantities moving throughout the stratosphere. If it were actually a layer, it would be less than 3 millimeters thick. The formation of ozone molecules is catalyzed by intense sunlight, and thus much of it is formed over the equator and only gradually migrates toward the polar regions of the planet.

Three decades ago, scientists hypothesized that the release of chlorofluorocarbons (CFCs) and closely related chemicals into the stratosphere could destroy these protective ozone molecules.[47] CFCs and their close relatives such as halons, carbon tetrachloride, and methyl chloroform, have numerous uses. For example, large quantities of CFCs have been used in refrigerators, air conditioners, sterilization processes, and the production of Styrofoam. But research has established that, once released, CFCs can move slowly from the Earth's surface into the stratosphere. Once they reach the stratosphere, they remain there for an average period of fifty years.[48] In the stratosphere, these molecules slowly break down and release chlorine atoms, initiating chain reactions that eventually destroy ozone molecules. It has been estimated that one chlorine atom can be responsible for breaking apart as many as one hundred thousand ozone molecules before sinking back into the troposphere.[49]

Although serious attempts to measure reductions in stratospheric ozone levels didn't begin until the late 1970s, ample evidence of decreases over almost all areas of the world has been gathered. It is estimated that the average concentration of ozone in the midlatitudes has been dropping at between 4 and 5 percent per decade.[50] Recognition that ozone depletion is a serious problem has also been given a boost by the annual autumn appearance of a large ozone "hole" over the Antarctic. In 2000, this Antarctic ozone hole became so large that it reached the Chilean city of Punta Arenas. And filaments of low ozone areas have reached Argentina, and perhaps the tips of South Africa, Australia, and New Zealand.[51] Although direct measurements of changes in the amount of destructive ultraviolet radiation actually striking the Earth's surface are difficult because of the lack of historical data, evidence that ozone depletion is accompanied by greater UV-B radiation penetrating to the surface, particularly in the Southern Hemisphere, is now accumulating.[52] There is also evidence of significant UV-B increase in the Northern Hemisphere.[53]

The decline in stratospheric ozone is having, and will continue to have, a significant impact on evolutionary processes and human health. Future likely risks to people include a much higher incidence of skin cancer and cataracts, and also infectious diseases because of suppression of immune systems. Although the extent of future damage remains uncertain, it has been suggested that every 1 percent decrease in stratospheric ozone will result in a 2 percent increase in skin cancer (nonmelanoma), and a 0.5 percent increase in cataracts. While a significant impact is also expected on the human immune system, there is as yet no basis for accurately quantifying the amount of this potential damage.[54] Ozone depletion will have similar destructive effects on the evolution of plants and animals.

A steady increase in the atmospheric concentration of carbon dioxide and other greenhouse gases is a second major threat to the atmosphere, and thus ecological security, linked to industrialization. These gases have historically provided a protective blanket that keeps the Earth's temperature at a level that can sustain the various existing forms of life. But now carbon dioxide, much of which is an anthropogenic (human generated) by-product of the worldwide spread of industrialization, and a number of other trace gases, threaten to increase global temperatures significantly as a result of their growing atmospheric concentration. Because of both deforestation and the large-scale burning of fossil fuels, the concentration of carbon dioxide in the atmosphere has increased from about 280 parts per million (ppm) at the beginning of the industrial period to about 370 ppm at present.

The physical basis of the global warming phenomenon has been understood for a long time. As early as 1827, Jean Baptiste Fourier argued that the chemical composition of the atmosphere was responsible for keeping the Earth's surface warm enough to support life. Without this "greenhouse effect," the Earth would be barren and cold. In 1896, Svante Arrhenius first theorized that human activities could be responsible for raising surface temperatures by increasing the amount of carbon dioxide in the atmosphere. He speculated that a doubling of carbon dioxide could increase temperatures by as much as 5 degrees centigrade. A permanent carbon dioxide monitoring station was erected at the top of the remote Mauna Loa volcano in Hawaii to check this theory as part of the International Geophysical Year activities in 1957. Since that time there has been an observed increase in carbon dioxide concentration from about 315 to 370 ppm.

Although the general circulation models used to project the future effects of greenhouse gas buildup are quite complex, the basic dynamics of greenhouse warming are not difficult to understand. Greenhouse gases capture long wavelength infrared radiation. Most of the broad spectrum of solar energy that strikes the Earth's atmosphere is unaffected by greenhouse gases. But much of the largely infrared radiation that comes from the Earth cannot easily pass through the blanket of greenhouse gases and escape into outer space. This long wavelength energy is captured by greenhouse gases—carbon dioxide, CFCs, methane, and nitrous oxide, as well as water vapor—and thus warms the atmosphere. Human activities are increasing the atmospheric concentration of these gases, thus leading to a steady warming of the Earth that could have a dramatic impact on the evolution of various forms of life.

The buildup of these trace gases in the atmosphere is now well documented, but there is controversy over the eventual impact of these increases on future global temperatures. Different assumptions programmed into general circulation models yield varying results. Thus, a variety of factors such as anticipated changes in cloud cover, precipitation, aerosols, snow and ice melt, and even such things as the release of additional greenhouse gases from warming arctic tundra can impact estimates of future temperatures. The possibility that people could one day alter their behavior to cut down on future greenhouse gas emissions is also a factor to be considered.

The most ambitious attempt to reach scientific consensus on the likely future impacts of these atmospheric changes is an ongoing study carried out as a joint effort of the World Meteorological Organization (WMO) and the UNEP. The Intergovernmental Panel on Climate Change (IPCC), composed of many of the world's best atmospheric scientists, published its first major assessment of climate change in 1990. Subsequent assessments were completed in 1995 and 2000. Although the estimates of the extent of global warming and associated sea level rise were refined over the decade, the earlier estimates have been largely substantiated by more recent research.

The 1995 assessment anticipated 500 ppm of carbon dioxide in the atmosphere in 2100, if 1994 emissions levels were to continue.[55] The assessment's "central value" estimate of the related increase in mean surface temperature was 2° C over the 1990 figure by the year 2100, although more pessimistic assumptions yielded increases of up to 4.5° C.[56] Such warming would increase the volume of sea water through thermal expansion of ocean water and the melting of polar snow and ice. The central estimate of sea level rise was 49 centimeters between 1990 and 2100.[57]

The 2000 study only slightly revised the earlier work. It found that the average surface temperature of the Earth has increased between 0.4 and 0.8° C since 1861. The last decade was likely the warmest in the twentieth century, and 1998 was likely the warmest year.[58] Snow and ice cover on land and sea has been substantially decreasing, as evidenced by the retreat of Alpine glaciers and disappearance of ice in the Arctic in the summer. Satellite data shows a likely decrease of 10 percent in snow cover since the 1960s in the Northern Hemisphere.[59] Because of ice melt and thermal warming, sea level is estimated to have risen between 10 and 20 centimeters in the twentieth century.[60] Looking forward, the 2000 report used different scenarios to project a range of carbon dioxide concentration in the atmosphere that would likely be between 540 ppm and 970 ppm by 2100, up from 367 ppm in 1999.[61] This would yield a global mean temperature increase of between 1.4 and 5.8° C.[62] Sea level is projected to rise between 0.09 and 0.88 meters over the 1990 level by 2100.[63] The mean ocean temperature and sea level are projected to rise for hundreds of years because of the long time scale on which the deep ocean adjusts to climate change.

Aside from the obvious physical discomfort and heat stress of living in a much warmer world, these projections suggest other serious consequences for human and ecosystem well-being. Efforts to model the environmental impact of global warming over the next century indicate higher maximum and minimum temperatures, and more heavy precipitation events, heat waves, droughts in midlatitudes, and intense tropical storms.[64] The projected temperature increases would likely lead to a substantial worldwide rise in sea level, a significant increase in precipitation in much of the world, and severe flooding. More than half of the people in the United States live in the 772 coastal counties that are adjacent to the Atlantic and Pacific Oceans, the Gulf of Mexico, and the Great Lakes, and obviously would be seriously affected.[65] Low-lying islands in the Caribbean and Pacific might simply disappear. Highly populated low-lying coastal areas ranging from Venice in Italy to cities in Bangladesh are likely to experience tremendous destruction of property, and possibly large numbers of deaths from tidal surges associated with stronger storms and higher sea levels. Venice already experiences significant flooding on an average of eighty days each year from the rising Adriatic Sea.[66] Coastline property around the world, ranging from exclusive beachfront resorts to fishing villages, would likely be eroded by future higher storm-driven tides leaving victims, governments, and insurance companies to pick up the tab for losses.

Recent violent weather events may be harbingers of things to come. In 1998, Hurricane Mitch slammed into Central America leaving over 10,000 people dead. India and Bangladesh have been repeatedly ravaged by strong storms and high tides that have drowned thousands of people in low-lying areas. In 1999, a storm packing 200-mile-per-hour winds and tidal waves of 24 feet killed more than 7,600 people and 193,000 farm animals in India. In 2000, monsoon floods beset the entire South Asia region, killing hundreds and forcing millions from their homes.[67] In the 1990s, major unexpected flooding hit the United States, Mozambique, and Venezuela. In the United States, catastrophic losses from storms, defined by insurance companies as storms causing insured losses over $5 million, have grown steadily from about $100 million per year in the 1950s to $6 billion per year in the 1990s (inflation-adjusted dollars). The number of such catastrophes grew from ten in the 1950s to thirty-five in the 1990s, causing great concern (and rising rates) among insurance companies.[68]

There will be a significant, but uncertain, impact on world agriculture from global warming. Current climate change models are not sufficiently refined to make specific forecasts for various agricultural regions. But hotter and drier summers are a good possibility for many of the world's currently productive agricultural areas. Many of the regions in which agriculture is now flourishing may become deserts, while currently cooler regions, such as Siberia, could well benefit from the warmer temperatures.[69] At a minimum, there will be heavy human and economic costs involved in shifting agricultural production from the presently very productive areas likely to be devastated to presently marginal areas that may have improved prospects.

Climate change will also likely increase the range of various pests and disease organisms that normally thrive in tropical climates.[70] Among the diseases most likely to spread and have a greater impact on the now temperate regions are malaria, schistosomiasis, and filariasis. Dengue and yellow fever are also likely to spread.[71] Seasonal malaria could lead to new epidemics among nonimmune populations, and might also be spread by anticipated "environmental refugees."[72] Small pockets of malaria-bearing mosquitoes already have been found near Washington, D.C., and the tropical West Nile virus has spread to much of the United States. Outbreaks of cholera related to warmer temperatures have been observed in South America and could become more frequent with global warming.[73]

Diplomatic Responses

In the face of these growing challenges to the integrity of the atmosphere and future ecological security, there has been a concerted effort to negotiate international agreements to deal with ozone depletion and greenhouse gas buildup. A flurry of diplomatic action aimed at protecting the integrity of the ozone layer came swiftly, quite likely spurred by vivid satellite images of a growing hole in the ozone layer over the Antarctic. In the late 1970s, the U.S. government responded to public pressure and took the precautionary step of banning the nonessential uses of CFCs, including use as aerosol propellants. The European Community (EC), a primary producer of CFCs along with the United States, did not adopt the U.S. approach that called for cutbacks based on the "reasonable expectation" of ozone depletion. European officials opted for a less precautionary standard that required more direct scientific proof that atmospheric change and health risks were directly related to the use of CFCs and halons. This difference over the kind of proof required before taking action remained at the center of many U.S.–EC disagreements that persisted throughout the ozone negotiation process.[74]

Scientific investigation of ozone depletion continued during these negotiations and new research produced some startling surprises. In May 1985, British scientists announced discovery of an ozone hole, or more accurately the thinning of the dispersed layer of ozone molecules, over Antarctica. None of the computer-generated models predicted this dramatic seasonal thinning experienced during the colder months. Other discoveries also indicated that the ozone depletion problem was worse than previously thought, and added impetus to political efforts to put limits on the production of CFCs and halons.

Continuing negotiations among the industrial countries that produced CFCs and other ozone-depleting gases resulted in the 1985 Vienna Convention for the Protection of the Ozone Layer, a significant step in building a scientific and political consensus that laid the foundation for later agreements. The Vienna Convention recognized that ozone depletion was indeed a problem and that stratospheric ozone should be protected. Signatories agreed to further research and policy coordination while endorsing the application of a precautionary principle where scientific uncertainty remained. Policymakers began anticipatory action to mitigate suspected problems, even though not possessing all the pieces of the scientific puzzle.

The Protocol on Substances That Deplete the Ozone Layer, better known as the Montreal Protocol, was signed in September 1987 by twenty-four countries. Building on an emerging scientific consensus that precautionary action should be taken to reduce the release of CFCs and closely related chemicals, governments agreed that there was a relatively high level of scientific certainty that CFCs and halons were depleting stratospheric ozone. The signatories agreed to specific targets and timetables for reducing the consumption of five kinds of CFCs and three kinds of halons. The initial targets for industrial country signatories called for a reduction in CFC consumption of 20 percent of 1986 levels by the year 1994, and for a reduction of 50 percent of 1986 levels by mid-1999. Halons were put on a less ambitious schedule. Less industrialized countries were given special consideration with delayed timetables (a ten-year grace period) for reducing CFC consumption. These countries were still hesitant to agree to proposed reductions until the anticipated associated economic costs were mitigated with provisions for North–South technology transfer. The protocol also put a prohibition on trade in CFCs with countries that weren't a party to the treaty. Signatories agreed that substitutes for CFCs should be developed as quickly as possible through cooperative research among signatory countries. A series of follow-up meetings in the early 1990s led to agreement that the problem was more serious than originally thought, and to accelerated phaseouts of most ozone-depleting substances.

While the Montreal Protocol is often hailed as a path-breaking model of anticipatory thinking that is much needed in an era of globalization, it is important to note that even accelerated phaseout dates do not mean that the depletion of stratospheric ozone will cease any time soon. CFCs reside for decades in the stratosphere, and continually break down into the chlorine atoms that destroy ozone molecules. There is still haggling over the timetable to phase out consumption of methyl bromide and the hydrofluorocarbons (HFCs), the latter having been developed as more benign ozone-depleting substitutes for CFCs. Some less industrialized countries have actually used their ten-year grace period to increase production of CFCs substantially. China, for example, increased its production from 12,300 metric tons in 1986 to 60,000 metric tons in 1996.[75] And CFC smuggling has become a profitable business that may slow the mending of the ozone layer.[76]

For many reasons, including the much greater magnitude of the challenge, the first international agreement to address global warming wasn't negotiated until 1992 at the UN Conference on Environment and Development. At this meeting, agreement was reached on a Framework Convention on Climate Change, a statement of general principles for dealing with greenhouse gases. The framework convention recognized the need for precautionary measures to protect the climate system and to stabilize greenhouse gas concentrations at levels that would prevent significant anthropogenic interference with the climate system. But the framework didn't establish any binding emissions reductions. It only suggested that the industrially developed countries, responsible for the bulk of cumulative emissions, take the first step and adopt measures to return greenhouse gas emissions to 1990 levels by 2000, a goal that many countries didn't take seriously. And the agreement required very little of the less industrially developed countries that will produce the bulk of future additions to greenhouse gas emissions.

Five years of continuing negotiations resulted in the Kyoto Protocol to the United Nations Framework Convention on Climate Change, which was completed for signature on December 11, 1997. The Kyoto Protocol included binding commitments for emissions reductions of six greenhouse gases by developed countries, but left unanswered the question of any reductions for less industrialized countries. The industrial countries initially agreed to reduce their overall emissions of greenhouse gases to at least 5 percent below their 1990 levels by the period 2008–2012. The protocol was to enter into force when at least fifty-five countries, including parties responsible for 55 percent of all carbon dioxide emissions by industrial countries, ratify the agreement. Since the United States is responsible for nearly one-quarter of the world's total emissions, U.S. ratification is very important to the success of the agreement. The Clinton administration signed the agreement, committing itself to a 7 percent reduction, but never forwarded the agreement to the U.S. Senate, where Senator Jesse Helms was waiting to lead an assault upon it. The Bush administration subsequently scuttled U.S. participation in the agreement, ostensibly because of its likely impact on the U.S. economy and its failure to include targets for less industrialized countries.

Subsequent conferences of the parties (COPs) have focused on controversial and complex issues related to compliance. Some industrial countries, including the United States, could not reach the promised levels of reduction solely by cutting back on greenhouse gas emissions. Thus, mechanisms have been explored for joint implementation of projects. Among these are project sharing among industrial countries, a clean development mechanism (CDM) giving industrial countries credit for related pollution reduction investments in less industrialized regions, emissions trading among industrial countries, and credits for carbon sequestration.

The CDM is aimed at building partnerships between industrialized countries in need of reduction credits and less industrialized countries in need of greenhouse gas–reducing development. Industrial countries can have emissions credits applied to their domestic reduction targets by creating joint ventures with less industrialized countries that will reduce greenhouse gas emissions in the latter. The CDM represents a cooperative approach to problem solving, and offers industrial countries a potentially cheaper way to reduce their greenhouse gas obligations, while offering the less industrialized countries a source of capital and technology to help reduce their emissions. There are still numerous technical issues that must be resolved in order to make certain that such reductions are real, measurable, and long-term.

Significant issues must be worked out to finance the transfer of technology to the countries where it would make the biggest difference in reducing greenhouse gas emissions. But the recent record of foreign aid from the industrial countries to the less industrialized world is not impressive. Incentives will have to be put in place to encourage private sector investment. For example, between 1990 and 1997, funding to less industrialized countries from the Global Environment Facility amounted to only about $5 billion. By contrast, private sector foreign direct investment flowing from the developed to the developing countries amounted to about $250 billion during the same period.[77] Much still needs to be done to create a vision for harnessing this private flow to meet the goals of the Kyoto accords.

Joint implementation and emissions trading among the industrialized countries is also permitted by the agreement. Industrialized countries may collaborate on initiatives and share credit, and those countries that exceed their reduction goals may sell excess emissions reduction credits to countries that are unable to reach their own targets. Creating such credits will obviously require careful measurement and verification to insure the integrity of the product. There is presently no agency that is equipped to do this. But the beneficiaries of such a mechanism would most likely be Russia and the Central European countries, both having cut their emissions as a result of the economic collapse of the 1990s.

Finally, the thorny issue of carbon sequestration must be addressed. The United States had been a strong advocate of credits for carbon sequestration in forests, soils, and wetlands during the pre-Kyoto negotiations. The U.S. State Department has calculated that nearly half of the carbon emissions that the United States would be expected to make beginning in 2008 under the treaty could be covered by carbon sequestration in U.S. forests and farmland. The State Department has calculated the annual removal of 310 million metric tons of carbon dioxide by forests and soils used for farming and livestock in the United States. When engaged in the negotiations, U.S. officials argued that this should be credited against the U.S. target, and other countries have demanded similar credits.[78] Skeptics argue that only sequestration from changes in land use taking place after the Kyoto Protocol was signed should count, and that there is little guarantee that the carbon will stay in these sinks for any substantial length of time.

After the Kyoto Protocol was opened for signature, there were several follow-up COPs in which these contentious issues were more fully discussed.[79] But the United States dropped out as a major player. In March 2001, the Bush administration announced that it would not treat carbon dioxide as a pollutant, and that as far as the administration was concerned Kyoto was dead. This effectively isolated the United States from the other industrial countries that decided to move ahead with refining the agreement at COP 6 in July 2001. Although the original agreement to reduce emissions by industrial countries by an average of

5.2 percent from 1990 levels by 2008–2012 has been reduced to less than an actual 2 percent through various negotiated schemes, the agreement represents a major step forward and demonstrates that the rest of the world is prepared to leave the United States behind. At COP 7 in Marrakech, Morocco, in November 2001, 165 countries worked out final details while the United States simply sent observers.

Summing Up: More Kyotos Needed?

The Montreal Protocol has proven to be a very successful agreement in confronting problems of the atmospheric commons. The key parties used science and anticipatory thinking, and acted swiftly in confronting the challenge. Much has been accomplished since 1987. At subsequent meetings of the parties the timetables for phasing out dangerous chemicals have even been accelerated. But dealing with global warming has been much less resolute, and this raises questions about the future applicability of the Montreal experience, particularly since the United States has reversed itself on the precautionary principle, and now refuses to take ongoing negotiations seriously.[80]

There are many reasons for differences in U.S. enthusiasm for these two agreements, including, of course, changes in domestic politics. The most obvious difference in the agreements is the cost of implementation. While the economic costs of phasing out ozone-depleting substances were not insignificant, the contribution of these substances to gross world product was minuscule. By contrast, the costs of making significant reductions in greenhouse gases are large, costs that the United States seems unwilling to consider. Burning fossil fuels has been at the core of the Industrial Revolution, and is still at the center of the dominant development paradigm. The Kyoto Protocol is really an initial attempt to redefine the direction of world economic development. This is no trivial undertaking.

The ability to reach a scientific consensus on ozone depletion was undoubtedly aided by the limited costs of dealing with the problem, and by the fact that the world's largest manufacturer of CFCs, Dupont, and a small number of other companies, were well on the way to developing substitutes that would be given long-term patent protection. And the graphic image of the hole in the ozone layer opening up annually in the Antarctic galvanized public opinion. The situation is quite different in dealing with greenhouse warming. A broad coalition of vested interests, ranging from OPEC to the automotive industry, initially launched a broad public relations campaign designed to discredit the science behind the Kyoto Protocol. The complex general circulation models used to project future conditions are not easily understood by the public. But most important, there has as yet been no equivalent of the hole in the ozone layer, no smoking scientific gun. Thus, an occasional cold winter or a cool summer gives ammunition to opponents of the Kyoto Protocol, who often argue that the science doesn't take sufficient account of nature's own climatic fluctuations.

The interests of key parties to these two agreements may also differ. The Montreal Protocol deals with a situation that has a harmful impact on everyone. People living closer to the polar regions may be more negatively impacted than those in the tropics, but there are few politicians touting the virtues of higher levels of ultraviolet radiation. Greenhouse warming, however, impacts different regions in dramatically different ways. People living on low-lying Pacific islands or in coastal areas near sea level might well have greater concerns than those living well away from water. And agricultural land in currently marginal growing areas, such as Alaska or Siberia, could well become more productive, while productive land could become desert. Thus, perceptions that there are likely to be winners and losers due to greenhouse warming can only get worse as more refined general circulation models indicate in greater detail the differential consequences of it.

Finally, there are unresolved fairness and equity issues between countries of the Global North and Global South to be addressed in climate change negotiations. These were more easily resolved in the case of ozone. CFCs initially were produced and consumed in the industrialized countries, and the United States took the lead in forging an ozone agreement. Although the less industrialized countries aspired to increase production and use of them, they were given significant side-payments in the form of technology transfer for making substitutes, and a significant delay in implementation. In the case of greenhouse gases, North America and Western Europe have been responsible for about 60 percent of the total human contribution since 1800.[81] While the Kyoto Protocol acknowledges the historical responsibility of the Global North for the bulk of greenhouse gas emissions by exempting the developing countries from binding targets, the focus of future reduction efforts remains divisive. The fact that there are now no future obligations for industrializing countries to control greenhouse gas emissions makes the agreement less palatable to many politicians in the United States. Because China is expected to overtake the United States as the largest producer of greenhouse gases over the next twenty-five years, an agreement that doesn't include eventual targets for the industrially developing world may not have the needed long-term impact.

Although bogged down by continuing negotiations over various compliance mechanisms and the failure of the U.S. Senate to ratify it, the Kyoto Protocol at least represents an initial step in what must be a long-term cooperative effort to confront the many challenges presented by greenhouse warming. Atmospheric scientists, for example, while calling the agreement a laudable and reasonable first step, point out that it would take as many as thirty more Kyoto-type agreements to deal resolutely with greenhouse warming.[82] The challenge is one of developing a governance process that can equitably improve the situation over a period of decades. This ongoing cooperative process must involve both the countries in the industrially developing world that will be responsible for much of the future increase in global greenhouse gas emissions, and the United States, the country now responsible for one-quarter of the world's current greenhouse gas emissions.[83]

CHAPTER FOUR

Global Energy Politics: Cycles of Insecurity

A N ADEQUATE and reasonably priced supply of energy is a crucial component of ecological security in the contemporary world. During the course of the Industrial Revolution, productivity has been greatly enhanced by burning ever larger quantities of coal, petroleum, and natural gas. In addition to heating homes, fueling vehicles, and powering factories, computers, and telecommunication systems, energy from fossil fuels has been used to transform ecosystems and enhance supplies of other kinds of resources. Food production, for example, has been increased through mechanized farming and the related application of energy-intensive fertilizers. Shortages of fresh water have, in some cases, been alleviated by using energy to desalinate seawater. And energy has been used to melt and recycle metals, thus easing demands for raw materials. But there are increasing limitations on the use of fossil fuels, especially given the growing environmental consequences of their use.

The fossil fuels that have provided much of the energy supply that created the abundance of the Industrial Revolution are now themselves becoming a source of insecurity. Acquiring, transporting, and burning fossil fuels is linked to significant political and pollution problems. The largest reserves of the more desirable fossil fuels, natural gas and petroleum, are found outside the countries that are now the biggest consumers, thus creating vulnerabilities that are a continuing source of potential conflict. And continuing to follow a growth path that depends upon using significantly larger quantities of petroleum and natural gas is not possible in the long term, given the twin constraints of resource depletion and global warming.

Twenty-five years ago, energy expert Amory Lovins called attention to the need to develop alternative, more ecologically secure, energy sources for the future. He warned of the security consequences of dependence on technologically complex and environmentally disruptive energy sources, and suggested the need to follow a "soft energy path," characterized by energy conservation and development of clean, renewable, and decentralized sources of energy.[1] While two energy crises led to progress in this direction, a subsequent glut of cheap oil and lack of a coherent energy policy in the United States have undone much of the progress that was made.

Over the long span of history prior to the onset of the Industrial Revolution, renewable energy from the sun in various forms—moving water, wind, biomass—was the soft power source that shaped the evolution of human societies. Economic growth and related sociocultural changes that took place within the constraints of this solar income were sustainable, as energy from the sun could be relied upon to be relatively constant for a very long period of time. But many of the huge subsequent gains in output during the Industrial Revolution involved the use of fossil fuels to do work previously done by human beings and draft animals. Over the last century, the growth of the automotive industry, factory production, and mechanized agriculture has begun to reduce ecological security by moving energy consumption in most industrial societies well beyond levels that could feasibly be supplied by current solar income, or even by domestic supplies of petroleum and natural gas. And this type of fossil fuel–dependent growth cannot be sustained indefinitely, particularly in densely populated developing countries, because supplies of the cleanest and most useful forms of these fund sources of energy are limited, and there are tightening environmental constraints on their use.

Energy from fossil fuels has been essential to the economic development that has accompanied the worldwide spread of an industrial way of life. Coal initially provided energy for factories, home heating, and rail and steamship transportation. Over time, cleaner-burning petroleum and natural gas gradually supplanted coal in many of these applications. But industrial growth and steadily increasing automobile ownership have strengthened demand for petroleum around the world, and have begun to put pressure on reserves that were once thought to be infinite. While world coal reserves are still quite substantial in relation to projected future demand, the less polluting fossil fuels, petroleum and natural gas, are in relatively limited supply in the face of projected future demand for them.[2]

Although the quantity and quality of the world's remaining fossil fuel supplies are clearly critical ecological security concerns, the nature of the worldwide energy industry is also of special interest in an era of globalization. The petroleum industry was one of the first to establish a global reach. It has seldom been free of attempts to limit production and fix prices on a worldwide scale, as first oil companies, and eventually exporting countries, used control of oil to build concentrations of political and economic power. Beginning with the Standard Oil Trust in the last quarter of the nineteenth century and continuing through the reign of the Seven Sisters and then the Organization of Petroleum Exporting Countries (OPEC), the global petroleum industry has been characterized by vertical integration, supply manipulation, and price-fixing agreements.

The paradox of the petroleum market is that while in the long term reserves are limited in relation to projected demand for them, in the short term there are many competitors seeking to quickly exploit seemingly abundant petroleum reserves. Petroleum markets have never been characterized by a long-time horizon, and this perceived abundance leads to periodic intense competition among producers, temporary oil gluts, and often plunging prices. As a result, from the earliest decades of oil production, industry participants have attempted to collude in order to control production and stabilize prices. The Standard Oil Trust dominated the fledgling U.S. market until the trust was broken up by government action in 1911. This shattered monopoly was soon replicated on the international level by a secret cartel controlled by the Seven Sisters, the seven large petroleum companies that conspired to control supply and set prices worldwide for nearly four decades. They were replaced, in turn, by the OPEC cartel composed of oil-exporting countries. From the mid-1980s until the turn of the century, there was no force well-organized enough to mediate among the various diverse producers and control the glut of petroleum making its way to market. But more recently, growing demand for petroleum and initiatives taken by a diverse group of exporters have resulted in a surplus reduction and higher prices.

No one, with the possible exception of commodity speculators, likes unstable oil prices. In fact, stable and reasonable oil prices could be considered to be a critical global public good. Over the last three decades, various kinds of oil price shocks have reverberated through the global economy, calling attention to both the resource vulnerabilities of oil-importing countries and the economic fragility

of oil exporters. The two energy crises of the 1970s and the brief spike in petroleum prices during Operation Desert Storm in 1990 forcefully called attention
to the vulnerabilities of the global economy in general, and petroleum-import-
ing countries in particular, to supply disruptions and related spiraling oil prices.
On the other hand, when oil prices have dropped precipitously, as they did during the 1990s, the oil-exporting countries have faced their own daunting economic challenges. Plunging oil prices in that disorganized market created
economic and political crises in many exporting countries. Russia, Mexico,
Indonesia, and Venezuela, among others, suffered significant economic and
political uncertainty, triggered at least partially by lagging oil prices.

Moving into the twenty-first century, there are three interrelated aspects of
this energy problematique that have different time horizons and degrees of
urgency. First, the most basic enduring problem is one of ecological insecurity
brought on by an imbalance between the likely future supply of petroleum and
natural gas and the projected needs of billions of future consumers. While there
is a spirited debate between somewhat Malthusian academic energy experts and
somewhat cornucopian economists over supply adequacy, there is general
agreement that at some point in the not-too-distant future alternative energy
sources must be developed. And it is obvious to all that, long before that time,
the bulk of oil and gas reserves will be found in only a handful of countries.

This is related to a second and more immediate strategic concern associated
with the geographic disequilibrium between petroleum supply and demand.
Most of the major consumers of petroleum products are now heavily dependent upon imports from only a few politically unstable oil-exporting countries.
Sporadic conflicts and political upheavals in the Middle East, political and economic uneasiness in Russia, and terrorist pipeline and oil field sabotage in many
other oil-exporting countries all focus attention on this more immediate geopo-
litical agenda.[3] Concern over the location of the bulk of world petroleum
reserves and the possibility that flows of oil from exporting countries could be
cut for strategic reasons still haunt policymakers in the industrial world, particularly given the prospect of rising imports by China, India, and other newly
industrializing countries.[4]

Finally, the persisting political and economic core of global energy insecurity is due to the peculiar nature of the global oil market, and the complex
interaction of economic growth, resource availability, energy cartels, and government policies. The oil business is becoming more complex and expensive as
much larger oil companies must now make sizeable investments in new technology, take bigger political risks, and drill in more inhospitable locations in
order to bring new reserves on line. And in an era when governments of some

industrial countries seem hesitant to promote long-term energy policies, and are actually deregulating energy markets, it is difficult to picture them playing a significant role in preparing for future crises, or a long-term transition to soft energy paths.

An Ecological Perspective

Anxiety over energy supplies now focuses on the global petroleum market for good reason. Just under 40 percent of measured world energy consumption comes from using petroleum, a figure that has remained much the same over the last decade.[5] This is projected to change very little over the next twenty years.[6] Although most trains and steamships once ran using coal-fired boilers, and some coal-fired "steamer" automobiles actually were produced in response to fuel shortages during World War II, the world's transportation fleet is now very much petroleum dependent, and cannot shift rapidly to alternative fuels. Furthermore, coal is a relatively dirty alternative fuel, and using a lot more of it is unlikely for environmental reasons. While natural gas is relatively clean burning, its worldwide distribution closely parallels that of petroleum. And difficulties in transporting it long distances, especially by sea, make it an unlikely candidate to supplant petroleum in many applications, at least in the near future.

The long term ecological security problem for the United States, and eventually the rest of the world, is one of an imbalance between future demand for and reserves of petroleum. Petroleum reserves in the United States are estimated to be about 21.5 billion barrels, down from about 27 billion barrels fifteen years earlier.[7] This would only be about five years' consumption if the United States relied solely on domestic supplies. Most other industrial countries face an even bleaker situation. Japan has no significant reserves, and those of France and Germany are very limited. Reserves worldwide, however, are still substantial and have fluctuated around the one trillion barrel mark for the last five years. If no additional reserves were to be discovered, and if all of this oil could be recovered, these reserves would support less than four decades of consumption at current rates. But more than one-half of oil known to be in the ground may never be lifted because of location, high development costs, and technical difficulties.[8]

Forecasting future world petroleum demand is filled with uncertainties. Future consumption will obviously be closely linked to patterns of economic growth. Based on a continuation of historical trends, world oil consumption is expected to increase from the current seventy-six million barrels per day to eighty-four million barrels by 2020. Petroleum consumption in the presently industrialized countries is projected to increase by only 1.1 percent annually over this period. This would yield a consumption figure in industrial countries of fifty-five million barrels per day by the year 2020. In the currently less industrialized countries oil consumption is expected to grow at 3.8 percent annually and reach twenty-nine million barrels per day in 2020.[9] But all of these figures are predicated on a global economy that continues to prosper. A lengthy recession (or depression) could have a dampening effect on oil consumption.

The future supply of petroleum is even more difficult to forecast. Experts differ considerably on what remains to be discovered, particularly given different assumptions about technological innovation and prices. Geologists tend to use physical models of reserves and see impending limits, while economists use price models and come to more optimistic conclusions.[10] While the world will never completely run out of oil, at some point the concentration of production in only a few areas and perceptions of scarcity will cause significant price instability and force an economically painful transition to alternative energy sources. It is difficult to predict exactly when this might occur, but since 1989 new oil discoveries have barely been adequate to replace the amount of oil consumed.[11]

Perhaps the most useful and respected perspective on the future of petroleum is that pioneered by noted geologist M. King Hubbert. Using his vast knowledge of exploration and discovery, Hubbert constructed a bell-shaped production curve in 1956 that tracked past and projected future petroleum production in the United States. His curve indicated that production would peak between 1965 and 1970. The U.S. peak came in 1970, and domestic production has been dropping steadily since then. In 1979, Hubbert went about constructing a similar curve for world production. It indicated a world production peak around the beginning of the twenty-first century. While his appraisal might have been slightly pessimistic, more recent estimates of the production peak now converge on the year 2010.[12]

Regardless of how optimistic or pessimistic future projections may be, there are certain characteristics of the world petroleum supply that make it unlikely to be the energy backbone for world economic growth for more than four more decades. A report from the M. King Hubbert Center for Petroleum Supplies summarizes the reserve situation:

Geologists know several things about the world's oil:

- Less than 5 percent of the world's oil fields originally contained about 95 percent of total world oil.
- The giant oil fields, because of their anomalous geology, are usually discovered early in an exploration cycle and provide enormous amounts of oil rapidly from a relatively small number of wells.

- The geology of the world's currently unproductive basins generally is unfavorable for the formation of giant fields, nor can many be expected to remain undiscovered in maturely explored basins.
- The unconventional oil deposits, such as tar sands and oil shales, cannot replace giant field production on a volume-per-time basis.

The report goes on to state that world oil reserves have increased by more than 300 billion barrels over the last 20 years, but the major factor in the increases was a growth of 250 billion barrels reported in Middle East reserves between 1986 and 1989. "Since OPEC production quotas are partly determined by reserve size, it was more than a coincidence that each country chose this time of market-share competition to increase reported reserves. A more important consideration, however, is whether the reserve increases were political or real."[13]

Fossil fuel reserves come from solar energy converted by photosynthesis into plant and animal life over time. Over the last three hundred million years, an exceedingly small portion of the planet's total dead plant and animal life has been transformed by rare geological circumstances into fossil fuels: coal, petroleum, natural gas, and various other hydrocarbons. These processes work at a glacial pace; the ongoing creation of new supplies can be considered insignificant in relation to contemporary demand for them. While deposits of coal are fairly common throughout the world, petroleum and natural gas have been produced by very unusual geological circumstances that have left limited quantities of these fuels concentrated in relatively few locations.

Coal was the first fossil fuel to be extensively exploited during the spread of the Industrial Revolution. A dirty and bulky fuel, coal is found in relatively copious quantities. Just under one trillion tons of coal are estimated to be in known reserves, and this quantity should be adequate for more than two centuries of consumption at current rates.[14] Much coal is the remains of trees and other plants once located in swampy areas at the edges of prehistoric seas. As seas periodically expanded and contracted, vegetation would flourish, die, and fall into swamps, where it was kept from oxidizing (rotting) by water and the deposition of sands and clays on top of it. Most coal fields have well-defined boundaries and are made up of seams found at various depths. The seams loosely represent various epochs in geological history, working from more ancient deposits to more contemporary ones in moving from deep mines toward the surface. This ancient vegetation, compressed by geological pressures over long periods of time, has become lignite, bituminous, or anthracite coal, depending on the source material, the length of time in place, and the amount of pressure to which it has been exposed.

Petroleum and natural gas are not nearly as abundant relative to present consumption as is coal, because the processes that have created them are much more specialized. Petroleum and natural gas are found to be associated (together) about 50 percent of the time in areas called fields, and in accumulations called pools. Most fields are only a few square miles in size, and even the largest fields seldom exceed 100 square miles. Similar to coal, the material that is now petroleum and natural gas was once organic matter, plants and animals that lived in or near prehistoric lakes and seas. These organisms died and precipitated to lake bottoms and seabeds, where clay sediments and similar materials covered them. Layer upon layer of compacting shale pressured and transformed this organic matter, over very long periods of time, into petroleum and natural gas.

These fuels are not always found where the creation processes began because they have been subjected to geological forces that have squeezed and moved them about. And much petroleum and gas has made its way to the Earth's surface where significant quantities have evaporated into the atmosphere. Much of the rest that remained in the ground migrated into porous source rocks, such as limestone or sandstone, and was kept in place under pressure in impermeable rock formations called trapping structures. Thus, it has been this very rare combination of events, including preservation of organisms in sedimentary basins, tremendous pressure on them over time, absorption into reservoir rocks, and containment within impermeable trapping structures, that has produced contemporary petroleum and natural gas fields. This simultaneous presence of so many necessary geological conditions is unusual, and explains why the world has so few significant petroleum- and gas-producing areas.[15]

Natural gas is somewhat more abundant than petroleum in relation to current demand. If fully exploited, known reserves would support present consumption levels for more than four decades. By contrast, those in the United States would only support about nine years of consumption at current levels.[16] The world's reserves of natural gas are highly concentrated. Russia alone has 36 percent of the world's estimated reserves, and another 36 percent is found in the Middle East. North America and Europe combined have only 8 percent of the world's total reserves.[17] Because of difficulties involved in transporting and handling natural gas, the market for it is far less global than that for petroleum. Natural gas is best transported by pipeline from regions geographically contiguous to markets. There have, however, been attempts to move gas on a continental scale. The former Soviet Union built long and expensive pipelines from Siberia to markets in Western Europe, and a regional network links the United

States, Canada, and Mexico. But much of the natural gas released incidental to petroleum production in the Middle East is still flared (burned) at the wellhead because of the difficulties and costs involved in moving it to potential markets.

Strategic Concerns

Ecological insecurity is not only a matter of diminishing reserves in the long term, it is also accentuated by a current imbalance between the location of contemporary reserves and the places where most petroleum is now consumed. The world's largest reserves are located long distances from the major markets for them. While the industrialized countries are by far the largest consumers of oil, none of them is among the top ten reserve countries. Most of the world's remaining oil is found in the unstable Middle Eastern countries and the former Soviet Union. And there is little indication that these realities will change in the foreseeable future.

The countries with the most significant petroleum reserves are indicated in table 4.1. These figures must be treated with some caution. They are estimated

TABLE 4.1. World Petroleum Reserves (in billions of barrels)				
Country	1978	1986	1994	2001
Saudi Arabia	113	167	260	259
Iraq	34	40	99	115[a]
Iran	45	37	59	99
Kuwait	71	92	95	97
UAE	30	35	62	63
Russia	—	—	—	54
Venezuela	18	56	65	50
China	20	19	30	30
Libya	27	23	37	30
Nigeria	12	16	17	30
Mexico	28	55	50	23
United States	28	27	22	22
Algeria	10	5	10	17
Norway	4	11	17	10
Indonesia	8	8	6	9

Source: "Annual International Outlook," *World Oil* (August of various years).
[a]Claimed by government but not verified

reserves given existing technologies and current prices. If oil prices should increase substantially for an extended period of time, there would be some increase in exploration and development that would likely increase these reserves somewhat. It also must be kept in mind that reserve estimates largely depend on assessments made by governments, and these can be significantly inflated for political and economic reasons. OPEC members, for example, have had an interest in claiming sizeable reserves in order to make arguments within the organization for bigger production quotas. Thus, Iraq's reserves mysteriously jumped from forty billion barrels in 1986 to ninety-nine billion barrels in 1994, and those of Iran jumped from thirty-seven billion barrels in 1986 to ninety billion barrels in 1997. In addition, some less economically developed countries have exaggerated reserve figures in order to try to protect the value of their currencies and attract foreign loans and investments. And estimated Russian reserve figures (and those of the former Soviet Union) have bounced around considerably during the post-communist period of political and economic turmoil.

While keeping the tentative nature of these figures in mind, several things are clear. First, world reserves have remained fairly constant in recent years, fluctuating around one trillion barrels. This lends some credence to estimates that oil production is likely to peak within the next ten to twenty years. Second, the vulnerability of many highly industrialized countries to Middle Eastern producers is highlighted by the fact that only two of them, the United States and Norway, are on the list of countries possessing significant reserves. And reserves are declining in both countries. Finally, the bulk of the world's known remaining petroleum is located in only a handful of countries. Saudi Arabia, now controlling more than one-quarter of world reserves, will be a dominant producer for decades. And the five Middle Eastern countries at the top of the list collectively control more than two-thirds of the world's known petroleum reserves. Russia is also once again becoming a significant producer, and has sizeable reserves that can be exploited.

The United States, Japan, and most European countries are now highly dependent on foreign sources of petroleum. In recent years Japan, for example, has been producing a meager thirteen thousand barrels of oil per day, less than 1 percent of daily consumption.[18] And most of these countries get little energy from other domestic sources. Table 4.2 highlights the total energy dependence of industrialized countries. Of all of the highly industrialized countries, only Canada, Denmark, Norway, the United Kingdom, and Australia produce more energy than they consume. The United States has become less self-sufficient over time. In a little more than a decade U.S. self-sufficiency dropped from 82 percent to 72 percent.

TABLE 4.2. Energy Dependence—Selected Countries (energy production divided by consumption)		
Country	1989	2000
Norway	3.66	5.70
Australia	1.57	1.97
Russia	–	1.54
Canada	1.20	1.39
Denmark	0.45	1.30
United Kingdom	0.96	1.14
China	1.07	0.95
Poland	0.96	0.83
New Zealand	0.85	0.80
United States	0.82	0.72
Netherlands	0.80	0.64
Sweden	0.63	0.62
Switzerland	0.48	0.52
France	0.47	0.49
Austria	0.44	0.40
Germany	–	0.37
Finland	0.28	0.35
Turkey	0.46	0.32
Greece	0.38	0.32
Spain	0.39	0.23
Japan	0.19	0.20
Belgium	0.23	0.18
Italy	0.17	0.17
South Korea	0.27	0.15

Source: U.S. Department of Energy Figures; www.eia.doe.gov/emeu/iea/tablef1.htm (September 8, 2002).

Although the United States is a large petroleum importer, because of substantial natural gas and coal reserves, it is relatively more energy self-sufficient than many other industrial countries. But the United States faces a continuing erosion of its petroleum reserves. The present total of 21.5 billion barrels represents a significant decline over the last fifteen years, but U.S. reserves were once nearly as large as those of present-day Saudi Arabia. Because the first wells were drilled as early as 1859, U.S. producers have worked their way through more than 170 billion barrels of domestic oil.[19] In recent years nearly all of the

United States, including areas offshore, has been scoured in a search for new reserves, but little of significance has been added. Therefore, U.S.-based oil companies have recently invested heavily in exploration for oil in more distant places such as the Alaskan North Slope, the Caspian region in the former Soviet Union, and parts of Africa.

The United States became a significant importer of petroleum in the late 1960s, and net imports of petroleum and petroleum products initially peaked at 8.6 million barrels per day in 1977, representing about 47 percent of consumption.[20] During the economic recession that followed, U.S. imports dropped sharply, reaching a low of 4.3 million barrels per day in 1985. But declining oil prices and economic recovery led to increasing imports in the 1990s. U.S. imports are currently just under ten million barrels per day, representing 54 percent of petroleum consumption.[21] United States oil companies used to be heavily dependent upon imports from the Middle East, but they have diversified sources of supply and now draw more heavily from the Western Hemisphere. In 1980, for example, 40 percent of all oil imports came from Arab members of OPEC. In recent years, this dependence on Arab countries has been reduced to less than one-quarter of all imports, as Mexico, Canada, and Venezuela have joined Saudi Arabia as major sources of supply (table 4.3). In the future Russia

TABLE 4.3. United States Crude Oil Imports (in thousands of barrels per day)	
Source	Amount[a]
Mexico	1,509
Saudi Arabia	1,503
Canada	1,454
Venezuela	1,106
Nigeria	537
Iraq	436
Norway	424
United Kingdom	402
Angola	353
Russia	220

Source: USDOE at www.eia.doe.gov/pub/oil_gas/petro...supply_monthly/current/txt/ Table_35 (September 2, 2002)
[a]May 2002

could also become a significant source of imports. Russia has ramped up production to nearly eight million barrels per day, and is now the world's number one producer. The United States and Russia signed an energy cooperation agreement in 2002, and it is possible that in the future Russia could provide as much as 10 percent of U.S. import requirements.[22]

The immediate security challenge for the United States and other industrial countries is to maintain access to the large supplies of petroleum coming from the unstable oil-exporting regions of the world. This requires not only diplomatic initiatives, but also willingness to use military force, as in the case of Iraq, in order to maintain access to and the security of oil fields, pipelines, tankers, and refineries.[23] For the United States, this also means continuing to walk a delicate political tightrope in the Middle East, trying to maintain good relations with Arab countries while simultaneously supporting its long-time political ally, Israel.

The Middle East remains a seething cauldron of political instability for many reasons. Palestinian–Israeli tensions regularly boil over into serious bloodshed. Iran and Iraq, two key OPEC members, fought a long war of attrition that periodically spilled over into world oil markets. In 1990, Iraq attempted to increase its oil reserves substantially by sending troops into fellow OPEC member Kuwait. And radical Islamic fundamentalists have periodically raised havoc in the region by targeting more conservative governments for elimination.[24]

The importing countries have now suffered through three learning experiences, otherwise known as oil crises, to help them prepare for future supply disruptions. The first of these began in late 1973 when the Organization of Arab Petroleum Exporting Countries (OAPEC) used the "oil weapon" selectively to embargo countries deemed to be sympathetic to the Israeli cause. Although the embargo was only a partial success, it demonstrated what could be accomplished through collective action. This first use of the oil weapon caught the industrial countries totally unprepared, and shook up global politics and economics. Leaders of Arab oil-exporting countries, who had been largely ignored in international political circles, suddenly found themselves being courted by diplomats from importing countries. And support for Israel quietly softened, particularly in oil-dependent countries such as Japan. Perhaps of greatest importance, industrial countries proved willing and able to pay much higher prices for oil, sometimes balancing these expenditures by exporting large quantities of arms to the unstable Middle East. The partial success of this embargo strengthened OPEC's hand and permitted the organization eventually to ratify a new price structure, which represented a fourfold increase in petroleum prices over those in place before the embargo began.

It has been estimated that in the first three years after the embargo, oil-importing countries paid an extra $225 billion into OPEC coffers, and lost $600 billion in productivity during the associated recession.[25] The gravest effects of the price shock were felt in 1974 and 1975 when industrial country growth rates plummeted from a pre-embargo average of 5.4 percent in real gross national product (GNP) to –1.4 percent in 1975. The less industrialized countries that did not export oil experienced a similar drop from a real GNP growth rate of 6.6 percent to 1.9 percent.[26]

The second oil shock was triggered in 1979, a direct result of the Iranian revolution and the overthrow of the shah. This sharp price increase was largely driven by psychological factors, rather than any real shortage of supply, since Saudi Arabia and Venezuela were able to increase production to overcome any general shortages.[27] Although the disruption itself was small and short-lived, a scarcity psychology pervaded the spot market for petroleum, and oil prices doubled. Once again the members of OPEC met and ratified this much higher price structure that was already in place. But the global recession that followed on the heels of this second disruption proved to be more enduring than the first. In the industrial countries there was only modest growth throughout the 1980s, and the non–oil exporting developing countries fared only slightly better.

The 1990 Iraqi invasion of Kuwait sent another price surge, albeit brief, through global energy markets, even though there still was excess production capacity worldwide. A multilateral coalition led by the United States quickly expelled the Iraqi forces from Kuwait during the 100-hour operation "Desert Storm." But Iraqi soldiers, later dubbed environmental terrorists, were able to start several large fires in the oil fields, thus inhibiting oil production for some time. After the fighting, however, oil prices rapidly fell back to their levels of a month earlier due largely to the excess capacity existing in other parts of the market.

In the late 1990s, a period of modest worldwide economic growth increased petroleum demand and OPEC was able to reduce production and thus increase prices. But a subsequent global recession pushed prices down once again. Even the onset of the war against terrorism and the military action in Afghanistan in 2001 did not have an appreciable impact on prices in a glutted market, although the prospect of a war in Iraq and a general strike in Venezuela increased prices sharply in 2003.

The United States and other Organization for Economic Cooperation and Development (OECD) countries obviously have a vital interest in maintaining political stability in the Middle East while continuing to find ways to diversify suppliers. But even the petroleum found outside the Middle East has certain risks attached to it. Russia has substantial oil and gas reserves, but in the past chronic political uncertainty, economic intrigue, and lack of investment capital have made dependence on Russian oil supplies somewhat problematic. After the breakup of the Soviet Union, the petroleum industry suffered major setbacks along with the rest of the economy. Between 1989 and 1994, oil production in the former Soviet Union fell 43 percent. In 1993 alone, capital investment in the Russian petroleum industry dropped by 46 percent.[28] More recently, however, Russia has reemerged as a major oil exporter. This country, which once produced 12.5 million barrels per day, increased production by 1.5 million barrels per day in both 2000 and 2001. The continued expansion of Russian production and exports could represent a long-term threat to the Saudi ability to manipulate oil prices.[29]

There is also considerable interest in oil from countries of the former Soviet Union surrounding the Caspian Sea. But these sources of supply are far from markets, and moving oil via pipelines and tankers through this part of the world is politically and environmentally risky. The infrastructure for the petroleum industry is poorly developed, and early estimates that claimed gigantic reserves in the region have only partially been supported by exploratory wells.[30] This oil, intended to flow westward from Azerbaijan, Kazakhstan, and Uzbekistan, must pass through areas of political and military turmoil on its way to market. There are various routes by which Caspian oil could move, but all are vulnerable to sabotage. A potential route through Iran to the Persian Gulf is unacceptable to the United States for obvious reasons. A proposed pipeline from Baku to the Russian Black Sea port of Novorossiysk passes through rebellious Chechnya. This oil would then be transferred to tankers and carried through the Bosporus to the Mediterranean. The Bosporus narrows to a width of 700 yards as it passes through Istanbul, and the Turkish government has vowed to reduce tanker traffic in the interest of safety. An alternate route passes through potentially unstable territory near Georgia on its way to the Black Sea, and this oil would still have to pass through the Bosporus. The route preferred by the United States and Turkish governments is by far the longest and passes through Turkish territory as it makes its way to the Mediterranean port of Ceyhan. But the involved oil companies are hesitant to spend the two to four billion dollars that the proposed 1,080-mile pipeline would cost.

The insecurities associated with pipeline politics aren't limited to these unstable parts of the world. In Colombia, for example, two guerrilla groups, the National Liberation Army and the Revolutionary Armed Forces of Colombia, are battling for control of the oil-producing region. A 470-mile pipeline that transports oil from the interior to the Caribbean was bombed 170 times in 2001.

In response, the Bush administration proposed $98 million in its 2003 budget to train Colombian troops in pipeline protection.[31] In Nigeria, various tribes have been able to close down oil production facilities as a result of feuds with the government and other ethnic groups, thereby cutting oil production at times by as much as one-third.[32] Such problems aren't limited to distant countries. In October 2001, a man fired a rifle bullet into the Trans Alaska pipeline, which carries 17 percent of U.S. domestic production. This resulted in the loss of 285,600 gallons of oil before the leak could be repaired.[33] And a small group of saboteurs has been at war with the oil and gas industry in Alberta, Canada. Tensions between energy companies and some landowners have escalated into significant violence including cementing in wells and blowing up pipelines and gas wells. More than 160 acts of vandalism were reported in one eighteen-month period in northwest Alberta.[34]

The World Petroleum Market

The oil industry has long had a global reach, and the fortunes of governments and countries have risen and fallen along with oil prices. In fact, the financial assets of many oil companies historically were often larger than those of exporter countries. And they frequently used their economic and political clout to influence politics in many countries. From the time of the Standard Oil Trust, through the heyday of OPEC dominance, and down to the present, the petroleum market has been shaped by political and economic machinations, and economies around the world have been buffeted accordingly.

The oil market has a checkered history, and many of its peculiar characteristics have persisted since the early years. The petroleum era opened in 1859 when Col. Edwin Drake drilled the first commercial well near Titusville, Pennsylvania. During the first decade of production, many of the problems that would characterize the industry over the years became apparent. The initial high prices for the seemingly precious fluid quickly gave way to cheap oil as speculators rushed to the Pennsylvania oil country and drilled more wells in order to cash in on the bonanza. Oil that sold for $20 per barrel in the first year of production was soon selling for less than 10 cents due to the production glut. In the early years, there were numerous conflicts among producers, all of whom were struggling to produce more oil, and the owners of downstream facilities: the transportation, refining, and marketing infrastructure. It was under these tumultuous circumstances that John D. Rockefeller stepped in and took an active role in shaping the market and controlling competition.[35]

Rockefeller got into the oil business in an unusual way. He didn't buy land, drill for oil, or do any of the usual things done by the early wildcatters. Instead, he bought a refining operation in Cleveland. Operating secretly, and sometimes using ruthless tactics, Rockefeller eventually was able to make large profits by controlling the downstream flow of petroleum after it left the wellhead. He cut deals with railroads and built refineries and retail operations as the industry moved west. By 1883, Rockefeller had consolidated his hold on a fledgling national petroleum industry through the Standard Oil Trust. He then bought oil fields in order to make his company fully vertically integrated from the wellhead to the customer, and subsequently moved into the international market. By 1885, over 70 percent of Standard's business was being done abroad.[36]

The size of the Standard Oil empire and the arrogance of its management inevitably led to a public reaction, which found political expression in the Sherman Antitrust Act of 1890. But it then took years for the government to attack successfully the well-entrenched business. In May 1911, the Supreme Court of the United States declared Standard Oil to be guilty of violating the antitrust laws and ordered it to divest itself of all of its subsidiaries, thus dividing it into nearly three dozen separate companies. While this dissolution ended the first near monopoly in the world oil industry, three of the Rockefeller progeny, Exxon, Mobil, and Socal, quickly became dominant forces in their own right, and joined with four other large companies to become the Seven Sisters, a group of oil companies that subsequently formed a new cartel to control the world oil business.

After the end of World War I, the chaos that followed the breakup of the Standard Oil empire slowly gave way to a more organized market controlled by the Seven Sisters. In the United States, Gulf and Texaco established a beachhead in Texas and joined the three Standard Oil offspring as major market players. Gulf Oil was financed by the Mellons out of Pittsburgh and grew courtesy of the huge Spindletop discovery in Texas. Texaco obviously also developed in Texas, marketing cheap oil from Spindletop and another discovery called Sour Lake. These five American companies were joined by Royal Dutch Shell, a British–Dutch company that made its mark in the Far East, and British Petroleum, which owed its origins to oil from Burma and the Middle East. These companies collaborated to form an oil cartel that, for the most part, controlled the world market for decades.

There was little love lost among the heads of these major oil companies and considerable intrigue took place among them. But they shared a common fear of the consequences of real market competition. By 1928, the Seven Sisters had knit together an organization that dominated the world market. This was accomplished partially during a meeting held in Ostend, Belgium, in July 1928, at which oil concessions in the former Ottoman Empire were divided up among four of the Seven Sisters. The so-called "Red Line Agreement" resulted from a red line being drawn on a map around former Ottoman territories, which included oil-rich areas in Saudi Arabia and Iraq. American and British companies agreed to operate through a joint venture, the Iraq Petroleum Company, in order to control production in and limit access to what were to become the great oil fields of the Middle East.

In the same year, the big three oil companies, Exxon, Shell, and British Petroleum, met secretly in order to discuss ways to dampen competition among them. Culminating in a grouse shoot at Achnacarry Castle in Scotland, the meetings eliminated a potentially explosive confrontation among the three. Price wars had broken out in various parts of the international market due largely to a glut of newly discovered oil. New production was coming out of Russia, Venezuela, Mexico, and Iraq. The Seven Sisters, in this distressed atmosphere, began flooding each other's markets with cheap oil. Executives from the big three settled in for two weeks of meetings, dining, hunting, fishing, and negotiating.

The two-week effort culminated in the secret Achnacarry Agreement, which laid out the key principles by which initially the three large multinational companies, and later the other four sisters, resolved to control the growing worldwide market, and thus deal with recurring petroleum gluts. Each company agreed to a quota, maintaining its current volume of production and accepting a similar proportion of any future production gains. New facilities were to be added only in response to increased demand for petroleum. Furthermore, worldwide prices were to be set artificially high by a "gulf plus" formula. This formula, designed to protect increasingly expensive American oil, priced oil delivered anywhere in the world as if it were expensive U.S. oil. Then imaginary freight charges were tacked on to the price as if the oil had actually come from ports in the Gulf of Mexico. Thus, oil being shipped from the Middle East to Western Europe would be billed at the Texas wellhead price, with freight charges added as if the cargo originated in Texas gulf ports.[37]

With small refinements, the Achnacarry Agreement put in place a cartel that persisted into the early 1960s. Although the world market was never completely locked up, because of oil production coming out of Russia and the emergence of several smaller petroleum companies, the Seven Sisters controlled enough of the world's oil and downstream facilities to effectively control prices. By the mid-1950s, the Seven Sisters, with their vertically integrated operations including exploration, drilling, transportation, refining, and merchandising, controlled about 90 percent of the downstream facilities outside of the Soviet Union.

The countries that actually produced oil were relatively powerless in their dealings with the global oil companies during the first half of the twentieth century. Most of them were not full-fledged countries, but confederations of tribes that were passed on as protectorates or colonies from one overseer to another. Even though formal independence came to many of them as part of a package of agreements carving up the Ottoman Empire after World War I, or as part of the more general independence movement following World War II, these fledgling states were in no position to assume a strong posture in negotiations with oil companies that were backed by the political and military clout of their powerful home governments. Mexico tried to deal resolutely with foreign oil companies in 1938, and Iran tried similar tactics under the socialist Mossadegh regime in 1951, but both countries were severely disciplined for their efforts. In each case the British broke diplomatic relations with the offending country, and foreign markets for their oil dried up. Mossadegh was replaced in a counterrevolution reportedly aided by "outside parties."[38]

The ferment that would eventually result in the dissolution of Seven Sister control and the rise of the oil-exporting countries as the controlling forces in the emerging global market began to emerge slowly in the 1950s. On the heels of World War II, small independent oil companies that had been very cautious in earlier years began to move more boldly to exploit new oil reserves outside the domain carved out by the Red Line agreement. These independents, such as Occidental, Phillips, Sun, and Atlantic Richfield, were able to get a toehold in the markets dominated by larger companies by buying and selling petroleum as cheaply as possible. The so-called "majors" were forced to confront the challenge of the independents by adjusting their own prices downward. This sudden vigorous price competition resulted in the "gas wars" of the late 1950s and early 1960s. In order to compensate for lower prices at the pump, the major oil companies, not about to absorb the full impact of the lower prices, forced producing countries to take a substantial cut in their royalties. In 1948, the posted price of a barrel of crude oil, upon which royalties paid to exporting countries were computed, was $2.17. By 1960, the majors had slashed this to $1.80 and subsequent cuts brought the posted price of a barrel of crude down as low as $1.30 by the early 1970s.[39]

The emergence of Russia as a major oil exporter in the decade following World War II also served to loosen up the market and drive oil prices down. Sitting on massive reserves of petroleum, the Russians needed to export large quantities of it in order to get hard currency to help rebuild a war-torn economy. The Soviets sold and bartered petroleum at prices designed to capture markets from established exporters. And the independents were only too happy to buy this cheap oil, which began to pour into storage tanks throughout the world.

The Rise of OPEC

The most important result of these developments was not necessarily cheaper gasoline and oil for consumers, but discontent among the oil-exporting countries that were forced to absorb much of the downward pressure on prices. Venezuela was among those most affected. Higher costs of production for Venezuelan crudes, long distances from European markets, and restrictions on U.S. oil imports combined to nearly drive Venezuela out of the oil business. In response to the price cuts, which made most production in Venezuela marginal, Venezuelan leaders undertook the task of forging producer states into an organization that they hoped would be able to counter the power of multinational oil companies. OPEC was officially founded in 1960 with Venezuela, Saudi Arabia, Kuwait, Iraq, and Iran as charter members.[40]

During its first decade, OPEC had relatively little impact where the vital interests of the oil companies were concerned. The oil companies controlled downstream transportation, refineries, and retail outlets, and remained in a strong position from which they could discipline unruly political leaders by selectively buying crude oil. Furthermore, during this period new oil discoveries in various parts of the world were adding to supply, thus giving the oil companies an opportunity to pit petroleum-exporting countries against each other in a scramble to sell as much oil as possible. Even among OPEC members, a series of meetings was required to formulate any action plan. At that time, the conservative Saudis, their neighbors in Kuwait, and the pro-American shah of Iran were not about to agree to any radical actions that might be suggested by Venezuela or Iraq.

OPEC became a powerful force in controlling the world petroleum market largely because of a confluence of events over which the organization had little control. The closing of the Suez Canal in 1967, as a result of Arab–Israeli hostilities, marked a watershed in relations between exporting countries and the oil companies. Although this closing resulted in no major oil crisis, it did reveal the vulnerability of the Western European importers who were substantially increasing their dependence upon Middle Eastern oil at the time. The canal closing led to only a slight increase in prices as supertankers were pressed into service to carry oil around the tip of Africa to European markets. But these temporary dislocations gave the OPEC countries a slight taste of power that served as a precursor of things to come.

Three factors, in addition to tightening markets, have been identified as ultimately leading to the OPEC price revolution. Inflation ran rampant through the industrial world in the late 1960s and early 1970s, turning terms of trade sharply against the oil exporters. While prices for manufactured products were rapidly rising, the price of oil remained constant or actually declined, thus diminishing the purchasing power of the oil-exporting countries. Second, a rising tide of Arab nationalism upset established political regimes in the area, and led to demands for a different type of relationship with the oil companies. Finally, the continuing Arab–Israeli dispute added a political dimension to events in the world oil market.[41] All of these factors combined to give OPEC more leverage in its relations with the oil companies and, in a meeting of exporting countries and oil companies held in Teheran in February 1971, the producers were able to get an increase in posted prices of 30 cents per barrel. Thus, at the beginning of the October Arab–Israeli war in 1973, the price of a barrel of Saudi marker crude had edged up to $2.55.

But the really significant increases in oil prices during the OPEC decade were catalyzed by the two major oil crises that originated outside of the organization. The first crisis was triggered by the 1973 Arab–Israeli hostilities during which the Organization of Arab Petroleum Exporting Countries (OAPEC), a subgroup within OPEC, declared a selective embargo based on politics. The countries agreed both to cut back oil production significantly and to deny shipments completely to the United States, the Netherlands, Portugal, and South Africa. Remaining countries were placed in one of three other categories and received oil in relation to their perceived sympathy for the Israeli cause.

The embargo and production cuts were only partially effective. The non-Arab members of OPEC continued to produce at capacity, thus easing the impact of the Middle Eastern cuts. There was also considerable transshipment of oil from non-embargoed to embargoed countries. In addition, the embargo really lasted only five months. In the two peak embargo months, November and December of 1973, only 10 percent of the noncommunist world oil supply was removed from the market. But the psychological and economic effects of the disruption were considerable. Countries and companies became locked in a race to get access to available oil supplies. Prices on the Rotterdam spot market for petroleum rose dramatically and, in this panic atmosphere, OPEC members had little trouble coming to agreement on higher prices. By the end of 1973 the price of a marker barrel of crude had gone to $3.60, and by the end of 1974 it had jumped to $10.46. Having ratified these dramatically higher prices, and feeling no repercussions from oil companies or importers, OPEC was then in a solid position to supplant the Seven Sisters in controlling the world market.

The rapid run-up of oil prices had a devastating effect on the international economy, resulting in a global recession that dampened demand for oil in both the developing and industrialized countries. In the twenty-one industrial countries that are members of the International Energy Agency (IEA), consumption of petroleum dropped from an average of 34.2 million barrels per day in 1973 to 31.8 million barrels per day in 1975. In the United States, the drop was from 17.3 million barrels per day in 1973 to 16.3 million barrels per day in 1975.[42] But the recession resulted in price stability in the oil marketplace. The Saudi Arabian marker barrel price edged only very slowly upward, reaching $12.09 in January of 1977.

The lessons of 1973–1974 were quickly forgotten as the international economy began to pick up steam again in 1976. A certain "happy days are here again" euphoria developed in the importing countries, and many experts argued that there could never be another oil crisis. For example, in January of 1974, the respected journal *The Economist* published an article forecasting an impending glut of petroleum.[43] Petroleum consumption rose significantly in the OECD countries and peaked at 41.6 million barrels per day in 1979. OPEC oil production increased along with demand and reached 30.9 million barrels per day in 1979.[44]

The price stability and accompanying economic euphoria lasted until September 1978 when political events in Iran set a second energy crisis in motion. Anti-shah violence erupted in the cities and oil fields of Iran during the last quarter of 1978, resulting in a slowdown of production and eventually a total halt in exports by the end of the year. By March 1979, the new revolutionary government resumed exports, but the panic had already begun. Similar to the first energy crisis, the initial signs of shortage pitted various consumers against each other in a rush to get supplies of petroleum and products. Even though the actual shortage of petroleum for all of 1979 was less than 2 percent of demand, panic drove prices up and OPEC was once again able to take advantage of the situation simply by ratifying the existing higher prices. By November 1979, the marker barrel price had reached $24 and many countries were selling oil at a significant premium over official OPEC prices. The price for a marker barrel of Saudi Arabian light crude hit an all-time high of $35 per barrel in October 1981.

In only a decade OPEC had been transformed from a relatively listless trade association into a powerful political and economic force capable of wresting control of the oil industry from the Seven Sisters and their associates. This sudden rise to power, however, covered over many significant differences among OPEC members that would subsequently limit the power of the cartel. OPEC would never have been able to raise oil prices substantially had it not been for the political and military events that shook the unstable Middle East, and the panic reactions that followed in the oil industry and importing countries. Once the higher prices were established, however, they provided a cement that held the disparate group together until the OPEC decade came to a screeching halt when oil prices plunged in the mid-1980s.

With the exception of a brief price spike associated with Iraq's invasion of Kuwait, petroleum prices continued to languish until shortly before the turn of the century. During this period, conflicts within OPEC, a feeble world economy, and increased petroleum production from non-OPEC countries kept production considerably above demand. The collapse of the Asian economies caused world-wide demand for petroleum to fall even further, from nearly seventy-six million barrels per day in 1997 to seventy-one million in 1998. By the beginning of 1999, the price of West Texas Intermediate crude oil had dropped to nearly $10 per barrel, a level not seen since the early 1970s.

The oil price collapse put severe pressure on the oil industry as well as the exporting countries. The oil companies responded by cutting back on explo-ration and shutting in less profitable wells. The low prices even set off a wave of "mega mergers" among the largest oil companies, further consolidating the industry. Among the larger mergers announced were a $50 billion merger of BP

TABLE 4.4. OPEC Profile				
Country	Reserves[a]	Production[b]	Population[c]	Oil Exports[d]
Saudi Arabia	259	7,750	21.1	56.1
Iran	99	3,661	66.1	20.7
Venezuela	50	2,855	24.6	19.2
UAE	63	1,995	3.3	17.2
Nigeria	30	2,008	126.6	15.3
Kuwait	97	1,665	2.3	14.9
Libya	30	1,408	5.2	10.3
Algeria	17	1,175	31.0	5.6
Qatar	14	828	0.6	5.6
Indonesia	9	1,431	206.1	1.3
Iraq	115	2,571	23.6	14.6

Source: Reserves and production figures from World Oil, "Annual International Outlook" (August 2002); population from Population Reference Bureau, 2001 World Population Data Sheet; oil export revenue from Wall Street Journal (December 31, 2001), 3(A).
[a]Reserves in billion barrels, 2001
[b]Production in thousands of barrels per day, 2001
[c]Population in millions, 2001
[d]Oil exports in billions of dollars estimated for 2001

and Amoco, a $74 billion merger between Exxon and Mobil, and a $13 billion deal between European companies Total and Petrofina. The economies of all of the significant exporting countries were also hit hard by the price decline. The downturn caused recessions, major increases in unemployment, and political instability in the affected countries.

These dire circumstances led the major exporting countries to gather in the Netherlands in March 1999 to discuss ways of dealing with their mutual problem. They reached agreement to slash production by nearly three million barrels per day. This created a gap of nearly 2.5 million barrels per day between the available supply and demand, and stocks were quickly drawn down. The resulting tight petroleum market had the expected impact on oil prices and the economies of importing countries. In response to the production cut, the price of a barrel of crude more than tripled to peak at $34 in March 2000. Gasoline prices at the pump rose accordingly, as did political pressures on leaders of importing countries.

In this environment, U.S. Energy Secretary Bill Richardson embarked on a pilgrimage to the major exporting countries, urging energy ministers to increase production and thus stave off higher energy prices and a potential global recession. These intensive lobbying efforts paid off in March 2000, as OPEC leaders agreed, over Iranian dissent, to boost output by 1.7 million barrels per day. Mexico, Norway, and Oman agreed separately to an increase of 400 thousand barrels per day, thus resulting in a total production increase of 2.1 million barrels per day.[45]

It is unclear whether the reverse price shocks of the 1990s were strong enough to impose discipline on OPEC and major non-OPEC exporting countries, such as Norway, Mexico, and Russia, and reinforce the lessons previously learned about the value of exporter collaboration. OPEC production in 2002 was close to 31 million barrels per day, almost the same as at its peak in 1977.[46] But its market share has dropped almost 20 percent since that time due to newcomers in the marketplace. It does appear that a new coalition of OPEC and non-OPEC exporters could be able to maintain negotiated management of future petroleum production, and thus prices, given a reasonable level of future economic growth. But the early years of the twenty-first century have been filled with political and economic uncertainty, a condition that is hardly conducive to rapid economic growth or stable oil prices.

Energy Crisis Cycles

The world petroleum market is still bedeviled by many of the same kinds of dilemmas that became apparent soon after Colonel Drake drilled his first well. Worldwide economic growth now depends on relatively stable and reasonable prices for petroleum and other fossil fuels. And stable petroleum prices, in return, depend on continuing economic growth. But the petroleum market remains highly unstable, being very sensitive to political events and changing economic conditions. The bulk of world petroleum reserves remains concentrated in only a few countries in the Middle East—the five Middle Eastern countries with the largest reserves controlling nearly two-thirds of the world total. There still is a significant amount of idle production capacity. If market forces were actually setting oil prices, most of the world's oil would be produced in the Middle East for only a few dollars per barrel. But the political reality is that countries as diverse as the United States, Russia, Mexico, Venezuela, and Iran have an interest in maintaining petroleum prices at levels far higher than a free market would dictate. Just as John D. Rockefeller initially solved an oil glut problem by building the Standard Oil trust, the management of oil production is now in the hands of a loose coalition that includes the OPEC countries and a small number of other key exporters.

The erratic behavior of the petroleum market over the last three decades suggests a crisis cycle model that can help explain large price changes and persisting problems of oversupply in the world oil market. The crisis cycle consists of five phases. First, economic growth causes an increase in demand for petroleum in the face of limited unused short-term surge capacity, thus creating a tight market. Second, this sets the stage for an unexpected political or military crisis in the Middle East (or elsewhere) to trigger a panic response, which quickly drives prices upward. Third, these higher prices, over time, elicit several responses: more exploration and production to close the perceived production gap, development of alternative energy sources, and tighter monetary policies intended to fight inflation in importing countries. Fourth, economic recessions, resulting from tight monetary policies in the importing countries, reduce demand for petroleum, resulting in excess production that drives down prices. The final stage of the crisis cycle occurs when the glut of oil and associated steady decline in prices leads to cutbacks in exploration and drilling and dampened enthusiasm for energy conservation. Attempts to develop and commercialize alternative energy sources are also devastated by these low energy prices. But these low prices also set the stage for economic recovery in importing countries, and eventually the creation of another tight market.

There have been two complete crisis cycles, one beginning at the end of 1973 and the other in 1979. Each of these previous crisis cycles began when political and economic conditions combined to produce a tight market for petroleum with oil supplies barely exceeding customer demand. The first cycle was set up by a long period of worldwide economic growth in the late 1960s and early

1970s that resulted in a steady increase in demand for petroleum. By 1973, OECD countries were consuming nearly 40 million barrels of oil per day. At the same time, supply was tightened by politically motivated cuts in supplies from North Africa. The second crisis cycle was set up by a quick spurt of economic growth in the late 1970s. Petroleum consumption quickly rebounded from the 1973–1974 shock, and OECD countries were guzzling nearly 42 million barrels per day by 1979. The trigger for the first crisis was the 1973–1974 Arab–Israeli war and the related OAPEC petroleum embargo. The second crisis cycle was triggered by the ouster of the shah of Iran and the related turmoil in the Iranian oil fields.

In both of these cycles, rising oil prices following political and military crises led to significant economic recessions in oil importing countries. During the first crisis cycle, the price increase was only a few dollars per barrel, very significant but still small enough that these economies only took a short time to recover. The second crisis cycle, however, resulted in price increases of more than $20 per barrel, and the world economy took nearly two decades to recover. As prices rose during the acute phases of these crises, oil companies invested new capital in exploration and development, eventually bringing new production to market. The combination of a recession in the importing countries and increased petroleum production, particularly during the second crisis cycle, led to a glut of petroleum and tumbling oil prices.

The last, and most destructive, phase of each of these previous crisis cycles emerged as a response to lower oil prices. During the first crisis, the price stabilization following the war led to complacency and greater petroleum consumption in importing countries, which then laid the groundwork for the second crisis. But during the extended recession and related long period of low prices following the second crisis, oil companies worldwide cut back significantly on exploration and well development. U.S. companies even shut in nearly 70,000 "stripper" wells, resulting in a loss of 300 million barrels of reserves.[47] The massive cutbacks also had a major impact on future investments by the U.S. industry. In 1981, there was a weekly average of 3,970 drilling rigs in operation. By the end of 1986, the number had dropped to slightly more than 800.[48] Similarly in 1981, 409 million feet of exploratory wells and development wells were drilled in the United States. Less than 200 million feet were drilled in 1986.[49] Thirteen years later, after more than a decade of low oil prices, fewer than 500 rigs were in operation, and less than 100 million feet of new wells were being drilled annually in the United States.[50]

These crisis cycles, with price spikes followed by periods of lower prices, have also had a devastating impact on efforts to become more ecologically secure through development of renewable energy sources. When energy prices have been high, there have been incentives to develop renewable alternatives. But when prices have declined precipitously, there has been little economic incentive to develop these seemingly more expensive alternatives to fossil fuels. In the United States only 12 percent of electric power is generated from renewable sources, most of that coming from hydroelectric. Less than 1 percent comes from either solar or wind power.[51] The development of the solar energy industry in the United States has been severely retarded by the long slump in oil prices that began in 1985. Even the so-called synthetic fuels industry, which was given a congressional mandate to develop limited capabilities in 1980, is now barely scraping by, nearly driven to the grave by low prices. The nuclear power industry is moribund; no new reactors have been ordered and built in the United States since 1978.

The situation is not nearly so bleak in other industrialized countries. In Europe, considerable effort has gone into building wind power, particularly around the Baltic Sea. But the nuclear industry is under political attack, and several plants have been scheduled to be removed from service. While energy conservation efforts have been somewhat successful in Europe and Japan, such efforts in the United States have been dismal: gas-guzzling sport utility vehicles and minivans have replaced compact economy cars on U.S. highways. And while cutbacks in fossil fuel consumption will be required of most countries that have ratified the Kyoto Protocol, the United States is unlikely to ratify it.

Given this situation, the relevant question isn't whether there will be another full-blown energy crisis, but when. Indeed, it could be argued that a worldwide economic downturn that began in 2000 was a direct result of the tight oil market created by the agreement among OPEC and friends to withhold production in 1999, which drove oil prices up to $34 a barrel by March 2000. The terrorist attacks on the Pentagon and World Trade Center in September 2001, and the subsequent military action in Afghanistan, occurred well after the recession-wracked world petroleum market had softened, and thus the attacks did not provide a trigger for a third energy crisis. But the military action in Iraq kept oil prices at high levels in a soft market in early 2003.

Summing Up: The Path Not Taken

Two decades ago, as a follow-up to the work suggesting the desirability of following a soft energy path, Amory and Hunter Lovins suggested that the United States and other oil importing countries were becoming overly dependent on complex energy systems that were increasing insecurity. They suggested that

"[T]he United States has for decades been undermining the foundation of its own strength. It has gradually built up an energy system prone to sudden, massive failures with catastrophic consequences. The energy that runs America is brittle—easily shattered by accident or malice."[52] Indeed, the United States and other countries are still held hostage to Middle Eastern politics, and nuclear power plants around the world are surrounded by "no fly" zones in an attempt to foil potential airborne saboteurs.

Energy systems have gradually evolved over the course of the Industrial Revolution into complex and brittle ones that often rely on fuels imported from distant parts of the world, create local and regional pollution problems, can be easily disrupted by accidents or deliberate sabotage, and are responsible for considerable greenhouse warming. Breaking out of these destructive patterns will require a sociocultural revolution. But in an era in which deregulation and privatization are being heavily pushed by corporate interests, from where will such initiatives come?

Energy security in the form of stable supplies and prices is now a crucial global public good. The political stability and economic fortunes of countries, both importers and exporters, now rise and collapse along with energy prices. Continued reliance on mythical market forces in the petroleum industry is a recipe for disaster. Someone needs to provide for spare production capacity, buffer stocks, pipeline protection and maintenance, and refining capacity. In the past, Saudi Arabia has been willing and able to play the buffer role, but in the future may be less able to do so.[53] In addition, someone must be willing to pay for research and development, as well as new infrastructure, if the harshest consequences of global warming are to be mitigated.[54]

In the long run, enhancing both energy and ecological security requires a process that will move all countries toward soft energy paths. Obviously, it is much more imperative for some countries to do so than others. Japan and Italy, for example, face a substantially different energy future than does Kuwait. This process will require long-term commitments from existing governments and creation of global institutions. Destructive energy price fluctuations can only be overcome through producer–consumer cooperation. For example, neither the United States nor Saudi Arabia has an interest in prices going too high or too low.[55] Prices that rise too high can trigger recessions, while those that fall too low can destroy efforts to commercialize alternative energy sources.

An orderly transition to alternative energy sources is in the interest of everyone. Some of these new energy technologies are already available at competitive prices, while others soon will be. In the United States, the operating costs of generating electricity from geothermal, biomass, and wind are now lower than electricity generated by advanced coal-fired plants.[56] And hydrogen systems could soon be developed to meet transportation needs.[57]

Since current energy choices have been shaped and limited by past generous government subsidies, and the present infrastructure supports these choices, government support of research, development, and creation of infrastructure, will be required to smooth a transition to new energy sources.[58] Writing about ethanol as a potential alternative to gasoline in the United States, Richard Lugar and James Woolsey contend that "Market forces seldom reflect national security risks, environmental issues, or other social concerns. The private sector often cannot fund long-term research, despite its demonstrated potential for dramatic innovation."[59]

The period of rapid fluctuating oil prices in 2001–2003 once again highlighted the inability of importing-country governments to cope with energy crises. At the onset of the war with Iraq in 2003, there was little spare production capacity left among exporters, and the Strategic Petroleum Reserve in the United States held only enough petroleum to make up for 53 days of imports, down from 151 days in 1985. And economies around the world were being battered by oil prices approaching forty dollars per barrel.[60]

In the early years of a new century, oil-exporting countries seem to once again have knit together a fragile coalition that may be able to agree to restrict production in order to keep oil prices high. A broad coalition of OPEC countries and major non-OPEC exporters seems to have learned that cooperation in restricting output yields higher prices that are to the benefit of all exporting countries. But there still is no producer–consumer dialogue that could lead to negotiated stable prices. Thus, world economic recessions continue to reduce petroleum demand and pummel prices, while periods of protracted economic growth lead to tight markets, crises, and skyrocketing prices. And the welfare of exporters, importers, and future generations suffers accordingly.

CHAPTER FIVE

The Political Economy of Feast and Famine

MAINTAINING AN adequate supply of food is critical to the security of human societies. Throughout history famine has been an important factor shaping evolutionary processes, wiping out countless numbers of people over the centuries. Inadequate diets have also been a factor, contributing to malnutrition and the related spread of disease. While the potential now exists to feed adequately the present world population, there are significant economic and political barriers to doing so. At present, hundreds of millions living in the Global North suffer from maladies associated with being overfed, while similar numbers in the Global South suffer from the ravages of malnutrition.

For thousands of generations, *Homo sapiens* lived mostly in small bands, hunting animals and gathering wild plants for food. About ten thousand years ago, however, people discovered how to cultivate grain and began to domesticate a small number of animal species. Few discoveries in human history have had a more profound impact on human well-being. Even with intimate knowledge of their environment, hunter-gatherer bands needed from 5 to 50 square kilometers to support each person. Early farming, by contrast, could support from twenty-five to as many as one thousand people on a single square kilometer.[1] The development of agriculture made large, organized societies possible by permitting a settled existence and denser populations. It was agriculture—a new set of techniques for wresting a living from the environment—that led eventually to the founding of cities, a more complex division of labor, and a sociocultural revolution.

Farming was independently discovered at least three times, in Southwest Asia between 11,000 and 9,000 B.C.E., in Southeast Asia between 10,000 and 9,000 B.C.E., and in Central America between 6,000 and 5,000 B.C.E.[2] It is also suspected that farming emerged at different times in at least three additional locations: Central Africa, North America, and South America.[3] In each society that discovered or adopted farming, a distinct agricultural system evolved to make good use of the local environment. In many cases, the evolutionary fate of societies rose and fell with the sustainability of their agriculture. Wet rice cultures in the Far East, Egyptian agriculture based on the regular flooding of the Nile, and the mixed farming cultures of Northern Europe all proved able to sustain themselves over centuries. In Mesopotamia, on the other hand, sustainability problems developed as vast networks of irrigation channels became silted. If not constantly maintained, these channels became useless. In other places, people cleared hillsides of trees and brush to grow crops, only to find such practices to be unsustainable. In a few generations rains washed away the soil. Soil erosion may have contributed to the decline of historical civilizations in Greece, North Africa, Italy, Australia, and Central America.[4]

Every persisting agricultural system is a product of sociocultural evolution. As with biological evolution, certain agricultural adaptations led societies up blind alleys while others were more successful. If a particular farming system proved to be unsustainable, eventually it would spell the dissolution of the society that depended on it. From the discovery of farming until the middle of the twentieth century, food production took place almost entirely within the constraints of current solar income. Human populations, like other animal populations on Earth, were sustained by the solar energy that living plants captured through photosynthesis. As the number of people grew, the area of cultivated land increased accordingly.

It was not until after World War II, when the Industrial Revolution accelerated its spread into agriculture, that food production per acre began to rise dramatically. New machinery, fertilizers, herbicides, pesticides, and seeds multiplied the yields obtained by traditional practices many times over. From the fuel that powered tractors to the mining and transportation of phosphorus and potash, modern agriculture came to rely on immense fossil fuel supplements to current solar income. This system has continued to spread worldwide, and it is no longer isolated populations, but the entire human race that would face serious peril if, for some reason, this industrialized farming proved to be unsustainable.

Just as agriculture has been transformed by the technologies associated with the Industrial Revolution, the nascent postindustrial revolution also is beginning to have an impact on farming. A host of new innovations in biotechnology, ranging from herbicide-resistant crops to cloned farm animals, is once again transforming the nature of farming. The impact of these innovations on food security, as well as the political economy of world agriculture, remains to be seen.

Elements of Food Security

In order to anticipate better the future of food security, it is necessary to assess three aspects of world food problems: the growing objective need for food, patterns of effective demand for food, and the likely impact of technology and climate change on future production possibilities.

The objective need for food refers to the nutritional intake required to maintain good health. For any given increase in population, the total objective need for food increases proportionately. Thus, the need for additional food production is increasing very little in the industrialized countries where population growth has leveled off. In the countries on the other side of the demographic divide, where populations are still growing rapidly, objective need is increasing sharply. In many cases, population growth has already outstripped local production capacity, and reliance on the world food market has increased. But depending on imported food can be a trap. It can undermine other aspects of development by diverting scarce foreign exchange, assuming a country has much foreign exchange to divert, from more important uses. Imported food can also have a negative impact on domestic agriculture, lessening economic incentives for increased production, thereby contributing to rural unemployment and poverty.

Throughout much of the Global South, the number of farmers is shrinking even as rapid population growth swells the objective need for food. Of the world's less industrialized regions, only Asia has shown a healthy increase in recent food production per person, with food production per capita there growing by an average of 2.5 percent annually in the 1990s. In Latin America, food production has barely kept even with population increases. In Africa, food production per capita has fallen slightly. In Sub-Saharan Africa, where the situation is far worse, only 80 to 85 percent as much food per person is grown now as compared to 1961.[5]

At present, the world's farmers collectively grow more than enough food to meet the objective needs of everyone. On a global scale food production per capita has risen for decades; at present the world's 6.2 billion people have 15 percent more food per capita than the global population of 4 billion had 20 years ago.[6] It has been calculated that a near-vegetarian diet for the world's entire population could adequately support 6.26 billion people, given contemporary production levels. By contrast, if 25 percent of required calories came from meat, only 3.16 billion people could be supported adequately by contemporary food production capacity.[7]

Given this rather optimistic record of past increases in food production, why do significant numbers of people starve and almost a billion suffer from malnutrition? The answer is found in the distribution of effective demand for food. Effective demand refers simply to the ability to purchase things. The fact is that in many places where objective need for food is growing most rapidly people frequently lack the money to buy it.

In an increasingly globalized economy, farming responds to world market forces. This means that producers in the less industrialized world now often divert acreage from food production destined for domestic consumption to grow food crops, raise livestock, or even grow flowers for export to the industrialized countries, where consumers wield greater purchasing power. Meanwhile, large numbers of people at home suffer malnutrition, hunger, and starvation simply because they do not have money with which to buy food. Without rapid and equitable economic development or massive increases in food aid, population growth, combined with a highly unequal distribution of the world's wealth, will condemn hundreds of millions to suffer from continuing malnutrition.

Looking beyond problems of effective demand, however, questions of whether worldwide food production can continue to keep up with population growth in the future remain. Soil erosion and water scarcity threaten to limit production, especially on presently marginal land. Even on better land, there is a point at which crop yields no longer respond positively to more fertilizer. In many countries, the dramatic yield increases of recent decades have reached a plateau. Perhaps more important, the heavy reliance of industrialized agriculture on fertilizers, pesticides, herbicides, and mechanized equipment ties food production to the availability of reasonably priced fossil fuels. As prices for fuels fluctuate, the costs of food production change accordingly. And, while innovations in biotechnology will undoubtedly influence total future world food production, it is unlikely that they will have a great impact on countries where objective need is rapidly increasing.

There is also climatological evidence that the last few decades were unusually propitious for farming in the world's temperate regions, but things may now be changing. Small shifts in climate have historically had a great impact on food production capabilities, and continue to have an impact on the global food outlook. The UN Food and Agricultural Organization (FAO) reported that the 1997–1998 El Niño/La Niña climate phenomenon had a large impact on crops, livestock, fisheries, and other food production, increasing the number of countries facing food emergencies from thirty-one to thirty-eight.[8] In the longer term, these cycles, combined with more fundamental shifts evident in global warming, could have a more substantial negative impact on future world food production.

Basic Food Needs

A healthy human diet requires a number of nutrients found in a variety of foods. The human body gets its energy by burning carbohydrates and fats. The amount of such potential energy in food is measured in calories. The number of calories human beings require varies greatly according to age, sex, and climate. The World Health Organization (WHO) estimates that an average adult needs to consume about 2,600 calories daily. Over the past two decades, the daily per capita calorie supply rose in the Global South and at the start of the new century averaged 2,650.[9] But the distribution of calorie consumption in these countries is highly skewed, with many people remaining malnourished. At the World Food Summit in 1996, leaders agreed to attempt to reduce by half the number of undernourished people in the world by 2015. Unfortunately, it is already evident that the rate of progress is woefully slow and that there is little hope of meeting this commitment.

In the Asian and Pacific regions, where 70 percent of the total population of the Global South lives, the food situation is serious. Two-thirds of the undernourished in the world live in this area. India has approximately 204 million undernourished people and China 164 million. In addition, Africa has 233 million malnourished and Latin America and the Caribbean 53 million. An estimated 26 million people are undernourished within the Eastern and Central European countries. And, despite relative wealth and food abundance, at least 8 million people in the Global North are presently undernourished.[10]

The gap between per capita calorie consumption in the Global North and South is significant (see table 5.1). While the world's population of underfed people is estimated at 1.2 billion, a similar number of people is now considered overfed. Overconsumption, the intake of excess calories, which is often accompanied by a lack of necessary vitamins and minerals, affects more than 1.2 billion

TABLE 5.1.	Average Daily Consumption—Developed and Developing Countries		
Totals	**Calories**	**Protein (gr)**	**Fat (gr)**
Developed	3,260	99	120
Developing	2,679	69	63
World	2,805	76	75
Vegetables			
Developed	2,403	43	58
Developing	2,331	49	37
World	2,347	48	41
Meat			
Developed	857	56	62
Developing	348	20	26
World	459	28	34
Fish			
Developed	45	7	2
Developing	23	4	1
World	28	4	1
Sweeteners			
Developed	415	-	-
Developing	195	-	-
World	243	-	-
Stimulants			
Developed	18	1	1
Developing	2	-	-
World	6	-	-
Alcohol			
Developed	151	1	-
Developing	37	-	-
World	62	-	-

Source: Year 2000 data compiled from the FAO's FAOSTAT statistical database (October 31, 2002).

people throughout the world.[11] And in much the same way that the under-nourished are vulnerable to specific diseases related to vitamin and mineral defi-ciencies, the world's overfed are vulnerable to diseases related to excess intake of alcohol, fats, sugars, and meat.

Analysis of U.S. consumption patterns reveals that Americans currently consume 17 percent more alcohol, 21 percent more fats and oils, 24 percent more caloric sweeteners, 114 percent more soft drinks, and 143 percent more cheese today than in 1970. And, although Americans recently have reduced red meat consumption, total annual animal consumption (red meat, poultry, and fish) averages 192 pounds per person, 15 pounds above the 1970 average.[12]

While some recent changes in diet, a shift to leaner meats, improved qual-ity, and increasing variety, are positive, the overall trend toward overconsump-tion is resulting in unprecedented levels of obesity throughout the industrial world. In the United States 55 percent of the adult population is considered to be overweight, in Germany 50 percent, and in the United Kingdom 51 percent.[13] Obesity, in turn, raises the risk of heart disease, stroke, cancer, and diabetes, the aggregate effects of which account for more than half of all early deaths in the Global North. In addition to these more lethal illnesses, obesity exacerbates con-ditions such as asthma, sleep disorders, back pain, infertility, and osteoarthritis.

In addition to an adequate intake of calories, people need protein in order to grow and develop, as well as to maintain and repair tissue. Various kinds of diseases and retardation result from protein deficiency. Foods vary in the nutri-tional value of the protein that they contain, and it is therefore difficult to be exact about daily requirements. In addition, most foods do not contain all of the kinds of proteins people need, so a varied diet is required for optimal health. When these factors are considered, an average adult needs to consume an esti-mated 65 grams of protein every day.

As with calories, worldwide consumption of protein is far from equal. People in the industrial countries, eating large quantities of meat, consume about one and one-half times the minimum protein required, while people in less industrialized countries often get less than the minimum—and in less desir-able forms. The average daily protein consumption in the industrial countries is 99 grams per capita. Sub-Saharan Africa has the lowest per capita protein con-sumption, with an average of 54 grams per day. Within Sub-Saharan Africa, in the Democratic Republic of Congo per capita protein consumption averages only 24 grams per day.[14]

Although not as commonly mentioned in international reports and statis-tics, vitamins and minerals are also essential components of the human diet. Thirteen vitamins are considered to be essential to well-being. Only small amounts of them are needed, but vitamin deficiencies can cause various diseases. People also extract seventeen essential minerals, such as calcium and iodine, from food. If a diet does not contain an adequate amount and variety of them, health suffers. Normal diets in the industrial countries contain the required vitamins and minerals, and if people have deficiencies they take pills to compensate. But in less industrialized countries, meager diets based on wheat or rice often lack the required variety of vitamins and minerals.

There are many different ways of categorizing the foods that produce the needed carbohydrates, fats, proteins, vitamins, and minerals. Normally, they are divided into six categories: cereals; roots and tubers; fats and oils; fruits, nuts, and vegetables; sugar; and livestock and fish. Three cereals—wheat, rice, and corn—are by far the most important food plants, accounting for nearly half of the food energy consumed around the world.[15] Wheat is the dietary staple in the cooler regions of the world, while in the more tropical areas rice is the mainstay of the diet. Rice is considered to be the world's most important food since it is essential to the diets of about half of the world's population. Corn, the third most important cereal, is fed mainly to animals, although the nutrients in it make their way indirectly into the human diet through meat and dairy products. Direct human consumption of corn has grown to include, in addition to the United States, Central and South America, the European Union (EU), and parts of Africa.[16]

The other half of energy from food comes from a wide variety of substances, none of which approach the cereals in importance. Meat, fish, and other animal products—foods that are very common in industrial countries—account for about 37 percent of the protein but only 16 percent of the calories consumed worldwide.[17]

Fish are an important source of protein around the world. Because of the global fisheries crisis and the continuing need for cheaper sources of protein, many countries have turned to fish farming (aquaculture). At present, slightly less than one-third of world fish production comes from aquaculture. Although a few industrialized countries are major aquaculture producers, 83 percent of all fish farming is carried out in China, India, the Philippines, Indonesia, Korea, and Bangladesh.[18] Although aquaculture has benefited these countries, there are mounting environmental concerns about the associated fundamental ecosystem modification and disruption.

Roots and tubers, especially the potato, are staples for many people, but their water content is high and their bulk somewhat restricts their movement in international trade. Potatoes also have a relatively low protein content, and thus are not desirable as foods in protein-deficient countries. Other types of roots and tubers, including yams, cassava, and sweet potatoes, remain important components of the diets of many people in poorer countries.

Fats and oils are derived from many plant species, including palms and sunflowers, but the principle source is legumes, such as soybeans and peanuts, which are also an important source of protein. Processed soybeans are becoming more important in the human diet as a protein supplement.

Of the remaining food categories, fruit and vegetable production is well dispersed around the world. These commodities have accounted for only about 15 percent of total agricultural trade exports in recent years.[19] Sugar, produced primarily from cane in the tropics, is an important export crop for many countries. But cane growers now face declining demand for their product because synthetic sugar substitutes have been developed in the industrial countries, where many people are attempting to reduce their calorie intake. In addition, the United States—as well as many other industrial countries—restricts the amount of sugar it imports in order to protect higher-cost domestic sugar beet growers.

Effective Demand

Before a world market emerged, societies experienced feast or famine locally, depending on their own harvests. Populations were trimmed by starvation and malnutrition when harvests fell short of needs. Famines were frequent, but many of them passed unnoticed by historians because they occurred in remote areas of the world. There is plenty of evidence that the grim reaper was regularly at work. In 1878, for example, Cornelius Walford published a study chronicling more than two hundred significant famines in Great Britain over the previous nineteen centuries. He also listed more than 150 major famines that occurred in other parts of the world.[20] More recently, Stephen Devereux identified thirty-two twentieth-century famines for which adequate information is available, including eleven that were responsible for more than a million deaths each.[21]

With the rapid growth of international trade in agriculture, food can now be made available almost anywhere. Famine and malnutrition, however, still occur either because bad harvests happen in a country that is too poor to purchase food abroad or because war or natural disasters keep food aid from reaching people. When food production or distribution is upset by bad weather or civil war, food prices rise, and it is the most impoverished groups that are most at risk.[22] Integration into the world market also brings pernicious forms of dependence that can aggravate famine. Cash crops for export often have replaced food crops for local consumption. Even food aid has, in some cases, diminished the incentives for local food production and contributed to long-term dependence.[23]

A growing global food market can thus be seen as both a positive and a negative development. On the positive side it has freed many countries from the necessity for complete food self-sufficiency, thereby making labor available for export crops or industrial development. It has also permitted food exporters such as the United States, Canada, and Australia to realize their agricultural potential. And the growth of a world market has smoothed out the impact of local weather disasters, since the affected countries can turn to this market for short-term relief.

On the other hand, the existence of a world market has seduced leaders of many less industrialized countries away from a prudent interest in domestic agriculture and exposed their people to potentially serious problems should higher food prices or balance of payments problems reduce future ability to import food. As people have swarmed from rural areas to cities, these countries have become permanent customers in the food market—permanent, that is, unless the currency with which to import food disappears. And, although worldwide availability of food for sale has curtailed the number and severity of local famines, an adequate diet still remains out of reach for many who cannot afford it. According to the FAO, there are currently eighty-three countries that it considers to be low-income food deficit countries.[24]

The bulk of the food now traded on world markets consists of grains, mainly wheat, rice, and coarse grains. Approximately 22 percent of total world production of wheat is exported annually, compared to 14 percent of coarse grains, and 7 percent of total rice production. Wheat is a dietary staple for large numbers of people living in temperate climates. Wheat grows well where winters are cool and summers are hot. It does not thrive in the tropics, where various plant diseases attack it. China and the European Union are the largest wheat producers, followed by the United States, India, Russia, and Canada. Wheat is the most significant commodity in international agricultural trade, with about one-fifth of total production regularly crossing national borders. The United States accounts for about 23 percent of all wheat exports, with most of the remainder coming from the European Union, Australia, and Canada[25] (see table 5.2).

Rice is the staple diet for half of the world's population. China and India together produce more than 66 percent of the world's rice, but both consume domestically most of the rice they grow. The United States, though not one of the biggest rice growers, exports almost half of what it produces. Most of the world's rice crop entering the international market at the end of the 1990s was exported by Thailand, Vietnam, Pakistan, China, and the United States.[26]

Corn, the most important of the coarse grains, is the only major crop that is indigenous to the western hemisphere. Corn grows well in the American

Midwest, and at the end of the 1990s the United States grew over 40 percent of the world's total corn crop. China, which grows over 20 percent of the world's corn, has moved into second place. The European Union, Mexico, and Argentina are the other major corn producers. In all, about 15 percent of world corn production is exported. The corn trade is highly concentrated, with the United States accounting for about 67 percent of total exports throughout the 1990s. The European Union is second, with 12 percent of the international corn market. Argentina has almost 10 percent, and China is the world's fourth largest corn trader with 4 percent of the market.[27]

The United States dominates the total world trade in grain. Exports recently have accounted for over one-third of all grain traded on the world market. Agricultural products also constitute a vital part of the U.S. export economy. In the late 1970s, agricultural commodities made up 20 percent of all exports. Even though agriculture's share of exports has now fallen to around 10 percent, they still make a major contribution to U.S. export earnings and help preserve some semblance of balance in U.S. trade figures.[28] But this dependence on foreign markets makes American farmers vulnerable to international competition, which is gradually eroding their share of the world food market. U.S. agricultural exports hit a peak in 1981 at nearly $44 billion, and then declined over the next five years, reaching a low of just above $26 billion in 1986. Exports then gradually increased, but again began dropping in the mid-1990s.[29] In 2000, total U.S. agricultural exports had regained some ground and stood at $49 billion. Optimists predict steady growth through 2009, when the value of exports is expected to be nearly $76 billion.[30]

Politics, Subsidies, and the World Market

The world food market, like the oil market, has long been plagued by boom and bust cycles. In the early 1970s, a preceding period of food glut was suddenly transformed into scarcity. Bad harvests, higher energy prices, and increased food demand due to population growth caused the world's carryover stocks of grain to plummet from 223 million metric tons in 1971 to a low of 186 million metric tons in 1972. This latter amount could supply only about fifty-seven days of world consumption at that time, a narrow margin against catastrophe. High food prices during the middle and late 1970s stimulated production, and world stocks gradually were replenished. American farm exports rose steeply as farmers were encouraged to plant fence row to fence row. By the early 1980s, however, continued expansion of production by the major exporting countries, coupled with stagnant demand in many of the importing countries, resulted

TABLE 5.2.   Major Cereal Producers and Exporters (in million metric tons)

WHEAT

Country	Production	Exports	% of Production Exported
EU-15[a]	105.2	38.8	36.9
China	99.6	0.6	0.6
FSU-12[b]	76.4	1.6	2.1
United States	60.8	28.9	46.6
Canada	26.8	17.3	64.6
Australia	23.8	15.9	66.8
Argentina	16.5	11.7	70.1
Subtotal	472.2	119.4	25.3
World Total	583.2	126.7	21.7

CORN

Country	Production	Exports	% of Production Exported
United States	251.9	49.2	19.5
China	106.0	7.3	6.9
EU-15	38.3	8.9	23.2
Mexico	17.7	0.0	0.0
Argentina	15.5	10.5	67.7
Southeast Asia	14.8	0.6	4.1
South Africa	7.5	1.3	17.3
FSU-12	7.5	0.2	2.7
Subtotal	459.2	78.0	17.0
World Total	585.7	86.0	14.7

[a]European Union
[b]Former Soviet Union

(Continued)

TABLE 5.2.   Continued

COARSE GRAINS[c]

Country	Production	Exports	% of Production Exported
United States	263.2	56.3	21.4
China	137.2	10.0	7.3
EU-15	103.0	27.6	26.8
FSU-12	40.5	2.0	4.9
Canada	26.8	3.5	13.1
Mexico	26.2	0.0	0.0
Argentina	21.5	12.9	60.0
Australia	8.7	3.6	41.4
Subtotal	627.1	104.9	16.7
World Total	876.4	122.1	13.9

RICE

Country	Production	Exports	% of Production Exported
India[d]	131.9	2.6	2.0
China	131.5	1.9	1.4
Indonesia	32.8	0.0	0.0
Vietnam	20.5	3.6	17.6
Thailand	16.9	7.5	44.4
Japan	8.6	0.6	7.0
United States	5.9	2.7	45.8
World Total	397.4	25.6	6.4

Sources:
For wheat and corn: All figures are estimated for 2000/2001. Compiled from data in USDA, *World Agricultural Supply and Demand Estimates* (WASDE) (March 8, 2002).

For coarse grains and rice: With the exception of rice estimates for India, data are estimated for 2000/2001. Compiled from USDA, WASDE (March 13, 2002).

[c]Coarse grains include corn, sorghum, barley, oats, rye, millet, and mixed grains (millet and mixed grains not included in data for the United States).
[d]Data for rice production in India are for 2001 and for rice exports are for 1999. These data are from FAO, FAOSTAT.

once more in overproduction. By 1986, the carryover stocks of grain had accumulated to an all-time high of 459 million metric tons. Then, in the last half of the decade, the world food situation came full circle. Drought in the United States and elsewhere caused production and carryover stocks to decline in 1987 and 1988.[31] Through the late 1990s, production increased once more, and global grain stocks recovered due to both an increase in productivity in the United States and elsewhere, and to a decrease in demand as a result of the global financial crisis in the late 1990s.[32] The future balance between world demand for food and production of it is uncertain, but the former Soviet Union (mainly Russia) and China will be pivotal players. The Soviet Union was always one of the world's top producers of wheat and coarse grains. In the 1960s, Soviet production expanded into the so-called virgin lands in Siberia. These marginal lands, subject to fluctuating rainfall and temperatures, can produce a good harvest one year and a crop failure the next. In good years, such as 1986, when the Soviets produced 210 million metric tons, there was little need to purchase grain abroad. But in bad years, such as 1975 when production was only 140 million metric tons, they were forced to import large quantities of grain.[33] Favorable weather and good harvests caused Russia to cut grain imports in the mid-1980s. The tumultuous politics following 1989 reduced imports into Russia even further. During these difficult years, meat became a luxury, fewer cattle were fed, and foreign exchange needed to import grain became scarce. In the late 1990s, however, corn imports increased and domestic production remained steady. Of the nearly 42 million metric tons of corn used annually, over half was used as feed for animals. At the same time, however, wheat production declined in Russia from just over 80 million metric tons in the 1997–1998 season to an estimated 56 million metric tons the following year.[34] But by 2002–2003 Russia had recovered and produced more than 85 million metric tons of grain, of which nearly 10 million metric tons were exported.[35]

The question of future Chinese food self-sufficiency also will be important in determining future world market conditions. It is a controversial topic. Lester Brown sees future Chinese affluence leading to diets that include more red meat. This, in turn, would drive demand for more feed grains and result in less cereal production for human consumption. Given limitations on Chinese food production, China would be forced to enter world food markets on a large scale.[36] Vaclav Smil, on the other hand, sees significant additional potential for China to use new farming technologies and techniques to beef up domestic production.[37]

In the industrialized countries governments intervene in agriculture because of market fluctuations, the structural transformation of agriculture accompanying industrialization, and related persisting political pressures from farmers. In the industrialized countries of Western Europe, North America, and the Far East, where this structural transformation is already far advanced, millions of people have moved out of farming. It is not surprising that remaining farmers, who once constituted a voting majority in all of these countries, have used their lingering political power to press legislatures to shield them from economic forces of change. Governments in almost all of the industrial countries have responded with protective legislation in the form of price supports, export subsidies, and import restrictions.

Pressure to protect farmers relaxed somewhat during the 1970s when rising world demand for agricultural commodities boosted prices. In the early 1980s, however, supply increased, demand contracted, and prices fell. Not only did protectionist sentiment resume, but the cost of such protection became much more burdensome on national economies. In 1990, consumers and taxpayers around the world paid an estimated $300 billion to protect farmers.[38] Each farmer in the United States received an average of $22,000 in income support, each Japanese farmer an average of $15,000, and each farmer in the European Union an average of $12,000. The average transfer of income from individual consumers to farmers ranged from $1,137 from every person in Finland, to $510 per person in Japan, $409 in the EU, $318 in the United States, and $70 in Australia.[39]

The farm crisis of the 1980s placed unprecedented demands on the U.S. farm program, which paid out billions of dollars to distressed farmers. The huge federal budget deficits of the late 1980s focused attention on the cost of these farm price support programs. It is estimated that farm subsidies cost U.S. taxpayers about $80 billion over the 1987–1989 period.[40] It was with these subsidies in mind that the U.S. government undertook a major overhaul of domestic farm policy through the passage of the Federal Agriculture Improvement and Reform Act of 1996.[41] In the same year, the United States negotiated to open foreign markets to its agricultural products during the Uruguay Round of multilateral trade negotiations. But subsidies to agriculture in the United States received a big congressional boost in 2002, and now remain contentious in domestic and foreign policy.

The Uruguay Round of the General Agreement on Tariffs and Trade (GATT) negotiations, concluded in Marrakesh in 1994, produced an agreement to reduce the volume of subsidized exports by 21 percent over six years for developed countries, and ten years for developing countries, with no subsidy reduction commitments by the least-developed countries. The agreement did not cover certain forestry goods such as rubber, nor did it cover fish or fish products, due to an inability to come to a consensus. Implementation of the agreement began in

1995 and includes trade rules related to export subsidies, market access, internal supports, and sanitary and phytosanitary regulations.[42]

Implementation of the agricultural agreement has been controversial. At the 2000 round of World Trade Organization (WTO) trade talks in Seattle, negotiations over agricultural policy stalled, even though agriculture was arguably the most important item on the agenda. The Seattle talks were meant to develop further the framework for trade in agricultural goods, and to negotiate the next round of reductions in tariffs, subsidies, and other domestic protection. But the talks failed as representatives from the Global South, feeling alienated and left out of key bargaining sessions, refused to agree on new reductions. They further argued that trade liberalization to date had unfairly hurt the farmers and economies of the developing countries, despite provisions in the agricultural agreement that allowed for differential treatment of them.[43] Before engaging in another round of reductions, the developing countries called for more effective implementation of the agreement concluded at Marrakesh in 1994, and specifically called for previously negotiated compensation to the least developed and net food-importing countries that had been hurt the most.[44] In preparing for the next formal round of agricultural trade talks, the WTO agreed to examine the effects of the recent reductions in subsidies and protection measures on developed and developing countries.[45] Ongoing negotiations have built on the progress made in Doha, Qatar, in 2001 and are scheduled to end by January 2005. The negotiations continue to focus on export subsidies, domestic support, and market access, while taking into consideration nontrade concerns and differential and special treatment for developing countries.[46]

Future Production Possibilities

In order to ensure adequate food supplies for the world's growing numbers, it is estimated that world food production will have to increase by more than 75 percent over the next thirty years.[47] Five factors will determine the long-term ability of farmers to feed this growing population: availability of land, availability of water, sustainability of energy-intensive farming systems, climate change, and technological innovation.

Arable land has been considered a primary factor potentially limiting food production since 1798, when the Reverend Malthus called attention to its relatively limited supply. Over the years, sophisticated measures, buttressed by imagery from satellites, have refined assessments of the extent of arable land. These measurements, combined with demographic data, have confirmed a steady rise in the number of people compared to the amount of land available to feed them. It has been estimated that in 1960, for every person on Earth, there was one acre of potential crop land. By the mid-1990s, that figure had shrunk to three-quarters of an acre per person, and it is projected to be one-half an acre by 2015.[48]

Data reveal little potentially arable land remaining unexploited in Asia, but significant amounts are still thought to lie in Africa and South America. According to the FAO, 92 percent of all potentially cultivable land is already being farmed in Southeast and Southwest Asia and 89 percent is being farmed in Central Asia. In Africa, however, only 21 percent of the potentially cultivable area is being farmed, and in South America the figure is a mere 15 percent.[49]

Nevertheless, these estimates must be viewed cautiously. Most studies overestimate the utility of unfarmed land by underestimating the difficulties of bringing it under cultivation. Much of this land is not likely to be economically viable for farming any time in the foreseeable future. Generations of farmers have learned which parcels are economically viable; that which remains to be exploited is marginal—less productive, more risky, or more expensive to bring into production. Even in the face of intense population pressures, not much of this hypothetically usable crop land can be counted on for conventional farming. More than half of it lies in remote tropical regions. Brazil, for example, is attempting to push back its tropical rain forest in order to create new farming and ranching opportunities for its burgeoning population, but farmers have been bitterly disappointed since much of the rain forest lies atop very poor soil that will not support normal agriculture.

There are other reasons why much of this theoretically arable land will never be turned under the plow. Most marginal land is found in areas where rainfall and temperature are erratic. Two or three years of good harvests may be followed by protracted droughts or early freezes, bankrupting any farmers who might settle there. Much of this land is best suited for grazing or forestry. Also, across vast stretches of potentially arable land in Africa, sleeping sickness carried by the tsetse fly would decimate farmers and livestock, while periodic locust plagues would devastate their crops. Finally, marginal land is often distant from markets and population centers. Developing the transportation infrastructure to bring crops to market would be prohibitively expensive in many of the poor countries where this land is found.

Not only is there limited potential for bringing more land under cultivation, much of the land already being farmed is now threatened. The two main dangers are soil degradation and competition from urbanization and industry. Together, these cause an estimated 10 million hectares of crop land to disappear worldwide each year.[50] Soil degradation—the diminishing of the land's productive potential through misuse—is by far the greater threat. Of the Earth's total vegetated surface, 17 percent had been significantly degraded by the late 1980s. Wind and water erosion did the most damage, accounting for 84 percent of the degraded land. Most of this erosion has resulted from unsustainable farming practices, such as deforestation, overgrazing, and the cultivation of marginal land. Former rain forest has become desert, irrigated land has become encrusted with salt, and productive soils have been compacted by heavy farm machinery.[51] At the turn of the century, only 11 percent of the world's total land was farmable without some kind of improvement because the soil was too dry, shallow, wet, frozen, or laden with chemicals.[52]

Despite constraints on expanding the total area under cultivation, world agricultural production continues to rise steadily. Most of these recent increases have resulted from higher yields on existing crop land, rather than from bringing new land under cultivation. From 1950 to 1988, land under cultivation increased by only 26 percent, while world food production grew by 160 percent. Over that time, the increase in acreage accounted for a shrinking portion of the increase in production.[53] But a significant question remains as to whether the substantial productivity increases of the last several decades can continue in the future.[54]

The availability of water may ultimately play a more important role than that of land in limiting world food production. Agriculture is by far the largest user of fresh water, accounting for nearly 70 percent of water used worldwide.[55] It takes approximately 1,000 tons of water to grow 1 ton of wheat. Unfortunately, even the present rate of water use may be unsustainable in many regions. Much of the world's irrigated land is supplied by wells. In many places continuous pumping is depleting the water table much more rapidly than nature can replenish it. Tube wells used for irrigation in India, for example, have a very short useful life since they dry up as the water table falls. New, deeper, and more expensive wells must be drilled to replace the old ones. Around the world groundwater reserves are shrinking in the face of increased demands from irrigation.[56]

Agriculture also faces competition for water in many regions. While 21 percent of the world's population lives in China, they have access to only 7 percent of the world's renewable fresh water. Disputes over which people, regions, and sectors should get priority during increasingly frequent water shortages regularly simmer. Water scarcity, combined with population growth, has resulted in a shift of irrigation water away from agriculture to industry and urban centers, where a cubic meter of water can generate more jobs and provide up to seventy times the economic value as it could if it were used in the agricultural sector. While 60 percent of the country's arable land is in the central and northern regions, only one-fifth of China's river runoff occurs in these regions, resulting in a heavy dependence on irrigation from wells.[57] Similar distribution problems affect food production in the former Soviet Union, where more than four fifths of river runoff flows into the Arctic and Pacific Oceans, away from the agricultural regions and population centers. Even in the United States, in places such as California and Florida, conflicts are growing among cities, industry, and farmers over rights to limited supplies of water.

Disputes over irrigation water are an increasing source of conflict among countries. Use of Colorado River water, for example, is a major irritant in relations between Mexico and the United States. As farmers in the United States have withdrawn larger quantities for irrigation, Mexico has been left with a brackish trickle on its side of the border. International conflicts related to water disputes often occur along rivers and around lakes that serve as political boundaries. Nineteen countries are now at least 20 percent dependent on surface water coming from outside their borders. Four countries—Turkmenistan, Egypt, Hungary, and Mauritania—are at least 95 percent dependent on water coming from outside their sovereign territory.[58]

At the turn of the century, about 40 percent of the world's food production was coming from irrigated land. In order for world food needs to be met in 2025, an estimated 2,000 cubic kilometers of additional irrigation water will be needed per year, an amount equaling the annual flow of 110 Colorado Rivers.[59] Yet, there is some reason to hope that future water supplies may be sufficient to permit food production to continue growing. The hope does not lie exclusively in tapping new sources of water, but in using existing sources with more efficiency. Less than 40 percent of the water now used to grow crops is actually taken up by plants.

Considerable waste comes from a tendency of governments to subsidize water consumption. For political reasons most governments in poor countries (and some in wealthier countries) price water at only 10 to 20 percent of the real cost of delivering it. Simply pricing water at its market value would encourage the use of drip irrigation and soil moisture monitoring, and would greatly increase the productivity of water, thus relieving pressure on limited local water supplies.[60] Improved efficiencies in crop production from irrigation water, dubbed "more crop per drop," have been the target of recent FAO research efforts. The FAO estimates that improved water management techniques could lead to a 34 percent increase in irrigated land area while increasing water inputs by only 12 percent. After 2030, worldwide demand for irrigation water is expected to decline with the slowing of global population growth, but regional water scarcities will endure.[61]

A third factor that may eventually constrain world food production is dependence on fossil fuel–intensive farming systems. The cost of farming and the price of food now fluctuate in tandem with energy prices. In modern agriculture, fossil fuels are used to produce fertilizers, herbicides, and pesticides, and to provide power for irrigation pumps and mechanized farm equipment. Estimates of worldwide energy use in agriculture reveal a dramatic surge in the second half of the twentieth century. In 1950, a total of 276 million barrels of oil equivalent were used in world agriculture. By 1985 this figure had grown to 1.9 billion barrels. Energy inputs per unit of production also increased. It is estimated that in 1950, 0.44 barrels of oil equivalent were used to produce one ton of grain. In 1985, an average farmer used 1.14 barrels to grow the same amount of food.[62] In 1950, only 14 million metric tons of chemical fertilizer were applied worldwide to agricultural land. By 2000 chemical fertilizer consumption had skyrocketed to 141 million metric tons— almost a tenfold increase.[63]

Climate represents the ultimate constraint on future agricultural production. Any significant deviations from what is now considered to be normal could severely disrupt world food production, and lead to large-scale food disasters. Climate change and variability can turn the most fertile agricultural regions into barren wastelands. The record shows that there have been considerable changes in climate over the centuries. For example, 90 percent of the last million years has been significantly colder than the present era.[64] More recently, starting in about 1310 and continuing until the middle of the nineteenth century, Europe experienced a "Little Ice Age," a period of unusually cool temperatures by contemporary standards.[65] Now there is every reason to believe that greenhouse warming will change the future climate in the world's major agricultural regions. Many of the world's current prime agricultural regions were once covered by glaciers. With greenhouse warming and potential changes in rainfall patterns, they could one day possibly become deserts.

As significant climate change does take place, it is possible that presently marginal farming areas initially would suffer the greatest damage.[66] Regions already subject to periodic drought could become unusable for crop production, and coastal lowlands used for agriculture could disappear as a result of sea level rise. And more extreme weather events could hurt farmers everywhere. Climate change could also increase the vulnerability of agriculture to pests and vector-borne diseases in areas not previously vulnerable.[67] But the greatest harm could come to poorer countries that continue to be major food importers, since any weather-related declines in world agricultural production likely would result in major dislocations in world markets and sharply higher food prices.

Feasting on Frankenfoods?

When Reverend Thomas Malthus wrote his famous *Essay on the Principle of Population as It Affects the Future Improvement of Society*, he did not foresee the scientific discoveries and technological innovations that would play a key role in keeping food production ahead of population growth over the following two centuries.[68] Malthus based his gloomy calculations on the observation that population grows exponentially while land under cultivation does not. He expected that hungry people would soon overwhelm the land's capacity to feed them. But innovations in farming have vastly increased agricultural productivity, proving the Reverend Malthus wrong, at least so far. Research has produced high-yield varieties of crops that, when properly fertilized, irrigated, and protected from pests, tremendously increase the productivity of each cultivated acre.

Technological advances in plant breeding, insect control, mechanical and chemical engineering, mapping technologies, and biotechnology promise more improvements in crop yields. Plant breeders continue to adapt major crops to specific local environmental conditions. The integration of discoveries in ecology and biology into farm management promises to generate new methods of insect and disease control while minimizing the use of environmentally harmful pesticides. Engineers are adapting production, harvesting, and processing equipment to meet specific needs in new areas. And new geographic information systems technologies are helping farmers to better locate crops in areas with higher quality soils in order to maximize yields and minimize soil degradation.

In addition to these more established technologies, scientists are now counting on innovations in biotechnology to greatly increase future food production. Whether genetically modifying plants and animals will actually increase food security or simply widen the current divide between rich and poor countries remains to be seen. Genetically modified organisms (GMOs), it is argued, hold the promise of increasing crop production and yields, providing self-sufficiency in developing countries, improving the health of people around the world, and arming people in the fight against disease by reducing malnutrition. One often cited example is the success of scientists in genetically engineering rice to include vitamin A. This new rice, often referred to as "Golden Rice" because the genetic modification process also turns the rice a golden color, could improve the health of millions of people around the world. Because of a plethora of intellectual property considerations, however, there has been great difficulty in getting it into commercial production.[69]

Bioengineering goes well beyond the more familiar selective breeding for specific genetic qualities. The most controversial techniques are transgenic modifications that alter plants and animals by adding genetic material from entirely different species. Current efforts range from inserting genes from Arctic fish into strawberries, in order to make them more resistant to frost, to inserting genes into salmon, trout, and other fish that make them grow to market size in half the time it would take without intervention.[70]

In 2001, an estimated total of 52.6 million hectares of bioengineered crops were grown by 5.5 million farmers in 13 countries. This compares to 1.7 million hectares in 1996. Of the 52.6 million hectares, 77 percent had been transgenically modified to incorporate a gene that made the crops tolerant to a specific herbicide, allowing the fields to be sprayed for weeds without harming the crops. Another 15 percent of the bioengineered crops grown in 2001 had been modified to incorporate the soil bacterium *Bacillus thuringiensis* (Bt). The incorporation of Bt in corn, soybeans, potatoes, and other crops causes the plant to manufacture toxins that kill caterpillars that normally feed on them. The remaining 8 percent of all bioengineered crops grown in 2001 were "stacked," meaning they had been genetically modified to produce both herbicide tolerance and insect resistance.[71]

Fears of potential harm to people and animals have fueled resistance to GMOs in Europe and Japan. There has been especially strong opposition in Great Britain, where the GMOs are commonly referred to as "Frankenfoods." These fears center on the belief that, since *Homo sapiens* has little evolutionary experience with such foods, ingesting food or drink containing them, or their processed by-products, could cause unanticipated allergic reactions. While concerns in the United States over genetically modified foods have been relatively subdued, the American public seems to be increasingly worried as more is learned about them. It has been estimated that two-thirds of the products in American supermarkets contain genetically modified ingredients.[72]

There are also environmental concerns that genetically modified crops might contaminate surrounding non-GMO crops and native species of plants and animals. Genetically modified corn has already leaped beyond its established plots and contaminated non-engineered corn in the United States, causing significant problems for farmers and exporters. It is also feared that a "superweed" could develop by naturally cross-pollinating with crops genetically engineered to resist the toxic effects of specific herbicides and pesticides. If such cross-pollination should occur, new species of such superweeds could emerge and consequently thrive while being impervious to the herbicides specifically designed to eradicate them. Although a case of GMO contamination such as this has yet to be documented, the experience with genetically modified corn argues for a precautionary rather than a permissive approach.

A second set of environmental concerns related to genetically manipulated crops is more controversial. These concerns echo earlier environmental debates over pesticides such as DDT. Fears center on the potential damage GMOs could cause to other species that eat them. Studies focusing on this possibility have had mixed results, but the impact of this research has been to cause many to criticize the U.S. Department of Agriculture (USDA) for allowing these crops to be so widely planted when questions of environmental safety remain. It has also resulted in arguments from critics and some scientists that additional research must be conducted before more GMOs are allowed in fields and on grocery store shelves.[73]

A third set of concerns about GMOs is related to the development of agriculture in the Global South. Critics argue that even if biotechnology proves to be ecologically safe, it will mainly benefit agribusinesses in the Global North and do little to increase food security in the Global South. "It's not the technology itself, it's who will control it and benefit from it that matters," according to Hope Shand, the director of research with the Rural Advancement Foundation International.[74] The distribution of GM crops planted in the North and South supports this position. With the sole exception of Argentina, most of the genetically modified foods produced throughout the 1990s were produced in North America.

One of the first genetically modified crops widely marketed to farmers throughout North America contained the now infamous "Terminator Gene." More formally known as the Technology Protection System, terminator technology was designed to create plants that produce infertile seeds, thereby forcing farmers to purchase new seeds each year. The owner of the system, Monsanto, has claimed that the terminator technology is essential to ensure that seed companies can recoup their research and development costs, and to continue to invest in future technological advances.[75] Those critical of the technology argue that the purpose of terminator technology is nothing more than to strengthen the economic position of agribusinesses at the expense of poor farmers. Because many farmers around the world, but especially those in poorer countries, depend on current crops to provide seeds for future years, the development and mass-marketing of any infertile seed poses what many perceive to be an unacceptable risk to their food security. Indeed, opposition to the Terminator Gene grew to the point that even a Monsanto spokesperson, Philip S. Angell, acknowledged that "there is something psychologically offensive about sterile seed in every culture," and he announced that Monsanto would not market the technology until more research can be conducted.[76]

From an evolutionary perspective, the terminator seed also could be seen as a long-term threat to food security. Widespread use of these genetically

engineered seeds could result in genetic simplification—a large-scale reduction in the variety of seeds available. But even more important, terminator
technology foils the evolutionary process of natural selection. In the natural
environment, each new generation of seeds represents a response to changing
conditions brought about through differential reproduction of plants.
Terminator technology freezes this critical adaptation process.

Despite any solid scientific evidence suggesting that genetically modified
foods are harmful to human health, opposition to GM foods is growing and has
affected world trade in food products. In 1996, the United States exported 305
million tons of soybeans to Europe. By 1999, that figure had dropped to only 1
million tons as a result of widespread resistance to GM foods.[77] In fact, the
European Union has passed strict rules to regulate GM foods, including labeling
provisions, an action supported by 86 percent of the public. Opposition has also
built in Canada, where 98 percent of those polled support mandatory labeling.
Labeling requirements have also been instituted in Japan, South Korea,
Australia, and New Zealand.[78]

Not surprisingly, the matter of GM technology and GM foods is on the
agenda of several international organizations. The WTO, the FAO, the WHO,
and the Codex Alimentarius, among others, have begun to address the disparate
concerns of the many groups with a stake in the GM debate. The WTO has
been asked to get involved in the GM debate at the behest of the U.S. government. The U.S. government has lobbied the WTO to interpret the Frankenfood
trade war between the European Union and United States as nothing more than
a strategy to protect EU markets from U.S. exports. Under the WTO Sanitary
and Phytosanitary Agreements, countries are allowed to restrict imported goods
on the basis of scientific uncertainty, applying the precautionary principle, but
only while additional information is gathered.[79]

Efforts are under way in other forums to expand application of the precau-
tionary principle to genetic modification technologies and food products. The
Biosafety Protocol, negotiated under the UN Convention on Biological
Diversity, addresses and regulates the transboundary movement of Living
Modified Organisms (LMOs) that have been altered using modern GM tech-
nologies. Unlike the WTO, which is heavily weighted with economists, the
Biosafety Protocol negotiators were primarily ministers of the environment.
The agreement, therefore, gives heavy weight to perceived risks to the environ-
ment and to biological diversity from GMOs. The Biosafety Protocol unequiv-
ocally embraces the precautionary principle. It also requires that all exporters of
LMOs that are to be directly released into the environment (such as seeds or
plants) provide prior notification of applicable biosafety information and try to

secure informed consent from the importing country. Alternative procedures also apply to products derived from or containing LMO materials and to LMOs intended for contained use.[80]

A consensus seems to be forming on two key strategies for dealing with genetic modification technologies and their products. First, there is a need for continued research and testing of GM foods, both those not yet commercially available and those already on the market. Second, products containing GM ingredients should be labeled in order to allow consumers to make informed choices. Whether these labels display the proportion of GM ingredients in the product, as in the European Union, or simply identify the product as having some GM content, remains to be seen.

While the debate over the safety of genetically modified cereal crops is important, the development of genetically engineered substitutes for many of the agricultural commodities currently exported by tropical countries may be more significant. Already chemical substitutes have captured much of the market for natural rubber, sugar, dyes, and fibers. Biotechnology is likely to expand this list to include other commodities, such as cocoa, edible oils, and vanilla. If production of these tropical crops is taken out of the fields in the South and put into biological factories in the North, both employment and exports will plummet in countries already struggling against poverty.

Thus, the likely overall impact of biotechnology on future ecological security is mixed. The good news is that it could give agricultural production a boost needed to keep up with growing world food demand. The bad news is that, in addition to the possible environmental risks, biotechnology threatens to squeeze out precisely those forms of agricultural production from which hundreds of millions of the world's poorest farmers derive their already marginal livelihoods. Biotechnology will also bestow a still greater competitive advantage on the well-capitalized farmers and agribusinesses already favored by a globalized agricultural system. Biotechnology could actually increase the potential for greater global food production while simultaneously increasing poverty and hunger in many parts of the less industrialized world.

Africa: A Malthusian Tragedy

Despite the favorable news about increased world food production in many areas of the world, there are still substantial pockets of starvation, malnutrition, and related disease. The specter of Malthus lingers over dozens of countries that cannot produce enough food for their rapidly growing populations, and that don't have the foreign exchange to make up for food shortfalls with imports. Of the eighty-three countries currently identified by the FAO as Low Income Food-Deficit Countries, and therefore considered at greatest risk of food insecurity, nearly half are in Africa. Chronic malnutrition persists throughout the less industrialized world, but it is in Africa that the Malthusian dramas of the twenty-first century appear most likely to be played out.

A number of factors contribute to the food disaster afflicting the region. The population of Africa is growing at 2.4 percent annually. In Middle Africa the population growth rate is 2.9 percent and in Western Africa it is 2.7 percent. Only in Southern Africa has the population growth rate dropped to 1.3 percent, but this is due to the impact of HIV/AIDS on the death rate. In Africa as a whole, however, 43 percent of the population is under 15 years of age.[81] Even if birthrates in the region significantly decline, the demographic momentum inherent in the young age structure of these countries could keep Africa's population growing for decades.

Furthermore, Africans are now leaving the countryside and crowding into cities, leaving a smaller proportion of the population on farms to meet the continent's growing food needs. In 1950, only 11 percent of the population in Sub-Saharan Africa lived in cities. By the turn of the century urban dwellers accounted for 32 percent of the region's population.[82] Rapid urbanization is expected to continue throughout the African continent, with 43 percent of the population projected to live in cities by the year 2010.[83] Even if migration to the cities could be slowed, Africa's food security problem would not be solved, largely because Africa is the only continent on which poverty is projected to rise in the twenty-first century.[84]

This Malthusian situation is compounded by the devastating impact of HIV/AIDS. Of the 42 million people living with HIV/AIDS throughout the world, 70 percent, or 28.1 million live in Africa.[85] People are becoming even more susceptible to the ravages of HIV/AIDS and other infectious diseases because of malnutrition. The economic impact of HIV and AIDS, particularly on the agricultural sector, has been great. Not only are many farmers dying from AIDS, but the disease often leaves other infected individuals too weak to tend to their crops.

Africa's uphill struggle with starvation and malnutrition is further exacerbated by the approximately three million refugees who have fled across borders to escape political turmoil, economic hardship, or famine. It is estimated that nearly a half-million people have been displaced from their homes but remain refugees in their own countries.[86]

Land degradation also limits future food production possibilities in Africa. Since 1950, an estimated 500 million hectares of land have been lost due to salinization, declining fertility, soil compaction, desertification, and pollution from heavy application of agrochemicals.[87] Limited rainfall and access to irrigation water make the situation worse. In Ethiopia, where over 90 percent of all farming depends entirely on rainfall, erosion has become so bad that it is estimated that an average of 2 billion tons of topsoil are blown away by the wind every year.[88] Almost two-thirds of Africa's land is arid or semi-arid, making the continent highly susceptible to droughts and desertification.

The decline in Sub Saharan Africa's agriculture is often blamed on a prolonged series of droughts, which, in turn, have been attributed to the lingering effects of La Niña. Recurring droughts throughout Sub-Saharan Africa have served to worsen soil degradation and make the land more susceptible to future droughts. These destructive processes are further reinforced by overgrazing, inefficient farming practices, and often civil conflict and war.[89] Where there is marginal land and erratic rainfall, a nomadic lifestyle can make the most efficient use of available resources. But nomadic cultures that have evolved in response to Africa's climatological irregularities are now thwarted by national boundaries, ethnic rivalries, and the pressures of overcrowding on fragile ecosystems.

In an ideal world, Africa would develop enough purchasing power to buy the excess food produced in the United States and Western Europe. But there are few indications that significant per capita economic growth will take place in Africa over the next few decades. And Sub-Saharan Africa's trade deficits have been increasing. From 1980 to 1995, external debt for Sub-Saharan Africa rose 50 percent, from 31 to 81 percent of the region's GNP.[90] Cereal food aid to Sub Saharan Africa, after increasing throughout the 1980s, declined from 3.3 million tons in 1994 to 2.2 million tons in 1999.[91] Food aid to Sub-Saharan Africa is expected to remain between 2.0 and 2.5 million tons. Thus per capita food aid and food grain consumption in the region are expected to gradually decline.[92]

Official international assistance of all kinds to Sub-Saharan Africa now amounts to more than 16 percent of the region's total GNP.[93] In order for these countries to avoid becoming permanent charity cases, it will be necessary for them to build more effective institutions and pursue economic and agricultural policies that encourage farmers to stay on the land. Better family planning programs will also be essential if Africa, as well as other food-deficit regions of the world, is to escape heavy dependence on food imports. But dealing effectively with the tragic HIV/AIDS pandemic also will be crucial to the success of any of these endeavors to increase food self-sufficiency.

Summing Up: Improving Food Security

The future of world food security remains precarious. On balance, progress has been made in increasing total world food production. More people are better fed than at any time in history. Yet, malnutrition and starvation persist in this world of seeming plenty. The greatest increases in total food production have not taken place in the countries in which objective need is growing most rapidly. And it is unlikely that, without new policy initiatives, innovations in biotechnology will have a great impact on future food production in the Global South.

Looking forward, it is very possible that the tight world food markets of the past could return because of the conjunction of a number of changes affecting consumption and production. Assuming that economic growth continues to take place in China and India, both of these countries could considerably increase food consumption and thus imports. At the same time, climate change related to greenhouse warming could begin to create major discontinuities in production. Even though some cooler and drier areas of the world might experience more favorable weather for agriculture, many of those areas that have been most productive in the past could experience much poorer growing conditions. And marginal areas might simply collapse. Future energy crises of various kinds are likely and will sporadically translate into higher prices for fossil fuel inputs into agriculture. Finally, globalization makes the rapid spread of pests and plant diseases much more probable, and the potential threat of future bioterrorism directed against agriculture cannot be ignored.

There have been numerous assessments of these and related issues, and there are ways to deal with them. But little actual progress has been made because the eradication of starvation and malnutrition, as well as provisions for future food emergencies, are not yet widely accepted as global public goods. Clearly more public sector funding for cooperative agricultural research that is transferable to countries of the Global South is essential. Removal of agricultural subsidies and barriers to imports in industrial countries is also critical to the development of agriculture and export earnings in the Global South. Increased aid to facilitate economic growth in poor countries would increase effective demand for food and give a boost to domestic agriculture there. Perhaps most important, however, is to learn from experience and anticipate the near inevitability of future sporadic tight food markets. Creating and maintaining a dependable buffer stock of food to be tapped in the case of food emergencies would be a global public good of utmost importance.

CHAPTER SIX

Globalization and Biosecurity

OVER THE long span of history, countless human societies have coevolved with plants, animals, and a variety of microorganisms in relatively isolated ecosystems. "The physical roughness of the Earth—its structural variety—has tended to hold its living communities in place. The barriers that surround any particular ecosystem help set the terms of life within it. They tie a particular assemblage of plants and animals together, and they tend to exclude predators, competitors, and diseases that evolved elsewhere."[1] Complex relationships have evolved among organisms sharing ecosystems, and between them and the natural systems that sustain them. Sudden changes, originating within or without, can destroy delicate equilibria that have evolved over time.

Many of the ecosystems within which these evolutionary processes have occurred have been buffered from significant external influences by formidable natural barriers: oceans, deserts, and mountain ranges. But technological innovation and the dynamics of globalization are now eroding the barriers that once protected these ecosystems from outside influences. People, plants, animals, and microorganisms are more freely crossing ecosystem boundaries, bringing with them the potential for destabilization. While rapid growth in human numbers and activities are significantly modifying many of these shared habitats from within, the dynamics of globalization are modifying them from without.

There is mounting evidence that numerous aspects of globalization and changes in human numbers, settlements, and behavior are upsetting many long-established relationships among *Homo sapiens*, plants, animals, and microorganisms. Rapid population growth in many parts of the world is leading to the displacement or elimination of many other species as growth pressures drive people to clear forests and settle in new territories. People also are more frequently moving plants and animals, sometimes deliberately and sometimes accidentally, from established habitats into new ecosystems, where some of them wreak havoc on their new environments. And many aspects of technological change and globalization are increasing the variety and mobility of pathogenic microorganisms that now threaten people, plants, and animals with new and resurgent diseases.

There has always been some extinction of species as well as a limited exchange of plants, animals, and microorganisms among the Earth's ecosystems. There is evidence of regular long-distance natural transport of many kinds of organisms from one continent to another. For example, hurricanes originating in Northwestern Africa have been responsible for transporting various kinds of African flora and fauna to the Americas. During one particularly strong hurricane, birds native to Northern Africa were observed in the eye of the storm over Florida. It is thought that the biologically diverse ecosystems of the Amazon owe much to the importation of nearly 12 million tons of nutrient and microorganism-rich dust annually from the Sahara and Sahel regions of Africa.[2] But, with the exception of a handful of periods of rapid large-scale transformation driven by planetary disasters, species extinction and replacement have been gradual, and the pace of species migration and ecosystemic change has been limited. Now, human population growth, large-scale industrialization, urbanization, and globalization are all increasing the frequency of species extinction, the migration of many kinds of organisms, and long-distance species migrations that were very rare in the past.[3]

Homo sapiens has played a significant role in determining the fate of other organisms and facilitating their movement. When groups of early *Homo sapiens* migrated across the face of the Earth, there was a nominal amount of collateral ecosystem change from smaller species that moved with them. From the time of the Roman Empire, through the age of European exploration and colonialism, and into the contemporary era of globalization, whenever there has been a significant movement of people, there also has been an associated flow of other species and microorganisms. In the emerging global system, population growth, increased industrial production, increasingly open societies and economies, and the related rapid movement of people and goods among and within regions are combining to make the extinction of species, the unintended introduction of nonindigenous species (bioinvasion), and an increase in the variety and mobility of pathogenic microorganisms major challenges to ecological security.

Vanishing Species

There have been five previous large-scale extinctions of species caused by natural catastrophes. Globalization could well be leading to a sixth. There is constant competition for the Earth's limited resources among the millions of species that share the global ecosystem. The rapid growth in numbers and movement of any species, including *Homo sapiens*, can have an adverse impact on others, as well as on shared ecosystems. For much of history other organisms, ranging from wolves to bacteria, have played a major role in checking the growth of human populations. But the tables now are turning. The size and activities of the world's growing and more affluent human populations are wiping out other species on a significant scale, potentially undermining an equilibrium that supports ecological security.

It is difficult to know precisely the impact of human activities on biodiversity.[4] Part of the problem is that the total number of species in the world is unknown. Without a reasonably accurate census of extant species, it is difficult to monitor the rate at which they are disappearing. A recent large-scale study of biodiversity makes a best estimate of the total number of existing species as about 13,620,000. Of this number, only 1,750,000 have been described (identified). Plants and chordates (fish, birds, mammals) have been intensely studied. About 270,000 of an estimated 320,000 plants and 45,000 of an estimated 50,000 chordates have been described. Of the estimated 8 million arthropods (crabs, spiders, insects), however, only about a million have been described. Viruses and bacteria are even more elusive. Less than 1 percent of the estimated 400,000 viruses and 1 million bacteria have been described.[5]

There is general agreement that the present pace of extinction is extremely high in relation to the "background" rate. In recent history, for example, for the 5,000 known mammals there has been about one extinction per 200 years. The current extinction rate for mammals is estimated to be at least 100 times as high.[6] Given the growing impact of contemporary human activities on other species, however, 18 percent of mammals, 11 percent of birds, 8 percent of plants, and 5 percent of fish are now defined by UNEP as "threatened."[7] There are inadequate data to make such judgments about other kinds of organisms. But an extensive report on biodiversity, to which more than 300 experts contributed, recently concluded that "It is obvious that the rate of extinction today is hundreds, if not thousands, of times higher than the natural background rate that prevailed before the beginning of rapid human population growth, a few thousand years ago."[8]

Deforestation is a primary cause of the loss of biodiversity. Forests are home to more than one-half of all species, and the bulk of them have not yet been identified. Population growth and the timber industry both are causing a substantial loss of forests. It's estimated that nearly one-half of the forests that once covered the Earth are already gone and that about 14 million hectares of tropical forests, an area about three times the size of Costa Rica, is being decimated each year.[9]

The loss of biodiversity raises some troubling and complex ecological security issues. It might be argued that human well-being could best be promoted by a scorched earth policy, using more herbicides, pesticides, and antibiotics to wipe out all potentially objectionable creatures. But there are numerous reasons to resist this temptation, and to value and nurture biodiversity. At the very least, it could be argued that *Homo sapiens*, being the wisest of species, has a moral, ethical, or stewardship responsibility for the welfare of others. This is particularly true for other large sentient mammals such as gorillas, dolphins, whales, and elephants that have much in common with *Homo sapiens*. It also could be argued that other species should be protected for their esthetic value: the beauty of birds, butterflies, or flowers. And all existing species are the product of natural selection, and thus should be valued as carriers of evolutionary wisdom.

But there also are reasons of very direct human self-interest to preserve biodiversity. Primary among these is the economic value of the services to people provided by existing ecosystems. Although it is difficult to quantify precisely the economic contribution of environmental services, an effort to estimate the annual value of "nature's services" by a group of thirteen ecologists, geographers, and economists, came up with a figure of $33 trillion.[10] Water and air are purified and distributed by natural systems. The grains that people eat are refinements of wild grasses found in nature. Much of the protein that people consume comes from fish and other animals. Timber and wood products are provided courtesy of natural ecosystems. And ecosystems and the species that occupy them are a vast genetic library of evolutionary information from which people can draw in order to solve problems and meet changing needs. For example, the active ingredients of at least a third of all prescription drugs have been derived from chemical compounds found in wild plants, fungi, or other organisms.[11]

Ecosystems also provide environmental services that are very central to ecological security concerns. The trees and other plants in tropical rain forests remove carbon dioxide from the atmosphere, produce oxygen, and, in a way, act as the lungs of the world. They also help to drive the world's climate by transpiring large quantities of moisture into the atmosphere. Soils are generated and maintained by the efforts of countless numbers of small animals and microorganisms. One gram of fertile agricultural soil could contain over 2.5 billion bacteria, 400,000 fungi, 50,000 algae, and 30,000 protozoa, all playing a role in converting nitrogen, phosphorous, and sulphur into forms usable by crops.[12] And a vast group of soil flora and fauna, called decomposers, breaks down wastes in soil and water into simpler constituents.

Perhaps the strongest argument for preserving biodiversity is that *Homo sapiens*, at this point, lacks an adequate understanding of the complex interdependence that exists among ecosystem components. The structure of contemporary ecosystems is the product of countless centuries of evolutionary experience. Each time a species is extinguished there is a small risk that it will be a keystone species, meaning "one whose impact on its community or ecosystem is large, and disproportionately large relative to its abundance."[13] Keystone species are facilitators that play crucial roles in maintaining ecosystem stability. Thus, animals as diverse as wolves, kangaroo rats, and seed-dispersing ants are essential in limiting the size of populations of some species or in facilitating the reproduction of others. To eliminate a keystone species is to risk the collapse of a significant part of an ecosystem, and perhaps the human beings dependent on it.

Because much research still needs to be done on the dynamics of diminishing biodiversity, there have been only limited attempts to deal with it politically. The international agreement with the greatest impact has been the 1973 Convention on International Trade in Endangered Species of Wild Fauna and Flora (CITES). This agreement among 146 parties restricts trade in species that clearly are threatened with extinction or that may become endangered if trade in them is not regulated. The parties to the agreement meet regularly to update the list of species in which trade is prohibited. A Convention on Biological Diversity also came out of the 1992 UN Conference on Environment and Development (UNCED). This agreement established a very broad framework for the conservation of biodiversity, equitable sharing of the benefits from using genetic resources, and the sustainable use of nature's components. It also recognized national sovereignty over biological resources. Unfortunately, this agreement has not yet had a great impact, partly since it has not been ratified by the United States Senate because of concerns about protecting the U.S. biotechnology industry and related intellectual property.

Bioinvasion

When people travel or trade, they inevitably transport other species, ranging from lice to mice. Contemporary globalization processes not only lead to more people traveling greater distances and a huge increase in the volume of trade, they dramatically increase the number of species hitchhiking from one ecosystem to another. This means that many species that have evolved within one ecosystem have more opportunities to relocate in others where, in some cases, they raise havoc. Many of these migrant species are innocuous, causing little harm in their new surroundings. But a portion of them, varying between 4 and 19 percent, can cause serious damage to the new habitats.[14] Many obnoxious species in the United States, for example, ranging from crabgrass and dandelions to gypsy moths and zebra mussels, have originated in other parts of the world.

Species move long distances via a variety of modes of transportation and for various reasons. Many species have been moved intentionally. New World colonists brought seeds, plants, and livestock with them, and sent other species back to Europe. At that time "acclimatization societies" sprang up in England having the intention of populating the Americas and Australia with European plants, birds, and mammals, including every bird mentioned in Shakespeare's works.[15] More recently a vigorous trade in species has developed, and exotic plants and pets are moving in large numbers from one country to another. Exotic pet stores are springing up in the United States, Japan, and many other countries. In Florida, more than twelve thousand animal shipments arrive annually at the Miami airport.

Many species have been resettled in the name of environmental improvement. In Australia in 1859, for example, a wealthy resident named Thomas Austin introduced European rabbits onto his estate in order to enhance his hunting experiences. Australians have been cursing him ever since because of the millions of descendant rabbits that have turned vast stretches of lush foliage into desert. To remedy this problem, in 1995 the Australian government began to experiment with a virus fatal to these rabbits. But the virus "jumped the fence" and killed millions of rabbits before its broader environmental effects could be tested. More recently, the same virus has been found in New Zealand, where it is suspected that farmers illegally introduced it in order to control the rabbit population.[16]

By far the greatest contemporary damage, however, comes from the unintended introduction of species. As travel and commerce have accelerated, so has the spread of species from one part of the world to another. In the United States, a wide variety of destructive plants, animals, and microorganisms, ranging from zebra mussels to the West Nile virus, have invaded from abroad. Ravenous

Chinese walking fish have been wiping out the other fish in U.S. ponds, and then walking to other locations.[17] Other parts of the world have been impacted similarly. As Yugoslavia fell into military quarreling in the early 1990s, scientists discovered a new enemy in a field near the Belgrade airport: the western corn rootworm apparently dropped in from the United States. The rootworm has now spread to much of Central Europe. South Africa has been invaded by varroa, a mite that destroys honeybees. It was first discovered near Cape Town Harbor in 1997, and has subsequently spread widely in South Africa.[18]

Bioinvasion creates significant economic, environmental, and health challenges. It is difficult to quantify precisely its economic cost. Approximately 50,000 nonindigenous species have been introduced into the United States. Many of these have been introduced intentionally, such as wheat, rice, and cattle, and are responsible for providing more than 98 percent of the domestic food supply.[19] But many other nonindigenous species do considerable economic harm to the food supply, forests, water, fisheries, and utilities. One study of seventy-nine harmful nonindigenous species introduced into the United States from 1906 to 1991 estimated a cumulative economic loss from them of $97 billion (1991 dollars).[20] A more inclusive study of damage from bioinvasion estimates a current annual cost of $138 billion in the United States for losses, damage, and control costs associated with invasive species. The most significant annual direct damage is caused by the zebra mussel, which arrived in the Great Lakes from Eastern Europe in 1986 and is now found in 20 states ($3.1 billion); the fire ant, which is found in the southern part of the United States and California ($2.0 billion); the Asian clam, which is fouling the water pipes of drinking water facilities in 38 states ($1.0 billion); and the Formosan termite, which is gnawing at buildings and trees in Louisiana ($1.0 billion).[21]

It is even more difficult to estimate the toll from invasive species on a global scale, but it is considerable. Chris Bright has made an estimate by using the following reasoning. The annual value of the world's eight most economically important crops is approximately $580 billion. Pests may destroy as much as 42 percent of these crops at a loss of $244 billion. Pesticide expenditures are as much as $31 billion annually, thus yielding a total crop loss and prevention cost of $275 billion. The percentage of pests in any country that is nonindigenous varies from 20 to 90 percent. Although a very rough estimate, the total crop losses to nonindigenous pests would lie between $55 and $247.5 billion annually.[22] Added to this, of course, is the enormous damage to people, nature, and infrastructure that is much more difficult to quantify.

The environmental damage done by nonindigenous species is less easily tallied. Freed from the competitors and predators that kept them in check in their old environments, and often tougher than the competition in the new ones, the invaders can expand rapidly at the expense of established species. In the United States, fishhook fleas native to Central Asia have invaded the Great Lakes region and destabilized the indigenous fish population.[23] European starlings have caused a major decline in Eastern bluebird populations. Invaders could also be at least partially responsible for the actual extinction of many existing species. It is estimated that of 613 threatened or endangered species in the United States, nonindigenous species have contributed to the decline of 160.[24]

Invasive species can also modify the chemical and physical features of the ecosystems that they invade. The zebra mussel has dramatically changed the aquatic community in the Great Lakes, and the Australian melaleuca tree has changed the soil characteristics and the topography of the Florida Everglades. And various kinds of invasive weeds have transformed vast stretches of the U.S. countryside.[25]

Invasive species also have a direct impact on human health. Animals such as killer bees or fire ants can sting and disable people. Many poisonous plants, such as foxglove, are also imported. Viruses and bacteria are constantly moving from one ecosystem to another, leaving victims of disease in their wake. Plants and animals also are seriously affected by traveling pathogens. It is estimated that there are more than fifty thousand plant diseases in the United States, most of which are caused by fungi. About twenty thousand of the pathogenic microbes that cause these diseases originated abroad. Livestock also are assaulted by hundreds of visitor microbes and parasites, and dozens more threaten to invade.[26]

The problem "does not lie with the exotic species themselves, but with the economic system that is continually showering them over the Earth's surface. Bioinvasion has become a kind of globalization disease."[27] But in the face of the challenges of bioinvasion, the institutional mechanisms needed to control the spread of nonnative species are relatively undeveloped. To date, agreements that are at all relevant to the invasive species problem have been designed to streamline trade rather than to protect the environment. The United States has been slow to respond to the invasion threat. An executive order was issued by former President Clinton in February 1999, setting up an Invasive Species Council charged with responsibility for coming up with a comprehensive plan for dealing with the growing economic and environmental threat. Not much has yet come from this, and little else has been done.

There are numerous international treaties that deal with invasive species in small ways, but these efforts have been aimed more at opening borders to commerce, rather than erecting potential barriers to migrating species. The most important of these agreements is the International Plant Protection Convention

(IPPC), which was signed by the United States in 1972. It provides a framework for agricultural cooperation in pest regulation, and to prevent the spread of pests that attack plants. But it doesn't deal with curbing invasive species in general. The Convention on Biological Diversity, which has not been ratified by the U.S. Senate, once contained a strong alien species article, but subsequent negotiations watered it down to a vague admonition to control and eradicate alien species that threaten ecosystems or other species. The creation of the World Trade Organization in 1994 was accompanied by an Agreement on the Application of Sanitary and Phytosanitary Measures designed to promote a common set of procedures for evaluating potential risks of contamination in internationally traded commodities. But this agreement also was aimed mostly at facilitating trade by requiring risk assessments to be done before any barriers are put in place to keep contaminated goods from entering a country. New agreements based on sound ecological principles are clearly needed to deal with the growing insecurity associated with invasive species.[28]

Microbes in Motion

The most dangerous and elusive organisms that are increasingly crossing borders are the various pathogens responsible for many of the serious diseases that sicken or kill human beings, animals, and crops. Many pathogenic microorganisms are indigenous, and populations of *Homo sapiens* have developed some level of resistance to them by virtue of having coevolved with them over time. And a large portion of microorganisms are not hazardous to human beings; in fact, many of them are quite beneficial. But there is now deep concern over the threat of new and resurgent diseases as significant changes in human behavior and the physical environment are giving viruses, bacteria, and other microorganisms new routes to travel within and among human populations.[29]

Human immune systems have been honed by thousands of years of coevolution with a variety of viruses, bacteria, and other small organisms, mostly within the confines of isolated ecosystems. For the most part, people and microbes have peacefully coexisted. But large-scale outbreaks of disease, called epidemics when they are localized and pandemics when they spread worldwide, can occur when something happens to disturb these equilibria.

Getting sick is a common experience, and most diseases do relatively little long-term harm. While some debilitating diseases have sporadically made major inroads into societies, human immune systems have evolved mechanisms to deal with most of them. Epidemics and pandemics break out when people, for one reason or another, encounter novel pathogens or new serotypes of old ones.

Many of the more serious diseases confer a degree of immunity to those who have been stricken. Thus, survivors of epidemics are likely to possess antibodies that offer some degree of protection against future assaults.

There are several ways, however, that people can be exposed to new pathogens against which they have few defenses. International travelers or people moving permanently from one country to another often experience a significant amount of illness when moving to or through new environments. Also, serious outbreaks of disease can occur when people trespass into previously unsettled areas. The pressures of population growth in the Global South are forcing significant numbers of people to move into formerly forested regions of the Amazon in Latin America and the edge of the tropical rainforests of Africa, where they can be exposed to novel pathogens such as the Ebola virus, lurking in the wilderness.[30] These pathogenic microbes can then move out of forests and into new and naive populations, riding along with people and animals.

There is overwhelming historical evidence that contact between previously isolated populations and ecosystems, or their integration into larger units, has created major evolutionary discontinuities and often exacted a tragic disease toll. William H. McNeill has observed that the expanding Roman Empire was repeatedly afflicted by strange maladies originating in the provinces. There were reportedly at least eleven microbial disasters during Republican times. A major epidemic struck the city of Rome in 65 C.E., but that paled in comparison with a widespread pandemic that began to sweep through the entire empire in 165 C.E. Mortality in this latter plague was heavy; it is estimated that one-quarter to one-third of those coming down with the disease died.[31]

In more recent history, contacts between expanding European populations and those in other parts of the world had similarly serious disease ramifications. By the middle of the fourteenth century, many of the small kingdoms of Western Europe had begun to increase commerce, not only with each other, but with countries of the Orient, courtesy of expanding trade routes between Europe and China. During this period of economic growth, urban expansion, and increasing trade, messengers, merchants, and mercenaries were moving more freely among societies. This increasing contact facilitated the spread of diseases to biologically naive populations, the most infamous of these diseases being *Yersinia pestis*, also known as the Black Death. Traveling with merchant caravans along trade routes from Asia, the black rat (*Rattus rattus*) carried disease-bearing fleas to Europe. The arrival of the bubonic plague in 1346 began a destructive pandemic, and successive waves of disease cut the region's populations by nearly 40 percent, the highest mortality being in urban areas.[32]

Contacts between previously separated people also resulted in heavy casualties during the age of European exploration and colonization. For example, the ships of Christopher Columbus, arriving in the Caribbean in 1492, were the first of a wave of vessels that brought Europeans, and the microbes that accompanied them, to the Western Hemisphere. Some of these microorganisms were responsible for eventually wiping out a significant portion of the indigenous peoples. The military history of the period is filled with tales of miraculous conquests of huge numbers of indigenous peoples by mere handfuls of European troops. But in reality there were no bonafide miracles. Most of the damage was inflicted by diseases, particularly smallpox, that for the most part were unwittingly launched by the European invaders. These new diseases killed approximately two-thirds of the people who encountered them, leaving societies in disarray and unable to muster a decent defense of their territories. In the words of McNeill, "From the Amerindian point of view, stunned acquiescence to Spanish superiority was the only possible response. . . . Native authority structures crumbled; the old gods seemed to have abdicated. The situation was ripe for the mass conversions recorded so proudly by Christian missionaries."[33]

In the more contemporary world, an accelerating movement of people and goods has also been accompanied by growing threats of disease. During World War I, influenza traveled from Kansas to Europe along with American troops, and eventually caused more casualties worldwide than did the military hostilities. And influenza pandemics have regularly spread around the world, sickening hundreds of millions, and killing tens of thousands.

There is now considerable evidence that pathogenic microorganisms are poised to launch new assaults on a global scale. Many diseases that were thought to have been beaten into submission are making a comeback. And some novel pathogens, to which few people are now immune, are emerging as serious threats to security. Since 1973, twenty well-known diseases—including tuberculosis, malaria, and cholera—have reemerged or spread geographically, and at least thirty previously unknown diseases have been identified.[34] Chief among these new diseases is the HIV/AIDS virus. In an unprecedented move, HIV/AIDS was declared to be a threat to national security by the Clinton administration in April 2000.[35] And, of course, the new threat of biological warfare, and the possible introduction of genetically engineered pathogens, worsens the situation. In spite of significant advances in medical technology, there are abundant indications that these new and resurgent diseases will be a continuing threat to ecological security.[36]

Growing Bioinsecurity

Infectious diseases are already a leading cause of death, accounting for nearly 30 percent of the estimated annual fatalities around the world. Traditional diseases such as respiratory infections, especially influenza and pneumonia, as well as diarrhea, currently exact the greatest number of casualties, but HIV/AIDS is rapidly growing in importance. In 2000, 3.9 million people died from respiratory infections, and 2.1 million people died from diarrheal diseases. At the same time 2.9 million people died from AIDS.[37] Some 42 million people are currently HIV positive. Five million people are newly infected with HIV each year.[38]

Tuberculosis (TB) and malaria are the next most significant disease threats to human well-being. The World Health Organization declared TB to be a global emergency in 1993. TB took the lives of 1.7 million people in 2000.[39] One-third of the world's population is infected with latent TB. Drug resistance is a growing problem, and nearly 50 percent of those with drug-resistant TB die despite treatment.[40] Malaria, a tropical disease that was thought to be under control in the 1970s and 1980s, is making a comeback. In 1998, 300 million people were estimated to be infected with malaria, and 1.1 million people died from the disease.[41] Most of the deaths occurred in countries of Sub-Saharan Africa where increases of 7 to 20 percent annually are expected for the next several years. Although they have not yet become major killers at this time, accounting for only about 600,000 deaths annually, hepatitis B and C pose a significant future threat. Nearly 350 million people are chronic carriers of hepatitis B and some 170 million people are estimated to be infected with hepatitis C.[42]

The impact of disease on the quality of life, economic performance, and life expectancy is enormous.[43] While the "healthy life expectancy," a measure of the number of years that a newborn can expect to live at full health, ranges between 70.0 and 74.5 for the 24 healthiest countries in the world, it is below 50 for the 51 least healthy countries. Poor countries as diverse as Bangladesh, Haiti, Afghanistan, and Nigeria fall into this latter category. At the very bottom of the list are countries such as Niger, with a healthy life expectancy of only 30.3 years, and Sierra Leone, where a child born today, on average, can expect a healthy life of only 25.9 years.[44]

The nagging question is why, despite numerous technological breakthroughs and repeated claims that the threat of disease would soon be eradicated, does bioinsecurity remain so pervasive? Both environmental degradation and changes in human behavior are making people more vulnerable to disease organisms.[45] There are at least seven kinds of environmental and behavioral changes that are now upsetting human–microbe relationship.[46]

Demographic Dislocation

Population growth and accompanying rapid urbanization continue to be critical factors in the spread of disease. The world's population will likely grow from the present 6.1 billion to nearly 8 billion over the next 25 years, and almost all of this growth will take place in the Global South, much of it in megacities.[47] The more people living in poverty in densely crowded urban areas, the greater the opportunity for viruses, bacteria, and other pathogenic microbes to spread.

Population pressures in poorer countries are forcing people to move onto marginal and previously unoccupied land. In both Africa and Latin America, isolated forest areas and their ecosystems are now under attack from this advancing army of human beings. In addition to millions of plant and animal species, these forests are also home to numerous potentially lethal pathogens. Before the recent human incursions, these potentially deadly microbes were limited to preying upon forest animals, and had little opportunity to move into large human populations. "These pathogens probably lurked relatively undisturbed in their animal hosts in the tropics, jumping to humans only in rare cases. They had little opportunity to adapt to humans, who usually were a 'dead end' host species, because the viruses would fizzle out once they swept through a small population at the edge of the forest. But once large numbers of humans moved into the forest, that picture changed."[48] The new settlements and highways that are being built in these areas offer routes for newly liberated pathogens to move to more densely populated areas. It is very likely, for example, that a large number of viruses, including hemorrhagic fever, yellow fever, the Marburg and Ebola viruses, and HIV/AIDS have jumped from animals to people.[49]

Ethnic violence and associated large-scale migrations are also factors in the spread of disease. There are presently some two dozen humanitarian emergencies worldwide that have created thirty-five million refugees and internally displaced people. Densely populated refugee camps are ideal incubators for diseases such as TB, cholera, dysentery, and malaria. Additionally, well over 120 million people live outside of their country of birth and millions more are migrating annually. These migrants often bring diseases with them to geographic locations where they haven't previously been found.[50]

Technological Innovation

Technological innovation is one of the most critical factors affecting many aspects of the coevolution of human beings and microorganisms. Technological breakthroughs in medicine obviously have greatly facilitated the detection and control of many infectious and noninfectious diseases. Paradoxically, there is a dark side to technological innovation that sometimes negates its positive impacts. Innovations in transportation, production and processing of food, and even in antibiotics can have a negative effect on human health. For example, a revolution in transportation has dramatically changed the environments within which microbes can spread. People crammed into a loaded 747 flying from New York to Tokyo are exposed to communicable diseases that are carried by other passengers. There is substantial evidence of significant disease risks in modern aircraft, which have been designed to be more heavily dependent on recirculated air in order to save fuel costs.[51]

There are other technology-related changes that facilitate the spread of disease. Mass production and large-scale distribution of food is facilitated by technological change, but brings with it new disease threats. Non-hygienic food production, preparation, and handling, as well as lax enforcement of standards, now spread diseases over a much larger territory both within and among countries. Like other sectors of the world economy, agriculture and food production have been subject to increased globalization. For example, nearly one-third of the fruit and vegetables consumed in the United States now comes from other countries. Public health officials have reported a sharp increase in disease outbreaks, including cyclospora, hepatitis, and salmonella, all linked to imported foods. This lengthy list of imports includes raspberries from Guatemala; strawberries, scallions, and cantaloupes from Mexico; coconut milk from Thailand; canned mushrooms from China; and pest-ridden oranges from Spain.[52] There are presently about nine million shipments of food and drugs coming into the United States yearly, more than four times the number only six years ago. At the same time, the staff of the Food and Drug Administration, responsible for monitoring this situation, has actually been cut back.[53]

Increased Travel and Commerce

The growing speed and pervasiveness of travel and commerce are now putting more people and microbes into motion. The world's airports are mixing bowls for people and traveling microbes. This dramatically increases the potential for maladies such as influenza to spread quickly around the world, often moving much faster than the incubation period of the diseases. Early in the 1990s, for example, a multi-drug resistant strain of *Streptococcus pneumoniae* originated in Spain and spread around the world in a matter of weeks. At present, more than one million people travel between developed and developing countries each week.[54] More than two million people cross an international border each day, up from only 69,000 in 1950. Between 1950 and 1998 the number of "passenger kilometers" flown internationally grew from 28 billion to 2.6 trillion, nearly a one-hundred-fold increase. World exports of goods grew in value from $311 billion to 5.4 trillion. This rapid export growth was accompanied by an enormous increase in air freight, which grew from 730 million to 99 billion ton-kilometers over the same period.[55] These traveling people and goods are frequently accompanied by bacteria, viruses, and other pathogenic microbes that can swiftly move through new environments. Thus, diseases such as the "Hong Kong" flu or the SARS virus may originate in distant geographic locations, but they can travel quickly to do their greatest damage in other parts of the world.

Microbial Adaptation

The technological innovations intended to control disease directly can sometimes rebound with detrimental effects. A flood of antibiotics is reshaping the microbial world in many unintended ways. Antibiotics are now employed in battling microorganism in human beings and farm animals, and even in keeping bacteria from feasting on military jet fuel. In 1954, 2 million pounds of antibiotics were produced in the United States. At present the figure is well over 50 million pounds.[56] And about 18 million pounds of antibiotics, about a third of the total sold in the United States, are fed to farm animals.[57] Such indiscriminate use of antibiotics can have dire effects on evolutionary processes. Slow mutations in viruses and bacteria are a natural part of evolutionary processes. But widespread and indiscriminate use of antibiotics and some medicines can hasten these natural processes, creating families of drug-resistant microbes. In 1998, the European Union banned the use of antibiotics similar to those used in human medicine to promote animal growth. And in 2000, the Food and Drug Administration announced plans to ban two poultry drugs in the United States for similar reasons.[58]

The processes that create these dangerous mutations are not difficult to understand. Suppose that an antibiotic kills in excess of 99 percent of a targeted bacteria in a disease victim. The minuscule portion of the bacteria that resists the drug can then replicate and pass on these resistance characteristics to ensuing generations. Over thousands of generations of rapid bacterial reproduction, the resistant strains begin to crowd out the original strain that was successfully attacked by antibiotics. This process is accelerated by indiscriminate use of antibiotics; patients who don't finish prescribed treatments; and by large-scale use of antibacterial agents in soaps, lotions, detergents, and a host of other consumer products.[59]

In the United States fourteen thousand people die annually from drug-resistant microbes that infect them in hospitals. Half of the people infected with the HIV virus harbor a strain that is resistant to at least one drug used to fight the disease.[60] Only a decade ago in India, typhoid could be cured by using three inexpensive drugs, but today they are ineffective. In Southeast Asia, 98 percent of gonorrhea strains have become resistant to penicillin, the leading defensive drug for decades.[61] Drug-resistant strains of tuberculosis are being found around the world. Although there are numerous countries that haven't encountered multiple drug-resistant TB, resistance to at least one anti-TB drug now ranges from a low of 2.9 percent of all cases in New Caledonia to a high of 40.8 percent in Hena Province, China.[62] Treatment of people with multiple drug-resistant TB can take up to two years and cost up to $250,000, a sum well beyond the reach of people in poorer countries.[63] The microbes causing other diseases, such as malaria, pneumonia, and diarrhea, are also becoming resistant to medicines traditionally used in treatment.[64]

Behavioral Changes

Changes in lifestyle are also increasing the ability of microbes to attack human beings. Changing patterns of sexual behavior, such as unprotected sex with multiple partners and increased intravenous drug usage, are part of a behavioral change that has been sweeping aside many biologically sound cultural constraints that have evolved out of past experience. Historically, changes to more permissive sexual behavior have had unfortunate consequences for people persistently ignoring evolutionary wisdom.[65] Recent shifts in sexual behavior have resulted in the proliferation of sexually transmitted diseases such as HIV/AIDS, herpes, syphilis, and gonorrhea. Similarly, it is difficult to conceive of a more efficient way to transfer diseases from person to person than sharing needles to inject intravenous drugs. Such needle sharing is a novel and destructive change in human behavior and accelerates the transmission of hepatitis, HIV/AIDS, and diseases that otherwise would not easily spread.

Persisting Poverty

Poverty is closely tied to the spread of disease. Good health and related medical care come at considerable economic cost. But a number of countries have actually experienced a decline in per capita income over the last decade. Unfortunately, infectious disease, including the HIV/AIDS virus, is most rampant in some of the poorest and least industrialized countries, where medical care is woefully inadequate. Increasing numbers of people living under conditions of squalor, without access to adequate medical care, are very vulnerable to disease outbreaks. In the United States, per capita health expenditures in the mid-1990s were slightly under $3,000 per person. By contrast, per capita expenditures were $4 per person in Ethiopia and Tanzania, $6 per person in Uganda, and $8 per person in Zaire.[66]

Pharmaceutical companies aren't easily enticed to develop drugs for diseases endemic in poor countries, and intellectual property considerations keep poorer countries from developing cheaper generic versions of drugs available in the wealthy ones. In the case of HIV/AIDS, the so-called drug cocktail used to fight the disease costs about $12,000 annually, far beyond the reach of most HIV/AIDS victims in Sub-Saharan Africa. About 95 percent of the people infected with HIV live in poor countries with almost no access to life-prolonging treatments because of institutional problems and cost barriers.[67] A concerted action plan for addressing the medical needs of people in poor countries is clearly needed, but it has been difficult to find adequate funding for such programs and to overcome, except temporarily, drug company resistance to permitting the manufacture of generic drugs there.[68]

Environmental Change

Finally, environmental changes of many kinds now under way, ranging from global warming to development of aquaculture, can lead to the emergence of new forms of disease as well as increase the range of existing ones.[69] Atmospheric changes, such as the loss of ozone or the buildup of greenhouse gases, can adversely impact biosecurity. The loss of ozone and related increase in destructive ultraviolet radiation reaching the Earth's surface can be expected to increase the rate of cancer and cataracts in people and farm animals as well as the rate of genetic mutations in microorganisms. Global warming will impact the health of vulnerable people suffering through future heat waves in large cities as well as increase the geographic range of serious diseases that are now mostly restricted to the tropics.[70] Among the most worrisome candidates are malaria, schistosomiasis, filariasis, cholera, and dengue and yellow fever.[71] Increased incidence of these diseases can be expected both in mountainous areas of the tropics, where they are not now common, as well as in less tropical areas where they are now rarely found.[72] Perhaps a harbinger of things to come, an outbreak of West Nile virus, likely being carried by the climate-sensitive mosquito *Culex pipiens*, emerged in New York in the summer of 1999, and subsequently has spread over most of the United States, killing 241 people and devastating wildlife.[73]

More localized environmental changes are also contributing to the emergence of new pathogens. For example, streams, lakes, bays, and oceans increasingly serve as dumping grounds for garbage, sewage, pesticides, and chemical wastes, thereby creating a kind of primordial soup within which viruses and bacteria can mutate and also infect a wide variety of other creatures. Even seemingly innocuous environmental changes, such as increasing dependence on fish farming in China and other parts of Asia, can lead to new disease threats, particularly to virulent forms of influenza such as SARS.[74]

There also is considerable evidence that a variety of new diseases is increasingly attacking plants and animals.[75] These diseases are a threat to biodiversity, economic well-being, and also human health, since many of them have the potential to be transferred to human beings. And the increased use of antibiotics as a precaution to ward off diseases in farm animals is giving rise to antibiotic-resistant disease strains that have the potential to jump to human beings, sometimes with fatal consequences.[76]

The HIV/AIDS Pandemic

Concerns about new and resurgent diseases are certainly justified, particularly given that a contemporary pandemic is now well under way. The current HIV/AIDS pandemic is in many ways similar to historical plagues, but there also are some differences. Many of the people who are now impacted by HIV/AIDS, living in Sub-Saharan Africa, are in many ways similar to those who were afflicted by the "Black Death" in the Middle Ages. For the most part, they are poorly educated, have little understanding of the causes of diseases, and have almost no access to medical care. Most are living in poverty, and their behavior is very much shaped by tradition. On the other hand, unlike the Black Death, HIV/AIDS spreads only with some difficulty, most frequently being transmitted among people who use shared needles or engage in unprotected sexual activity with more than one person, and from infected mothers to their unborn children. Unlike the plagues of the past, which quickly moved through vast numbers of people, the HIV virus can remain in incubation for considerable periods of time, both masking the true extent of the plague and allowing victims unwittingly to pass the disease to others.

The HIV virus has been quietly spreading around the world for more than two decades, but is only now gathering significant momentum. There are now in excess of 42 million people living with HIV/AIDS (see figure 6.1). In 2001, 5 million people were newly infected with HIV, and 3 million people died of HIV/AIDS.[77] Although HIV/AIDS has spread to all countries, it is now most

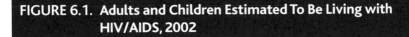

FIGURE 6.1. Adults and Children Estimated To Be Living with HIV/AIDS, 2002

Western Europe
570 000

Eastern Europe
& Central Asia
1 200 000

North America
980 000

East Asia & Pacific
1 200 000

North Africa
& Middle East
550 000

South & South-East Asia
6 000 000

Caribbean
440 000

Sub-Saharan
Africa
29 400 000

Latin America
1 500 000

Australia
& New Zealand
15 000

TOTAL : **42** MILLION

Source: UN Cartographic Section, *AIDS Epidemic Update,* December 2002, p. 34.
Used by permission.

devastating in countries characterized by high degrees of poverty and illiteracy. Thus, of the 40 million people living with the disease worldwide in 2001, 28.1 million were in Africa and 6.1 million in South and Southeast Asia.[78] The total of AIDS deaths since the pandemic began now stands at about 25 million, with 4.8 million of these being children under 15 years of age. In addition, nearly 15 million children have been left without parents by the disease.[79]

The pandemic is having its harshest impact on the countries of Sub-Saharan Africa. In the region as a whole, 8.4 percent of the adult population now is living with HIV/AIDS.[80] In Botswana, a startling 36 percent of all adults fall into this category, meaning that the country could soon come apart without dramatic remedial action. The largest number of people within a country who are

HIV positive, 4.2 million, live in South Africa, where one in every five adults is infected. Many other countries in the region are similarly affected; Zimbabwe, Swaziland, and Lesotho have one in four adults infected, Namibia and Zambia have one in five, and Mozambique, Malawi, Kenya, and the Central African Republic have one in seven.[81]

In these troubled countries, the HIV/AIDS pandemic is having a demographic and sociocultural impact similar to that of the historic plagues. In many of these less developed countries, the so-called "population pyramid" with large numbers of people in the younger age categories at the base and relatively fewer people at the top is being transformed into a "population chimney."[82] In Botswana, for example, in twenty years there likely will be more adults in their sixties and seventies than there will be in their forties and fifties. At present, a fifteen-year-old boy in Botswana has an 85 percent lifetime chance of dying of AIDS, while in South Africa the risk is 65 percent.[83] There are now seven countries in Sub-Saharan Africa with life expectancies under forty years. In Botswana, HIV/AIDS has decreased the life expectancy from the seventy-two years it would have been before the disease, to thirty-nine years at present.[84] In the southern region of Africa, life expectancy at birth rose from forty-four years in the early 1950s to fifty-nine years in the early 1990s. But it is now expected to drop back to forty-five years between 2005 and 2010.[85]

Aside from this incredible toll in human lives, the economic impact is also severe in a region of the world that already had limited prospects before the onset of HIV/AIDS.[86] A majority of those infected are in their prime working years, and their loss will be a substantial economic blow.[87] Most Sub-Saharan economies depend heavily upon agriculture. Although the agricultural sector may produce only one-quarter of a country's gross domestic product (GDP), it might provide a living for as much as three-quarters of the population. In Zimbabwe, the output from communal agriculture has reportedly fallen by 50 percent over the last five years, a significant portion of this due to HIV/AIDS. Warnings have been issued that a food crisis could develop there within twenty years due to inadequate farm labor. Other production has also been significantly impacted. Managers at a sugar plantation in Kenya report a huge increase in absenteeism and much lower productivity due to HIV/AIDS.[88] The mining sector in South Africa has been hit especially hard by a shrinking labor supply and lost productivity. An official at Anglo Coal, for example, reports that the number of shifts lost due to AIDS-related illness has doubled over the last six years, and that HIV/AIDS will cost the company nearly $25 million over the next ten years.[89] At the gold mining firm AngloGold, estimates are that one-third of its 44,000 mineworkers are infected with HIV.[90]

The HIV/AIDS pandemic in Sub-Saharan Africa, as well as in other parts of the world, raises important questions about processes of sociocultural evolution and ecological security. Old ways of addressing such problems may not work in a new world. For example, the nature of the disease was known for two decades and the potential for its explosive spread for at least a decade. But aside from laboratory research in the wealthy countries, comparatively little was done in an anticipatory mode to head off the disease in these poor countries.[91] To deal effectively with the spread of the disease requires political action and open discussions of sexual behavior and methods of having safe sex. But these are taboo subjects in many social and religious traditions. And HIV/AIDS isn't the type of issue that politicians are willing to embrace for a wide variety of cultural and strategic reasons.

The HIV/AIDS pandemic represents a major discontinuity in sociocultural evolution, with some aspects of traditional patterns of behavior leading people to contract the disease. In Sub-Saharan Africa where these sociocultural problems are severe, sex is rarely discussed. There are also African social customs that facilitate the spread of this disease. The Luo tribe in Kenya is typical of many in Africa. Widows are expected to wed a relative of the dead husband, a type of "social security" initiative that has made sense over the ages, but that now often spreads HIV/AIDS. Even Luo burials can spread HIV/AIDS. Funerals are followed by feasting, dancing, and occasionally by sexual relations among those partaking in the festivities. In many African countries, AIDS creates widows who have no means of support. These women often turn to prostitution, thus accelerating the spread of the disease.[92]

HIV/AIDS is also a politically sensitive issue, particularly in the embryonic democracies of Sub-Saharan Africa. In South Africa, in particular, the government has had a difficult time engaging the issue in the post-apartheid environment. It seems that leaders of the African National Congress made better revolutionaries than AIDS activists. Leaders such as Nelson Mandela and Thabo Mbeki have not distinguished themselves by publicly confronting the disease. It wasn't until 1998 that Mandela even mentioned HIV/AIDS in his public remarks in South Africa. More recently, President Mbeki shocked AIDS activists by questioning whether the HIV virus actually causes AIDS![93] There are some exceptions in other parts of Africa, however. In Uganda, an active government-backed anti-AIDS campaign began in the late 1980s, and the prevalence of HIV/AIDS among adults has dropped to about 8 percent as opposed to 14 percent in the early 1990s.[94]

Perhaps the most contentious set of issues brought on by the African tragedy is the clash between moral imperatives and North–South political and economic realities. At the same time that the Clinton administration was preparing to declare the AIDS pandemic a threat to national security, it was also trying to head off plans by African leaders, particularly in South Africa, to produce their own generic versions of anti-AIDS drugs. The drugs that delay the onset of AIDS have been developed at considerable cost by governments and the drug industry in the industrial countries, and carry very high price tags.

According to the Agreement on Trade-Related Aspects of Intellectual Property (TRIPS), these drugs have patent protection for at least twenty years, meaning that poorer countries theoretically have little choice but to pay high prices for medicines. But the TRIPS agreement also has an escape clause for certain circumstances, such as national emergencies, and allows governments faced by an emergency to grant the right to third parties to produce and sell a product without the consent of the patent holder.[95] Indeed, on May 10, 2000, then-president Clinton ordered a special exemption from patent laws for HIV/AIDS drugs for African countries, and promised not to invoke U.S. trade laws against Sub-Saharan countries related to protection for patents on HIV/AIDS drugs.[96] Almost simultaneously, five of the world's largest pharmaceutical companies announced their intention to slash dramatically the prices for HIV/AIDS drugs sold to Sub-Saharan countries.[97] The political economy of patents and prices for these crucial life-prolonging drugs remains murky, with governments, drug companies, and philanthropists searching for formulas to deliver these much-needed drugs effectively to victims at an affordable price without challenging the existing system of intellectual property rights.[98]

The HIV/AIDS pandemic now threatens to accelerate in Nigeria, Ethiopia, Russia, China, and India. It is estimated that the number of people with HIV/AIDS in these countries will grow from the present fourteen to twenty-three million to fifty to seventy-five million by 2010.[99] China now officially estimates at least one million people to be living with HIV/AIDS, and India nearly four million, but experts contend that the numbers are too low.[100] Ignorance about the virus is widespread in both countries and neither government has been anxious to confront the problem.[101]

Summing Up: Building Biosecurity

The threat of new and reemerging infectious diseases, buttressed by the specter of bioterrorism and the obvious devastation of the HIV/AIDS pandemic in Sub-Saharan Africa, has finally focused the attention of policymakers on the need to deal with these most basic threats to ecological security. But building biosecurity requires going beyond a simple U.S. declaration that infectious disease is a threat to security interests. The amount of money flowing into disease detection and prevention in the United States and abroad was minuscule compared to the amounts being poured into military weaponry before the 2001 anthrax episode. Since then there has been a frenzy of efforts to prepare for a bioterrorism attack, but these broader disease issues are still much ignored.

The HIV/AIDS crisis, the emergence of new diseases, and the reemergence of old diseases in poorer countries raise some very fundamental questions about relations between rich and poor in an increasingly global system. The poor countries are the most seriously impacted by infectious diseases, yet have the fewest resources to deal with them. The pharmaceutical industry, based largely in the wealthy countries, prices drugs and vaccines to maximize profits in a global marketplace, thus leaving them out of the reach of the bulk of the world's population living in poor countries. And intellectual property considerations, spelled out in the TRIPS agreement, discourage poor countries from creating their own generic versions of these much-needed drugs. In the case of HIV/AIDS, the combination of drugs that can most effectively prolong the lives of victims costs about $12,000 per year, about what government and insurance plans will bear in the economically developed countries. While there is a tremendous need for such drugs among the millions of poor HIV/AIDS victims, there is little purchasing power available to buy them. It is estimated that a generic version of these drugs could be provided for as little as $200 per person per year. Brazil gives state-of-the-art treatment to 90,000 of its 530,000 HIV-infected citizens at a cost of $4,500 per person. But 81 percent of the cost goes for drugs that Brazil must import because of patent protection.[102]

The HIV/AIDS pandemic thus sharply focuses attention on the marketplace morality that determines life and death outcomes for millions of disease victims, and the lack of any global governance mechanism that could levy taxes to remedy the situation and supply needed medicines to the global poor. There is a series of similar issues related to affordable vaccines for a number of other diseases that wreak havoc in poor tropical countries. Affordable vaccines are essential for future human well-being in poverty stricken countries, but the prospect of meager profits there makes pharmaceutical companies hesitant to develop and test them.[103]

The increasingly visible tragedy in Africa finally has occasioned piecemeal responses from governments, international agencies, companies, and philanthropists. Pharmaceutical companies have grudgingly responded to political pressures with promises of some free drugs to help HIV-infected pregnant women. The United States and the European Union once suggested to the World Trade Organization that poor countries should be allowed to produce their own generic versions of AIDS drugs.[104] But on December 20, 2002, the Bush administration, bowing to pressure from pharmaceutical companies, moved the other way, and the United States blocked a proposal before the World Trade Organization that would have permitted distribution of generic versions of patent medicines to less developed countries. The measure was sidetracked when 143 members voted for it, while the United States voted alone to veto it.[105] The Bill and Melinda Gates Foundation has given hundreds of millions of dollars to address AIDS-related problems in the developing world. The World Bank belatedly came up with $500 million for HIV/AIDS programs for African countries. And the former Clinton administration initially requested $254 million to combat HIV/AIDS abroad.[106] In January 2002, UN Security General Kofi Annan suggested the establishment of a global fund to fight HIV/AIDS, TB, and malaria. In its first year the fund received a billion dollars in pledges, including $500 million from the United States. But the fund projects that it will need at least $20 billion annually in five years to fight those diseases.[107] The problem is that these actions are much too little and too late. As economist Jeffrey Sachs has put it, "How could the world have stood by for the first twenty years of this pandemic, letting it reach 35 to 40 million people before any real funding started?"[108] And the fundamental issue of the world's poor gaining regular and affordable access to patented drugs still remains to be addressed.

Building biosecurity requires moving beyond the wake-up call represented by HIV/AIDS and emerging bioterrorism, and addressing a series of long-term security issues raised by infectious diseases. Existing institutions have been shaped and pruned by decades of complacency and budget-cutting in the mistaken belief that the battle against disease has been won.[109] The World Health Organization (WHO) was created in 1948 as the UN agency responsible for creating and disseminating international health regulations and guidelines as well as to provide technical assistance to member countries. But the WHO has been far from anticipatory or flexible in dealing with the changing disease challenges. It wasn't until 1995 that a division was created to deal with emerging and contagious diseases.[110] New leadership promises change, but member support will be essential to an effective response.

An effective biosecurity policy requires continuing surveillance and rapid response to disease outbreaks. Two surveillance networks have been established in order to monitor and assess disease outbreaks. The WHO has set up a network called WHONET that links microbiology labs around the world to a central database devoted to detecting reservoirs of drug-resistant microbes and preventing their spread. And a group of scientists in the United States has set up a Program to Monitor Emerging Diseases (ProMED), an electronic mail network that facilitates reporting on and discussions of disease outbreaks around the world.

While these are positive developments, it is of little use simply to report on disease outbreaks if no response capability exists. The Centers for Disease Control and Prevention in the United States do send teams of epidemiologists to various countries where disease outbreaks occur, but the agency has had inadequate funding to broaden its role. While the WHO would in theory be a logical choice to carry out the response function, it now lacks authority, funding, staff, and facilities to do so. Clearly, much remains to be done in addressing diseases that can quickly move through all of the neighborhoods of the emerging global city.

CHAPTER SEVEN

Technology and Ecological Security

P REVIOUS CHAPTERS have focused on imbalances in the first three relationships defining ecological security. The emphasis has been on industrialization, globalization, demographic change, and their combined impacts on environmental systems, resource availability, and other species. In the remaining chapters, the emphasis shifts from the challenges to equilibrium presented by the growing demands of dynamic populations of *Homo sapiens* to their sociocultural responses. *Homo sapiens* is different from other creatures by virtue of being able to understand these mounting challenges to ecological security and to collectively respond to them. Scientific research, technological innovation, and societal governance are important evolutionary products that can help deepen understanding of growing problems and create and implement ways of dealing with them. Science, technology, and good governance have a critical role to play in maintaining the first three equilibria that define ecological security. And they are absolutely crucial to maintaining the fourth: addressing the growing agenda of issues associated with increasingly intense interactions among societies.

The focus here shifts to socioeconomic and political processes and institutions: examining both how societies attempt to maintain these three equilibria and how they manage the increasingly complex interactions and potential conflicts among them associated with deepening globalization. While globalization brings with it a novel series of ecological challenges, it can also intensify socioeconomic insecurity, and feed more traditional kinds of conflict within and among societies. Technological innovation and related globalization are changing many of the rules governing the enduring quest for power, privilege, and prestige. In the contemporary world, as throughout history, traditional worries, such as keeping the economic wolf from the door, are still vital concerns.

Homo sapiens shares much in common biologically with other animals. This includes profiting from survival-relevant information that is passed on through processes of natural selection. Other primates, such as gorillas or chimpanzees, may pass rudimentary social skills from one generation to the next. They don't engage, however, in scientific research, nor do they make use of complex forms of governance. Their genetic inheritance pretty much determines their potential. A major difference between people and other animals, therefore, is the ability of the former to learn from the rich flow of information carried by sociocultural evolution. *Homo sapiens* engages in collective decision making, gains from scientific research, and makes extensive use of technological innovations. These attributes have been crucial in the adaptation of human societies to changing environments, and have helped to elevate an otherwise fairly nondescript primate to premier status. But while *Homo sapiens* has used these social and mental skills to reach this pinnacle, it is also the only species that has developed the potential to use sophisticated weaponry to annihilate itself.

Scientific research, technological innovation, and governance have an enormous impact on the coevolutionary processes that shape ecological security. Their past influence on biological and sociocultural evolution has been significant; their future influence will be enormous. They also have a critical impact on relations among societies. For example, science and technology play a crucial role in shaping traditional military power relationships among states. They are also critical factors in the emerging intense economic competition associated with globalization.

Governance, science, and technology have been and continue to be major factors altering human relationships with nature. For example, innovations in medicine have had a major impact on the length of the life span and human reproduction, and thus, the human genome. Innovations ranging from eyeglasses to kidney dialysis now permit people who probably would have died young in an earlier era to survive long enough to reproduce, and thus make a contribution to the future gene pool. And future innovations in genetic engineering will expand significantly the human impact on biological evolution.[1]

Similarly, the printing press, radio, television, computers, and telecommunication satellites have already had, and will continue to have, a tremendous influence on sociocultural evolution, expanding dramatically the dissemination of ideas within and among societies.

Technological innovation is a powerful force that can help people live in greater harmony with nature. And it has, in many ways, strengthened ecological security by enhancing nature's productivity. Thus, the observation made by the Reverend Thomas Malthus at the end of the eighteenth century that future population growth would outrun the ability to grow food seems somewhat erroneous, at least to this point, because of a technological revolution in agriculture. Technology has dramatically reshaped relationships between people and other organisms. Various kinds of weapons, ranging from mousetraps to rifles, have shifted the balance between people and a wide variety of pests and predators. Advances in medicine and sanitation continue to keep most pathogenic microorganisms in check, even as people expose themselves to more risky situations.

Technology is also a force that creates and redistributes power and wealth. It has been a key factor in historical power shifts both within and among societies.[2] It has been a driving force behind major sociocultural transformations and social paradigm shifts. It is currently the force that is changing the rules and concerns of warfare and diplomacy. From clubs and spears to thermonuclear warheads, innovations in weaponry have shaped the fortunes of peoples, nations, and empires. Technology and engineering have played an equally important role in wealth production, economic competition, and related stratification within and among societies. They have also been major factors in creating a large and persisting development gap between rich and poor, both within and among societies.

Scientific discovery and technological innovation are processes that generally have had a positive impact on human welfare. But many innovations have had unforeseen side effects, creating new problems while ostensibly remedying existing ones.[3] Although essential to supporting billions of people at ever-increasing levels of consumption, many of the same innovations responsible for increased well-being have also had serious negative impacts on nature. For example, antibiotics have cut a wide swath through the ranks of pathogens, but in doing so have given rise to antibiotic-resistant organisms. Fertilizers have greatly increased agricultural productivity, but run-off has often polluted nearby lakes and streams. And while pesticides have helped to save crops from hordes of insects, many of them have had unforeseen effects on people and ecosystems. It is the management or stewardship of technology, carefully assessing and monitoring the uses to which it is put, that is most critical in determining its long-term impact on ecological security.

Good governance, therefore, is crucial to ecological security. The interaction of societies with nature is mediated by public policy. Science and technology policy can move in any number of directions. It can be driven solely by market forces, influenced by government funding, or tightly controlled by governments. Technological innovation can augment resources, increase the diversity of available products, enlarge markets, and enhance productivity.[4] During the course of the Industrial Revolution, the main thrust of technological innovation has been to increase the efficiency of human labor. Progress has come to be defined as increased economic output per hour worked. But there have been significant consequences of following this path, a critical one being substantial increases in environmental pollution. There is no reason, however, that future patterns of innovation can't be shaped to enhance ecological security by focusing on ways to use resources more efficiently, thereby eliminating much of the environmental pollution associated with economic growth.

Innovation: A Double-Edged Sword

Not all technological innovation and diffusion has a benign impact on ecological security. While innovations often help to remedy imbalances between people and nature, they also can have unforeseen side effects. Technology is thus a double-edged sword, helping to resolve some critical environmental problems associated with globalization, while also creating new challenges. Sometimes innovations can reduce substantially the impact of human activities on natural systems.[5] The development and use of stack scrubbers in electric power plants has played a positive role in clearing the air. But in other cases innovations have been environmentally disruptive. For example, the automobile has given unprecedented mobility to large numbers of people, but at the expense of countless environmental insults ranging from urban pollution to global warming.

The worldwide spread of biomedical technologies has had, and will continue to have, significant and somewhat unexpected impacts on demographic change. A population explosion in the Global South was originally facilitated by the spread of health care technology, which reduced infant mortality and lengthened life spans. It wasn't until the development and diffusion of new family planning technologies, such as birth control pills, that population growth there began to slow. But now other kinds of innovations are creating new kinds of demographic challenges. For example, the spread of diagnostic ultrasound machines, capable of detecting the sex of a fetus, is significantly distorting sex ratios in many countries, particularly in Asia. In China, sex-selective abortions prompted by the use of the new machines are reflected in statistics that show that 117 males now are born for every 100 females. There are now forty-one million more males than females in China, and the disparity continues to grow in spite of laws against such practices. A trade in kidnapped women is now booming, and Chinese gangs traffic in Vietnamese and North Korean women for potential Chinese husbands.[6] Sex-selective abortions in China and other Asian countries are creating demographic bulges of males, who then have a reduced likelihood of marriage or children, a situation that could impact the future stability of the Asian region.[7]

Technological innovation can reduce the environmental pressures of economic growth by facilitating a process called dematerialization. This ongoing process is reducing the quantity of raw materials needed to produce a unit of economic output. Some dematerialization is related to the general structural shift from the production of goods to provision of services in the economies of advanced industrial countries. But dematerialization can also result from technology policies that lead to reduced material requirements. The earliest computers were based on vacuum tube technology and were so big that large rooms were required to house them. The same functions are now performed by laptops that can be carried to and from the office. Similarly, contemporary automobiles are much lighter and more fuel-efficient than their predecessors, due to the use of plastics and composites to replace the heavier metals previously used. The weight of the average car (excluding SUVs) in the United States has fallen by 660 pounds since the early 1970s.[8] The overall material intensity per unit of gross domestic product (GDP) in the United States has dropped significantly in recent years. Unfortunately, this decline has been more than balanced by increases in GDP, thus resulting in a slight increase in the total amount of materials used.[9]

Technology has also played a key role in increasing resources available to enhance human nutrition, thus avoiding some of the worst Malthusian predictions. The application of industrial era technologies to agriculture has enormously expanded world food production. The increasing use of man-made fertilizers in agriculture has fostered a rapid expansion of food production over the last fifty years, particularly in the wealthy countries where farmers can afford to apply them. Nitrogen is important in increasing crop yields. The current world production of nitrogenous fertilizers is greater than the total amount of nitrogen deposited on farmland from all natural sources.[10] But the downside is that the biosphere has become glutted with nitrogen. The land can no longer absorb or break down all of these nitrogen compounds, and much nitrogen winds up in rivers, lakes, and oceans, creating algae blooms and similar problems.[11]

A new generation of biotechnology holds the potential to once again transform world agriculture. This nascent revolution in genetically modified organisms also has both positive and negative implications for ecological security. The first wave of commercially available genetically modified seeds has been designed to be herbicide tolerant or pest resistant, possibly reducing the amount of conventional pesticides and herbicides to be applied to crops. But at the same time, there are significant risks associated with becoming dependent on genetically modified crops. These include innocent creatures being adversely impacted by them, insect pests developing tolerance to the built-in insecticides, or these foods harming people.[12] And it is unclear what role, if any, such innovations might play in improving agricultural production in the poor countries that are in greatest need of more food.

In the energy field new technologies are helping to meet the world's growing energy needs. Novel drilling and recovery techniques in the oil and gas industries are opening up previously inaccessible areas for production, and extending the lives of existing fields. But now, the twin specters of fossil fuel depletion and greenhouse warming require conservation and decarbonization, necessitating a new mix of energy sources including renewables and nuclear power.[13] But nuclear energy is very much a Faustian bargain, producing relatively clean power, but also increasing the risk of potential future disasters, like Chernobyl, as well as creating seemingly intractable problems of transportation and long-term storage of highly radioactive waste.

Antibiotics and other medicines have become critical in maintaining the health of the more than six billion people in the world living under increasingly crowded urban conditions. But excessive use of antibiotics, disinfectants, and antiseptics is leading to increased bacterial resistance. For example, many strains of *Staphylococcus aureus*, which can cause blood poisoning and pneumonia, are now resistant to all antibiotics but vancomycin. Strains have recently been detected that also are resistant to vancomycin, foreshadowing the day when no current antibiotics will be effective against the bacteria.[14] Excessive use of antibiotics in animal feed, where they are employed for prophylaxis and growth promotion, makes a significant contribution to the resistance problem. In Denmark in the mid-1990s, for example, 24 kilograms of vancomycin were used nationwide for all human therapy, while 1,000 times as much of its close relative, avoparcin, was used in agriculture.[15] In 1995, Denmark banned avoparcin from animal feed, and a second antibiotic, virginiamycin, was banned in 1998. Danish farmers also voluntarily removed all other antibiotics from their feed. As a result, in chickens the prevalence of one type of intestinal bacteria resistant to vancomycin dropped from 73 percent to 6 percent between 1995 and 2000. Similar results were found in a sample of pigs.[16] In the United States, the Food and Drug Administration (FDA) in 2000 banned two antibiotics used in poultry farming, but Bayer Corporation, the maker of one of them, challenged the ban in court. The FDA issued new draft guidance to deal with the problem in late 2002.[17]

Perhaps the greatest impact of technological innovation and diffusion on ecological security, however, has been the profound transformation of living standards, cultures, and relationships among people and societies. Technology has been a stratifying force; those who have mastered it usually have dominated those who have not. Most obvious is the role that more sophisticated weapons have played in transforming military hierarchies. The world's great empires have been built on a foundation of superior technologies. The Romans, for example, not only possessed more sophisticated weaponry than those societies that they conquered, but the Roman legions had enhanced logistical capacity including engineering, road building, and organization. The British Empire was also forged through use of sophisticated weapons, and it was maintained by improvements in transportation and telecommunications.[18]

Warfare has also shaped evolutionary processes, principally through either the assimilation or the elimination of societies and associated cultures as a result of combat. But the Industrial Revolution gave birth to large-scale industrialized warfare and related world wars that reshaped both nature and societies. Thus, World War I resulted in 26 million total military and civilian deaths and World War II in 53.5 million. The latter war dramatically shifted the demographic face of Europe. The Holocaust eliminated much of its Jewish population. In Russia there is now a significantly greater number of elderly women than men, a legacy of World War II. The major powers now have at their disposal thermonuclear, chemical, and biological weapons that, if used in the future, could wipe out a significant portion of the human race, as well as dramatically change the global ecosystem.

In the contemporary world, however, the emphasis on a hierarchy maintained by military force has gradually been supplanted by a hierarchy shaped by economic competition. This is not to claim that the major powers are on the verge of disarming. Indeed, the United States has been particularly committed to the use of high technology weaponry in wars of various kinds. But for many reasons, including the threat of mutual annihilation, large-scale warfare among the affluent countries of the Global North seems increasingly unlikely.

Technology and Sociocultural Revolutions

Technological innovation and diffusion also have been forces responsible for shaping sociocultural evolution and transforming relations among people.[19] There have been two major clusters of innovation leading to revolutionary transformations within and among the impacted societies.[20] The first of these technology-driven transformations, now known as the Agricultural Revolution, apparently took root in several places around the world beginning around 8000 B.C.E. The second transformation, the Industrial Revolution, began gathering momentum in the fifteenth and sixteenth centuries in Europe, and is still spreading to the more remote areas of the planet. Both of these revolutions dramatically transformed relations among peoples and between them and nature. Each of them was both driven and enabled by bursts of technological innovation that diffused from one country to another, creating new social paradigms; dismantling existing cultures; reshaping worldviews; redefining human values and purpose; and transforming political, economic, and social life.[21]

The revolution in agriculture got its initial impetus from the domestication of plants and animals, which, over time, permitted people to move from hunting and gathering to a more secure livelihood in farming. This shift resulted in better diets and more dependable supplies of food. The development of this more sedentary way of life was accompanied by modest population growth, the emergence of small cities, and eventually by a more complex division of labor. As this revolution gathered momentum, it produced subsequent clusters of related innovations and growing social surplus (capital) that was eventually large enough to support substantial military adventures, some of which culminated in the growth of empires of significant size.[22]

The more recent Industrial Revolution, the latter stages of which are marked by its spread to the Global South, gained much of its initial momentum from innovations that first harnessed wind and water on a large scale to do work that previously was done by people and draft animals. It subsequently enhanced productivity through much more complex industrial technologies that fed on a generous energy "subsidy" stored in coal, petroleum, and natural gas.[23] Agricultural cultures have been dramatically transformed as this modernizing Industrial Revolution has spread worldwide. As a result, people have been liberated from traditional social constraints; slavery and serfdom have been gradually reduced; and political and economic freedoms have been enhanced. New political and social institutions developed, and economic capitalism laid the foundations for even more intense technological innovation, economic activity, and, eventually, globalization.

This spread of industrial activity has had a mixed impact on ecological security. Initially, populations in industrializing societies grew slowly, but then increased rapidly in size as improved medicine, nutrition, and sanitation cut mortality rates substantially. Indeed, living standards have increased sharply, over time, in many countries. But, on the other hand, growing numbers of factories have released a torrent of pollutants that have fouled the air and streams and have adversely impacted human health. Nature has been "technoformed," as forests and farmland have given way to pavement and factories in order to meet the material needs of growing numbers of people. Other species have felt the brunt of human expansionism as well, as significant numbers of them have been banished from their habitats or even vanished in this increasingly uneven competition with people. But more ominous, the material successes of the industrial period have given rise to the arrogant belief that *Homo sapiens* is now wise enough to be exempt from the laws of nature, and can ignore the wisdom produced by the coevolutionary processes that shape ecological security.[24]

While the industrial way of thinking and organizing continues to move fitfully into the more peripheral areas of the world, there are ample signs of yet another massive technology-driven sociocultural transformation emerging in the affluent countries. This nascent postindustrial revolution hasn't yet been properly named, but it is being driven and enabled by clusters of innovations in transportation, telecommunication, and digital-, nano-, and bio-technologies.[25] As in the other two revolutions, these emerging technologies have the potential to transform human relationships with nature as well as the social paradigm shared by people in industrialized societies.

Each of the two previous revolutionary periods gave rise to larger sociopolitical units. The Agricultural Revolution provided the economic capital essential to the formation of early states and ultimately the military ventures that led to empires such as the Egyptian, Roman, or Macedonian. The Industrial Revolution eventuated in the rise of powerful states and then in networks of colonies that brought people from around the world into much closer contact. This nascent third revolution is, in turn, creating units well beyond the state and shaping a global system in which much larger numbers of people are in increasingly frequent physical and mediated contact.

This third revolution in human affairs represents a similar discontinuity in evolutionary processes. Scientists are now deciphering the genetic codes of people, plants, and animals. They are developing the capabilities to redo the work of millions of years of natural selection. Similarly, the dynamics of sociocultural evolution are at risk, as the institutional templates for passing accumulated social wisdom from one generation to the next are disintegrating. Whether *Homo sapiens* is wise enough and well-governed enough to understand and deal with the consequences of these changes in an anticipatory fashion, or must suffer the consequences of a devastating loss of biological and cultural wisdom, remains to be seen.[26]

Economic Globalization

This emerging period of discontinuity promises to change dramatically relations among peoples, as did the previous two. Postindustrial technologies are enabling rapid globalization, and challenging the powers of states. Economic globalization has come first, and the problems of governing a nascent global economy now are becoming obvious. But economic globalization inevitably brings with it ecological and sociocultural globalization, and a growing agenda of related harmonization issues.

Globalization has many positive aspects. Theoretically, a much more refined worldwide division of labor and the expansion of global markets should maximize production of goods and services. A worldwide flow of images, information, and ideas could produce greater understanding among peoples. But contemporary globalization also forces revolutionary changes in the lives of many. Like all revolutions, there are unforeseen costs, and these costs often are paid by those who have little voice in globalization processes.

Economic globalization lies at the core of a complex of changes that carries differential costs and benefits for the people involved. For the fortunate, economic globalization is a consensual process driven by a belief that worldwide markets and a global division of labor offers them the potential for greater wealth. The political and economic elites who control worldwide capital flows are eager participants in this process. But economic globalization is contentious, as it not only creates wealth for the fortunate, but marginalizes those without the intellectual or financial resources to profit from it.

Economic globalization can be a positive force in addressing many material aspects of human insecurity. The logic behind it is that an emerging world market maximizes the potential for exploiting comparative advantage, thus advancing productivity and promoting economic growth. As borders and barriers disappear, capital should flow to the most productive parts of the world. While the mix of attributes that attract capital varies across industries, it includes factors such as low wages, abundant natural resources, political stability, an educated labor force, and access to transportation.

More frequent interaction among peoples brings with it the need to harmonize practices, customs, institutions, and values that have evolved separately over time in myriad diverse cultures. Economic harmonization, including agreements aimed at reducing tariff and non-tariff barriers to trade, has been the first step in this process. During the last fifty years of trade liberalization, tariffs on manufactured goods entering industrial countries have been reduced by 90 percent. As a result, in industrial countries imports and exports as a share of GDP rose from 12.8 percent in 1970 to 21.0 percent in 1999.[27]

Economic harmonization is now moving beyond tariffs on manufactured goods and into more politically sensitive areas such as services and agriculture. "As a consequence, open trade can conflict with long-standing social contracts that protect certain activities from the relentlessness of the free market. This is a key tension generated by globalization."[28] The process of harmonizing domestic economic practices, standards, values, and institutions with those that have evolved elsewhere under other circumstances understandably creates tensions and raises controversial issues, particularly since it is the views of American economists that have predominated.

In democratic societies, such important questions normally are subject to public scrutiny. But it is peculiar to the nature of economic globalization that it is frequently distant bureaucrats, economists, and lawyers, who have never stood for election, who make critical harmonization decisions. Thus, very crucial issues of how rules governing economic and other aspects of globalization are set, who participates in these processes, and how these people are selected remain controversial, and give rise to unruly demonstrations when international financial institutions hold their annual meetings.

There are several systemic perils associated with deepening economic globalization that potentially could have a very negative impact on the young global economy. Primary among these is the risk of economic contagion as the barriers separating the world's diverse economies are brought down. In a world composed of more tightly linked economies, economic "viruses" can spread rapidly through the expanding links that connect them. Thus, the seemingly perpetual concern with the economic health of developing economies such as Argentina, Brazil, Turkey, and Thailand or even with the larger Russian and Japanese economies.

A second kind of peril associated with deepening economic globalization is the vulnerability of marginal countries in the global economy, and their ecosystems, to rapid capital movements and speculation leading to currency destabilization. Economic predators can profit by periodically attacking weak currencies, but at a heavy cost to the countries under assault. Recent examples are the rapid fluctuation in value and the wholesale destruction of several Asian currencies. Currency devaluation and a related economic crisis in Indonesia in the late 1990s led to a wholesale assault on nature as people fought off starvation by eating or exporting almost all living things of any value. As one observer put it at the time, "The Indonesian Crisis is jumping species. It's well known that people are hungry, hurting and scared. Now, down the food chain, elephants, monkeys and other wildlife are dying."[29]

Finally, economic globalization can be accompanied by the twin tragedies of exploitation and dislocation. In many ways, exploitation is old wine in new bottles. People and resources in poor areas of the world have been exploited for the benefit of those in wealthy countries for centuries. But globalization can accelerate this exploitation of cheap labor and devastation of natural resources in a so-called race to the bottom. The other face of exploitation is the dislocation of workers in the countries from which industries migrate in search of cheap labor, abundant resources, and lax environmental standards. Thus, tens of thousands of blue collar workers in the United States and elsewhere have paid a "globalization penalty" in the form of unemployment and declining living standards in recent years due to growing imports, as well as the migration of blue collar, and even white collar, jobs to other countries.[30]

In the aggregate, the extent to which globalization is making people more economically secure or insecure is unclear; there are winners and losers. Large protests against globalization would seem to indicate that there are significant numbers of people who are being made more insecure. As economist Dani Rodrik has put it, "In practice, however, trade becomes contentious, when it unleashes forces that undermine the social norms implicit in domestic practices. . . . Trade usually redistributes income among industries, regions, and individuals. Therefore, a principled defense of free trade cannot be constructed without addressing the question of fairness and legitimacy of the practices that generate these distributional 'costs.' How comparative advantage is created matters."[31]

Deeper Harmonization

The early stages of economic globalization have focused on harmonizing trade policies, primarily by reducing tariff barriers, but more fundamental questions must be confronted as countries continue to attempt to establish a level playing field for international commerce. Pressures to harmonize domestic environmental standards and policies regarding genetically modified organisms are a logical extension of these economic negotiations. But deeper globalization also implies increasing pressure for sociocultural harmonization. Questions of minimum wages, child labor, human rights, cultural autonomy, and political democracy get mixed into the discussion.

There is an ongoing discussion of the extent to which states should be allowed to exploit the global commons or domestic environments in order to gain a competitive trade advantage. There is a related controversy over the extent to which trade agreements should be permitted to supercede domestic environmental standards.[32] Given the priority that the industrial countries give to economic globalization, the World Trade Organization (WTO) now has the power to adjudicate such disputes. Because the organization is staffed mainly by economists, there has been a tendency to give priority to trade when in conflict with environmental concerns.[33] For example, in 1998 a WTO appeals panel initially overturned an American law protecting sea turtles. It is estimated that up to 150,000 turtles a year drown in nets used to catch shrimp worldwide. U.S. law stipulates that any shrimp imported into the United States must be caught with nets that allow trapped turtles to escape. But India, Pakistan, Malaysia, and Thailand charged the United States with erecting a non-tariff barrier to trade.[34] After considerable maneuvering, the Appellate Body of the WTO recognized the relevance of the CITES agreement protecting endangered species in this case, and cautiously sided with the United States.[35] A similar situation is developing out of attempts to encourage better forest management by certifying "green timber." These wood products are certified as having been harvested using environmentally acceptable techniques. But the issue arises as to whether U.S. federal, state, or local governments are permitted to require purchase of green timber for governmental use.[36]

Other issues of environment and health have also become snarled in trade disputes.[37] There is an ongoing dispute between the United States and the European Union (EU) over the American practice of dosing beef cattle with hormones in order to hasten their growth. EU officials claim that hormone residues in beef represent a threat to young children, and have banned the import of hormone-laden beef. U.S. officials claim that the ban, in place since 1989, is really designed to protect European farmers from competition and represents an unfair trade practice.[38]

Disputes among countries are also growing over genetically modified foods. Again, the United States, the largest producer of such foods, is pitted against the European Union and several other countries. Europeans argue for a ban on all such imports on safety grounds, but this could also be construed as a violation of free trade. The struggle over such crops has also moved to Asia, where genetically modified foods have previously been well received. Many Japanese consumers refuse to buy genetically modified foods, Indian farmers have ripped up fields of modified cotton, and politicians in the Philippines have delayed field trials of such crops.[39] Continuing negotiations over these issues resulted in the Cartagena Protocol on Biosafety, which was opened for signature in 2000.[40] The United States only participated in the negotiations as an observer and is not likely to ratify the agreement.

The amount of increased contact among cultures generated by economic globalization naturally creates its own momentum for cultural harmonization.

But even among the industrial countries there is growing discomfort over the leveling demands of global capitalism.[41] Many of the traumas associated with opening up economies are paralleled by those of opening up societies. Creating a level playing field economically requires addressing many social and political questions ranging from government support of industries to child labor and human rights.

A *BusinessWeek* article on increased competition in the world wine industry offers an apt metaphor for the impact of globalization on cultural diversity. Commenting on the changing nature of competition in the world wine industry, the article points out that a flood of cheap wine from the United States, Chile, and Australia is decimating the traditional French wine industry. While the French have an ancient wine culture that has maintained a complex system of 450 labeling regions and very strict rules on how grapes should be grown and wine should be made, the new foreign competition is not bound by any such traditions. Thus, the French may produce very distinct regional premium wines that can be clearly identified by their *appellation d'origine*, but the "modern" foreign companies often produce cheap, uniform, generic wines. While French winemakers often age their wine in oak barrels to add flavor, many new world wineries simply throw oak chips into the brew fermenting in steel barrels. While the best-known French chateaux will certainly continue to sell to the high-end market, a large portion of the smaller and less well known producers simply will be eliminated by the lean and mean competition.[42]

The similarities with more general sociocultural globalization issues are obvious. Globalization is seen by its critics as a large-scale assault by a technologically overdeveloped and increasingly uniform industrial culture on the storehouse of wisdom that traditional cultures represent.[43] The homogenizing influence of Westernization is steadily extinguishing these surviving evolutionary products, and the rich wisdom that they may contain. As Benjamin Barber has put it, "McWorld is a product of popular culture driven by expansionist commerce. Its template is American, its form style. Its goods are as much images as materiel, an aesthetic as well as a product line. It is about culture as commodity, apparel as ideology."[44] It remains to be seen whether, in the long-run, this McWorld can evolve into a more complex and resilient culture with the potential to endure.

Intellectual Property

There are few areas in which harmonizing of practices cuts more deeply to the core of cultures than treatment of intellectual property. Intellectual property laws determine developments in broad areas of social activity ranging from treatment of literature and music to the organization of research and development. Safeguarding intellectual property has emerged as a serious point of contention between the United States, the country responsible for much of the world's research and development, and many less industrialized countries that don't share the U.S. perspective. There is general agreement that the rights of creators of intellectual property must be protected in order to encourage invention and creativity in increasingly market oriented societies. There is also at least theoretical agreement that these rights must be balanced by obligations to make such property available to people at a reasonable price.

Using patents and copyrights to stimulate technological innovation and literary expression originated in the Venetian city-state and gradually spread to other European countries, where it assumed a variety of forms and functions. Initial attempts to reach international agreement and harmonize intellectual property standards resulted in the Paris Convention for the Protection of Industrial Property, which was signed in 1883. The agreement set no minimum standards of patent protection, but it did obligate the signatories not to discriminate against foreigners when providing intellectual property protection. Shortly thereafter, in 1886 the Berne Convention for the Protection of Literary and Artistic Works was negotiated to protect the intellectual property rights of artists, writers, musicians, and other creators of literary and artistic products. Both of these basic agreements have been much amended in subsequent negotiations. A World Intellectual Property Organization (WIPO) emerged in 1893 out of the secretariat set up to administer these two basic agreements.[45]

Prior to the 1990s, the business of harmonizing patent, copyright, and trademark policies was carried out by WIPO. Starting in the 1970s, however, discontent with WIPO and the framework provided by the Paris and Berne Conventions began to build in some of the industrialized countries, particularly the United States. In the late 1970s, representatives of U.S. pharmaceutical companies and the U.S. Patent and Trademark Office began to pressure WIPO for a new diplomatic conference that would fundamentally reform intellectual property rules. The director general of WIPO refused the request, pointing out that the less industrialized countries were adamantly opposed to changing the status quo.[46] WIPO, having become a part of the United Nations system in 1974, was much more driven by the interests of the less industrialized nations that made up the bulk of UN membership than it was by those of the United States.

In a stroke of hegemonic genius, the United States devised a strategy for circumventing the WIPO "problem" by dragging intellectual property issues into a forum that it and other industrialized countries dominated, the Uruguay Round of trade negotiations within the framework of the General Agreement on Tariffs and Trade (GATT). The less industrialized countries opposed this gambit, arguing that WIPO was the appropriate forum for such talks, but the United States rounded up a coalition of forty countries that agreed to the inclusion of intellectual property concerns in the Uruguay Round.[47] At the conclusion of the Uruguay Round in 1994, an agreement on Trade Related Intellectual Property Rights (TRIPS) had been fully integrated into international trade agreements.

The ways that societies approach intellectual property is a product of sociocultural evolution. Historically, the concept of intellectual property has been almost irrelevant in many societies. In writing about biological innovations, Vandana Shiva notes,

> Central to the privatization of knowledge and biodiversity is the devaluation of local knowledge, the displacement of local rights, and simultaneously, the creation of monopoly rights to biodiversity utilization through the claim of novelty. It has sometimes been argued that monopolies exist even in traditional communities. Yet, in the case of agriculture, for example, seeds and knowledge are freely exchanged as gifts. Similarly, knowledge of medicinal plants is a local common resource.[48]

In the past, no one has collected royalties for inventing bows and arrows or for developing cooperative techniques to hunt game. In many societies, music and poetry have been treated as public goods, freely shared among all members. And inventors and creators have seldom been solely motivated by greed, but have also subsisted on the prestige associated with their work.

The pace of change and the pressures for harmonization in an increasingly complex global market system have focused attention on several contentious intellectual property issues that divide people within and among societies. The first, and perhaps most crucial, of these is the question of who is afforded an opportunity to participate in making intellectual property policy. In most countries elections don't turn on intellectual property issues. And the delicate balance between the rights of creators and the well-being of society seems to be tipped in the direction of creators, and their small army of lawyers that dominate policy making. In international forums, economic interests take precedence over sociocultural and developmental concerns. The TRIPS negotiation within the GATT framework is clearly a case in point. Given the strong role played by the United States within GATT, economic concerns of industrial countries were dominant, and deeper moral, philosophical, and developmental issues were largely ignored.[49] But the rules laid down by powerful economic interests that control policy in industrialized countries may well have little legitimacy in other settings.[50]

A second set of issues concerns the amount of protection given to innovations and artistic works in relation to the needs of society to have access to them. The global system is composed of countries with different developmental needs, different value systems, different economic systems, and much different stakes in the long-term protection of intellectual property. Countries of the Global South have little interest in harmonizing standards on industrial country terms. Even in the industrial countries, however, a case can be made for reducing, rather than increasing, protection of intellectual property. Over time, governments in these countries have played a very significant role in education, as well as in financing research and development, and a strong argument can be made for increased public access to products derived from government-sponsored research.[51] But ever since socialism was overwhelmed by market ideologies, such arguments find little resonance in political processes increasingly dominated by corporate interests.

A third set of issues concerns the kinds of incentives that are required to induce people to innovate. Market oriented societies emphasize the importance of patents and copyrights in insuring that individual and corporate creators are amply rewarded economically for their innovations. But this neglects the fact that people innovate and create for a number of reasons. Some of the greatest literary and artistic contributions have been motivated simply by a concern for improving the human condition. Thus, Aristotle had no need for a literary agent, and there is little evidence that Tolstoy wrote mainly in order to meet mortgage payments. Physicians have historically developed innovative techniques to operate on the sick as part of what is considered to be their moral obligation, and in most countries such medical procedures cannot be patented. But in the United States, some surgeons have broken ranks and attempted to patent certain kinds of simple medical procedures, suing their colleagues for using them without permission.[52] While financial considerations are certainly important in countries increasingly dominated by research bureaucracies within large corporations, deeper questions must be raised about the wisdom and efficacy of such policies.

Finally, there are a number of persisting ethical and developmental issues concerning the kinds of innovations that should be protected by patent and the duration of such protection. While there are significant measurement problems in determining exactly where the world's brainpower is concentrated, most attempts at quantifying research and development come to the logical conclusion that more than 90 percent of technological innovation occurs in the Global North. From the perspective of many countries in the Global South, the existing intellectual property regime offers them few benefits and has little legitimacy, particularly given

that many presently industrialized countries, including the United States, pur-
loined technology freely from other countries as they industrialized.

Perhaps more important are specific disagreements over what kinds of products should receive extensive patent protection, and what are reasonable prices to
be charged for them. Pharmaceuticals are a case in point. In the early days of the
HIV/AIDS epidemic, AZT was the only drug that offered much hope to victims.
And the manufacturer took full advantage of the situation by setting high prices for
the life-prolonging product, knowing that much of the income was going to come
directly from public treasuries. More recently, a combination of very expensive
drugs has been found to be effective in fighting the HIV/AIDS virus, but the pharmaceutical companies, based in industrial countries, originally priced the combination well beyond the reach of millions of poor HIV/AIDS victims in Sub-Saharan
Africa. This resulted in a delicate political game in which pharmaceutical companies searched for stop-gap "aid" solutions that could dampen the resulting moral
outrage, and thereby avoid a damaging assault on the intellectual property regime.

A different set of challenges to harmonization of traditional intellectual
property practices is presented by the novel and complex challenges raised by
the speed with which cutting edge postindustrial technologies are moving.[53]
Foremost among these is a series of pivotal ethical and ecological issues raised
by the fast-paced developments taking place in biotechnology. Geneticists and
biologists are now unlocking many of the most basic secrets of life, and patent
offices, courts, and international negotiators increasingly find themselves applying industrial precedents to postindustrial issues.

In a precedent that has shaped the course of a worldwide debate, the U.S.
Supreme Court decided by one vote in the *Diamond v Chakrabarty* case in 1980
(444 US 1028) that genetically modified organisms could receive patent protection. Subsequent biological research has raised a host of more complex issues.
One of them concerns the desirability of granting patents for nature's own
products and processes. Patents are now being issued for the so-called "discovery" of existing human, animal, and plant genes whenever scientists can describe
them and their functions. Thus, a worldwide search is now under way for plants
and animals with economically useful characteristics, much to the chagrin of
the less industrialized countries where many of these species are found. Often,
the usefulness of these plants and animals is well known to indigenous populations, but they have never had the money or inclination to file for patents. Thus,
in the mid-1990s, two scientists of Indian origin working at the University of
Mississippi Medical Center were granted a patent for the medical uses of
turmeric, the spice used in making curry. A subsequent challenge from India's
Council of Scientific and Industrial Research pointed out that the medical use of

turmeric was mentioned in many Indian writings including one in ancient Sanskrit, and thus was hardly original. In this case the U.S. Patent Office actually reversed itself in 1997.[54] But the appropriation of folk knowledge continues as large corporations scour the world searching for new biological materials.

Developments in other fields raise similar challenges to the existing intellectual property regime. A flood of supposed innovations in computers and telecommunications keeps patent offices and court systems working overtime. The patent and copyright dominance of industrial countries is further cemented by corporations that make bold intellectual property claims in the hopes of striking it rich in the courts. There is abundant evidence that corporations are trying to lock up future intellectual property rights by making very broad claims. For example, in the mid-1990s, the company TRW attempted to obtain a patent on a wide band of outer space, claiming that its idea of placing satellites in orbit there was a patentable idea.[55]

The intellectual property regime that evolved out of an industrial era is now being challenged by the pace of change and complexity of issues in the postindustrial period. But the less industrialized countries have played little role in shaping this regime and can do little to protest it and the related large scale appropriation of intellectual property tied to it, since these agreements are now closely tied to preservation of trade privileges. It is common knowledge that presently industrialized countries ignored intellectual property laws to jump-start their own industries. More than two centuries ago, U.S. officials willfully ignored British patents on industrial machines in order to spur the domestic industry. But as Seth Shulman has put it, "The intellectual property laws favored by the United States make it extremely difficult for these (developing) countries to establish their own base in emerging fields such as biotechnology or software development. In such a regime the fledgling local industries have to contend with a daunting array of royalty payments and legal permissions, not to mention the formidable technological hurdles involved."[56] Harmonization of intellectual property policies in a diverse global village will remain a contentious process for the foreseeable future.

Technology and Conflict

Technological innovation and diffusion have always played a crucial role in defining the nature and scope of conventional security threats. Beginning with knives and continuing through bows and arrows to tanks, planes, and nuclear-tipped missiles, innovations in weaponry have greatly increased the potential for both wartime loss of human lives and environmental damage. At present, the major powers have accumulated a substantial arsenal of nuclear and thermonuclear weapons that, if ever used in substantial quantity, could bring on a "nuclear winter" that would have a major impact on the evolution of all forms of life.[57] Even the fallout from a nuclear conflict between lesser nuclear powers, such as India and Pakistan, would have devastating ecological consequences.

Given this situation, the threat of large-scale conventional or nuclear warfare among the industrial powers is now receding. But it is being replaced with new security threats from smaller countries, terrorist groups, or even demented individuals. In the words of Martin Libicki, "Today, almost every element of power can be acquired in the global marketplace. Information technologies have given nearly everyone a voice in the world arena. And so it seems that the small have caught up with the strong and that size does not matter, at least as it once did."[58]

This change in the source of threats is at least partially due to perceptions of the huge number of casualties and tremendous damage to the environment that would result from another major war. But it is also due to the growing vulnerability of ever more complex societies to terrorist activities. As Thomas Homer-Dixon has put it, "Modern societies face a cruel paradox: Fast-paced technological and economic innovations may deliver unrivaled prosperity, but they also render rich nations vulnerable to crippling, unanticipated attacks. By relying on intricate networks and concentrating vital assets in small geographic clusters, advanced Western nations only amplify the destructive power of terrorists—and the psychological and financial damage they can inflict."[59] It is now possible for individuals and small groups to get access to destructive power capable of killing thousands of people, as the destruction of the Federal Building in Oklahoma City in 1995 and the World Trade Center in New York in 2001 illustrate. Even the U.S. Postal Service has been paralyzed by dissemination of weapons-grade anthrax, possibly the work of only one individual.

The accelerating development of postindustrial technologies is creating novel security threats to increasingly complex societies. A new generation of deadly biological weapons is emerging as a by-product of useful research. But this explosion of research in biotechnology is opening up the possibility of cheap biological weapons being developed and used by rogue states or even terrorist groups.[60] Even seemingly innocent chains of innovations in computers and telecommunications are having indirect effects on security by making complex societies vulnerable to cyberattacks and related telecommunications chaos (see table 7.1). Growing dependence on computer networks, the Internet, communications satellites, and related telecommunications systems makes complex societies increasingly vulnerable to "electronic Pearl Harbors," information warfare designed to disable electronic communication, control, and information systems.[61]

Rapid progress in biotechnology undoubtedly will have a positive impact in the struggle against disease, but it also will increase the potential for the diffu-

TABLE 7.1. Personal Computers per 1,000 People				
Countries		GNI[a] $ billions 2000	Population millions 2000	GNI per capita $ 2000
Less than 5.0	30	684	1,729	400
5.0-19.9	32	1,583	2,021	780
20.0-49.9	24	1,660	684	2,430
50.0-199.9	38	3,704	507	7,300
200.0 or more	29	23,430	834	28,090
No data	54	254	282	900

Source: 2002 World Bank Atlas, International Bank for Reconstruction and Development/ The World Bank, 2002.

[a]GNI = Gross National Income

sion of biological weapons to smaller powers and terrorist groups. This "dual use" problem results from the fact that many of the techniques and instruments used in contemporary biological research can also be used to build weapons. Over the last fifteen years the amount of information that is easily available to make biological weaponry has grown enormously as have the number of people who possess it. Whereas in the 1960s and 1970s, aspiring young science students were experimenting with chemistry sets, in the contemporary world their counterparts are experimenting with genetic engineering kits. Recipes for producing botulinum and anthrax have been posted on the Web, books describing biological warfare assassination techniques are readily available, and even some private militia groups are training to use biological weapons.[62]

It is thought that there are currently ten countries that possess biological weapons, and another four are under suspicion of making them.[63] Other countries could soon possess them because the costs of equipping and staffing a biowarfare facility are very small, especially compared with those of creating a nuclear weapons facility. And the expertise required to make bioweapons is readily available, particularly given the availability of large numbers of unemployed and underemployed scientists who had experience in such programs in the former Soviet Union.[64] The dual use problem has recently escalated as viral genetic codes are being sequenced and the Human Genome Project has produced large quantities of information about the human genetic code. This makes the creation of a virus hybrid, combining the worst aspects of two or more viruses, possible.

The United States and other industrial countries are ill-prepared to deal with this new kind of challenge to both conventional and ecological security.[65] There are dozens of potential toxins that could be used to create biological weapons; smallpox, anthrax, plague, and botulism lead the list. Smallpox is perhaps the most dangerous since there have been outbreaks of it as recently as 1971, and samples are kept in storage. A large-scale outbreak would probably kill about 30 percent of those infected. At the time of the anthrax scare in 2001, the United States only had 15.4 million doses of smallpox vaccine in storage, enough to vaccinate less than 7 percent of the American population. And the time required for vaccination and for antibodies to develop would be weeks, during which millions of people could be infected.[66] The subsequent war on terrorism subsequently sent officials scampering to increase the amount of available vaccine.

A much different kind of threat to the security of complex societies is emerging out of their growing dependence on telecommunications and information systems.[67] The most obvious source of new challenges would be attacks by computer viruses and worms that spread rapidly via the Internet. Eight to ten new viruses and worms appear daily on the Internet, but only a few survive to do extensive damage.[68] In 1999, the "Melissa" worm virus infiltrated thousands of corporate computers and did more than $1 billion damage. In 2000, a much more destructive "Love" virus emerged from the Philippines and spread rapidly around the world, doing as much as $10 billion damage.[69] This damaging virus was particularly noteworthy because it was the creation of a young computer student in Manila. At that time, the Philippines had no applicable laws against this type of cybercarnage. In fact, only thirty-seven countries did have any laws addressing unauthorized access to computer systems, and they differed greatly.[70]

In April 2001, a cyberskirmish broke out between hackers in the United States and China.[71] Apparently, incensed by the collision of a Chinese fighter and a U.S. reconnaissance plane, U.S. hackers hit and defaced dozens of Chinese websites. Chinese hackers responded by wrecking nearly one thousand websites in the United States. A possibly related political worm, named "Code Red," appeared on the Internet on July 12, 2001, and attacked nearly twenty thousand computer servers. After lurking quietly for five days, it reemerged in a much more virulent form and infected 359,000 servers in less than fourteen hours. Then it suddenly switched tactics and attacked one of two White House servers. This attack forced the Pentagon to block public access to its websites and the White House to change its numerical Internet address.[72] By the time the worm was purged from the Internet, it had become one of the most expensive attacks in history, costing several billion dollars to repair the damage.[73]

The proliferation of these computer viruses, so far apparently created mostly by amateurs, raises the question of the potential for military or dissident political groups to use similar techniques to wage full-scale "cyberwar" or "netwar."[74] Tremendous damage could be done by an adversary penetrating complex telecommunications and computer systems, as well as computer-dependent infrastructure, such as hydroelectric dams. Sensitive information could be stolen, computerized control systems could be hijacked, viruses could disable important systems, and codes to be activated at a later date could be embedded in systems that control strategic assets.[75] Indeed, the United States and its allies apparently effectively targeted Saddam Hussein's telephone exchanges and radio links as a key part of their strategy in the Gulf War.[76]

As societies become increasingly dependent on the Internet and related cybertechnologies, a very steep price could be exacted by small adversaries. Viruses and worms could be designed to cause the Internet to crash. If this were to happen, the increasing numbers of businesses using the World Wide Web to order parts for "just-in-time" manufacturing would be left without components. Many banks that use the Internet to provide services wouldn't be able to do so. And the increasing number of telephone calls that travel over the Internet wouldn't get through. Even the U.S. Department of Defense has become very dependent on the Internet for unclassified communications.[77]

Summing Up: Conflict or Cooperation?

Scientific discovery and technological innovation hold the potential to increase or diminish both conventional and ecological security. Technological innovation has been a prerequisite for sustaining the more than six billion people in the world at current levels of living. But technological innovation can also be a destabilizing force. This is particularly true of the growing array of "dual use" technologies that can increase well-being or be employed in various kinds of warfare, killing millions with biological weapons or disabling complex societies with electronic attacks.

The future directions in which scientific research and technological innovation move will reflect the policy priorities of the Global North. Investments in research and development can be made in areas that will foster North–South cooperation and reduce the gap between rich and poor countries, or they can be made in areas that sharpen competition or conflict in the emerging global system. In the end, it is the uses to which scientific research and technological innovation are put that will determine their future contribution to ecological security.

CHAPTER EIGHT

Ecologically Secure Development

ONE OF THE greatest challenges associated with the rapid pace of technological innovation and associated globalization is narrowing the persisting economic gap between the Global North and Global South. Resource-intensive industrialization and accompanying sociocultural modernization developed slowly over an extended period of time in Europe and in the United States. Population growth during this process was modest, and natural resources were relatively abundant. Living standards, for the most part, rose slowly, but steadily. And there was little sense of urgency to "catch up" with other more developed countries. There were none.

Industrialization and associated modernization take place under much different circumstances in the contemporary world. Globalization gives urgency to the pace of economic change in the Global South. The advent of global telecommunications is sparking a revolution of rising material aspirations. In the industrializing parts of the world young and old are now increasingly exposed to a barrage of advertisements intended to increase demand for consumer goods ranging from jeans and cosmetics to washing machines and automobiles. But while the increased potential for automobile sales in China may be good news for Detroit, it's not good news for the environment.

Past industrialization clearly has made a substantial contribution to social progress and has had an overall positive impact on ecological security. Although utopian images of conditions in imaginary, pristine pre-industrial environments are seductive, they gloss over the periodic famines and plagues that often made life there brutish and short. There can be no question that the economic abundance created during the Industrial Revolution has permitted a much larger number of people to enjoy higher standards of living. The abundance it has created also has facilitated innovations of many kinds, particularly those in medicine, that have directly reduced mortality rates and lengthened life spans. On the other hand, industrialization has exacted heavy environmental costs, many of which have fallen more heavily on the poor.

Entering the twenty-first century, it is no longer clear that, on balance, traditional forms of industrial growth will continue to enhance ecological security. As large-scale industrialization spreads to China, India, Indonesia, and other densely populated countries, increasing local and global environmental costs associated with it may well exceed economic benefits. Resource-intensive industrialization, as traditionally experienced, may be unworkable. But while the window of opportunity for this kind of development is now closing, other windows promising different kinds of progress are opening. Ecologically secure development can be promoted by emphasizing environmentally benign aspects of sociocultural modernization while avoiding the heavy industrialization that has large environmental costs. Improvements in telecommunications, medical care, education, nutrition, and a host of other enhancements in the quality of life can take place without paying heavy environmental costs. But this requires devising strategies to "leapfrog" the traditional industrial experience.[1]

In the immediate postcolonial era economists generally assumed that traditional industrialization would spread worldwide and narrow the gap between rich and poor. An emerging global market, free of barriers to trade, would be the vehicle enabling this transformation to take place. "But the evidence paints a different picture. Average incomes have indeed been growing, but so has the income gap between rich and poor countries. Both trends have been evident for more than 200 years, but improved global communications have led to an increased awareness among the poor of income inequalities and heightened the pressure to emigrate to richer countries."[2] Ironically, while industrialization has been spreading to the periphery, inequality has continued to increase.[3] For the quarter century between 1970 and 1995, real per capita income for the richest one-third of countries went up annually at a rate of 1.9 percent. The middle third saw an increase in income of only 0.7 percent, while the bottom third showed no increase at all.[4] These trends have persisted into the twenty-first century. Thus, old ways of thinking about development are under scrutiny, and a search has begun for a new development paradigm that would be sustainable and ecologically secure for a more densely populated future world.

There are now nearly five billion people living in crowded and polluted less industrialized countries, and their numbers are rapidly growing. Past industrialization and the persisting high levels of consumption in industrial countries have severely taxed the global ecosystem and thinned the world's natural resource base. The ecological consequences of the spread of an industrial way of life to a future world with a population of between eight and nine billion people are frightening to comprehend.

As the North–South economic gap has been widening, the less affluent countries of the Global South have, in many ways, become more ecologically insecure.[3] Continuing to transfer the shopworn industrial growth paradigm to these densely populated countries may only compound their environmental problems. Thus, it is highly questionable whether the less industrialized countries can or should follow a developmental path similar to that originally marked out by the more affluent ones. Instead, it now is essential to create new ways of defining progress that will safeguard future ecological security while shaping a new kind of development that will meet basic human needs. This holds the best hope for the people of the Global South to avoid the environmental and human pitfalls of traditional industrialization and begin to close the North–South economic gap.

Part of this process of creating a more ecologically secure model of progress involves clarifying the language used to describe it. Economic growth refers to changes in production that are conventionally measured by an increase in gross domestic product (GDP). But growth can be of many different types, some of it much more useful in meeting human needs than others. Industrialization is a particular type of resource-intensive growth that has historically been associated with significant natural resource requirements as well as substantial environmental pollution. Modernization refers to a package of positive psychological and sociocultural changes that historically have been associated with advanced industrialization. Development is a more elusive term encompassing many of the positive changes in societies that have been closely tied to economic growth. Sustainable development is a concept that has come into use to stress the need for modernization and social progress that can endure over the long term without destroying the Earth's nonrenewable resource base or substantially degrading environmental services. Sustainable development here refers to long-term ecologically secure development that meets the needs of human populations while maintaining equilibria among them, and between them and nature.

Keeping these ideas in mind, a strong case can be made that traditional industrialization was a limited success in the countries that industrialized early, certainly raising levels of living, but also generating significant inequality, and leaving a trail of environmental devastation at home and abroad. For many countries that began industrializing later, attempts to replicate the early successes and compete in a globalizing economy have had very mixed results. And the prospect of a future China, India, and Indonesia industrializing and growing economically in this traditional manner certainly brings trepidation to those concerned with future sustainable development.

A Persisting Gap

The contemporary world is still a very inegalitarian place.[6] People in the wealthy countries generally over-consume, while people in the poorest countries often survive in very dire straits. At present, the 20 percent of the world's population living in the richest countries is responsible for 82 percent of global export trade and 68 percent of foreign direct investment, and uses 74 percent of the world's telephone lines. The poorest 20 percent, by contrast, are responsible for little more than 1 percent of each.[7] An estimated 2.8 billion people, slightly less than one-half of the world's population, live on less than $2 a day; of these, 1.2 billion survive on less than $1 a day.[8] By contrast, between 1994 and 1998, the net worth of the 200 wealthiest people in the world, almost all of them in the Global North, increased from $440 billion to more than $1 trillion, although a more recent meltdown in equities markets has somewhat reduced this figure. In fact, the assets of the wealthiest three of these people alone, at that time, exceeded the combined annual gross national product (GNP) of the 48 least developed countries.[9]

Development has traditionally been measured by income levels expressed in GDP per capita. By this measure, there are large economic disparities among countries and regions. For example, the average per capita income for Organization for Economic Cooperation and Development (OECD) countries is nineteen times the average for the least developed countries (see table 8.1). In 1990, the United Nations Development Program (UNDP) cautiously decided to supplement this rudimentary measure of well-being by creating a Human Development Indicator (HDI). The HDI aggregates life expectancy, adult literacy, educational enrollment, and GDP per capita into a more robust indicator. This measure represents at least a small step toward acknowledging that social progress consists of more than just economic growth.[10]

TABLE 8.1. Regional Development Disparities		
Region	HDIV[a]	GDP/Capita[b]
World	0.716	6,980
OECD Countries	0.900	22,020
All Developing Countries	0.647	3,530
Eastern Europe/CIS	0.777	6,290
Least Developed Countries	0.442	1,170
Sub-Saharan Africa	0.467	1,640
East Asia/the Pacific	0.719	3,950
South Asia	0.564	2,280
Latin America/Caribbean	0.760	6,880

Source: UNDP, Human Development Report 2001, 144.
[a]Human Development Index Value for 1999
[b]GDP measured in dollars (purchasing power parity) for 1999

The data in table 8.2 paint a somewhat more refined picture of development disparities. The development gap between the affluent OECD countries and the very poor countries in Africa is glaring. Were other kinds of data related more closely to ecological security, such as disease, factored into the HDI, the gap would become even larger. These disparities also are reflected in lack of access to the basic tools of future development. For example in 1998, there were an average of 557 telephone lines for every 1,000 people in the United States, Japan, and Germany, while there were just 3 for every 1,000 people in Bangladesh, 4 for every 1,000 people in Nigeria, and 19 for every 1,000 people in Pakistan.[11] Not only is the gap between rich and poor not closing, there are 18 countries that have had a declining HDI for a period of more than a decade. The HDI for Zambia has declined from levels reached in 1975, and the HDIs for Zimbabwe, Romania, and Russia have declined from 1980 levels.[12]

Given these large and persisting disparities, there have been significant efforts over the years to close the gap through various kinds of foreign assistance. Aid has taken many forms, the most common of which has been outright grants and concessional loans provided by governments bilaterally and through multilateral organizations. But an overview of recent trends in official development assistance paints a gloomy picture (see table 8.3). Although the world's population and its needs for aid have been growing, the

TABLE 8.2.   Human Development Index—Highest and
              Lowest Scores

Country	1980	1990	1999	Rank
Norway	0.875	0.899	0.939	1
Australia	0.859	0.886	0.936	2
Canada	0.882	0.925	0.936	3
Sweden	0.872	0.892	0.936	4
Belgium	0.861	0.895	0.935	5
United States	0.882	0.912	0.934	6
Iceland	0.883	0.910	0.932	7
Netherlands	0.872	0.900	0.931	8
Japan	0.876	0.907	0.928	9
Finland	0.854	0.894	0.925	10
Mali	0.277	0.310	0.378	153
Central African Republic	0.349	0.370	0.372	154
Chad	0.255	0.321	0.359	155
Guinea-Bissau	0.254	0.306	0.339	156
Mozambique	0.303	0.311	0.323	157
Ethiopia	–	0.294	0.321	158
Burkina Faso	0.263	0.294	0.320	159
Burundi	0.308	0.344	0.309	160
Niger	0.253	0.254	0.274	161
Sierra Leone	–	–	0.258	162

Source: UNDP, *Human Development Report 2001*, 145–48.

data illustrate that some key donors actually have been reducing their commitments over the last decade. Within the United States, congressional support for nonmilitary foreign aid has waned, in part due to a lack of commitment to helping poor countries, and in part due to the end of the Cold War. While the robust U.S. economy in the 1990s created an opportunity for giving more aid, this didn't happen. The United States in 1990 contributed $11,262 million in official development assistance, including debt forgiveness. By the end of the decade, however, this assistance had declined to $9,145 million. It represented a paltry 0.10 percent of U.S. GNP.[13] And even this aid was largely used to benefit U.S. businesses. Approximately three-quarters of it was tied to the purchase of goods and services in the United States.[14] While it has

TABLE 8.3. Official Development Assistance (ODA)—Large Donors (in millions of dollars)						
Country	1960	1970	1980	1990	2000	%GNP[a]
Canada	65	337	1,075	2,470	1,722	0.25
Denmark	5	59	481	1,171	1,664	1.06
France	823	735	2,889	7,163	4,221	0.33
Germany	224	599	3,567	6,320	5,034	0.27
Italy	77	147	683	3,395	1,368	0.13
Japan	105	458	3,353	9,069	13,062	0.27
Netherlands	35	196	1,630	2,538	3,075	0.82
Sweden	7	117	962	2,007	1,813	0.81
United Kingdom	407	482	1,854	2,638	4,458	0.31
United States	2,760	3,153	7,138	11,394	9,581	0.10
World	4,676	6,713	26,195	52,961	53,058	0.22

Sources: www.oecd.org/dac/htm/dacstats.htm#dactables and www.oecd.org/media/release/nwo1-37a.htm (July 23, 2001).
[a]2000 ODA as percentage of GNP

been argued that private sector foreign direct investment in poorer countries can make up for the lack of aid, the reality is that more than two-thirds of such investment remains within the Global North, moving from one wealthy country to another.[15]

Past loans to poorer countries, in many cases, have only worsened their current financial plight. Given the slow pace of economic growth there over the past four decades, many of these countries have been unable to repay loans and have fallen more deeply into debt. There are now fifty-five countries considered to be heavily indebted. In recognition of these growing debt levels in impoverished countries, the World Bank, International Monetary Fund, and several governments have undertaken an initiative to reduce the debt of the world's poorest countries. The Heavily Indebted Poor Countries (HIPC) Initiative was launched in 1996, and has been aimed at relieving unsustainable debt burdens and spurring poverty reduction efforts. Reviewed in 1999, the HIPC Initiative was broadened to include more and deeper debt and poverty reduction efforts.[16] But there is little indication that the twenty-two countries that are now receiving debt relief, amounting to $34 billion over time, will see a basic change in their economic situations.

The Colonial Legacy

An uneven diffusion of technology and related economic growth has been responsible for shaping this world characterized by sharp and growing inequalities between the early industrializers and the poorer countries that are now attempting to catch up. Fossil fuel–based industrial technologies first refashioned Western European economies and societies, and then diffused slowly outward to other areas of the world. The uneven pace and manner in which industrialization has spread have given rise to numerous differences and inequalities between the early and late industrializers. Innovations in transportation and weaponry permitted the early industrializers to establish extensive colonial networks that were used to meet growing needs for cheap labor and natural resources. Technological innovation continues to create an overwhelming competitive advantage for them in the global economy. Most of the late developers, by contrast, largely remain, as they were in colonial times, exporters of labor, minerals, and agricultural commodities.

During the colonial era minimal attention was paid to the future political and economic welfare of the colonies that were eventually to become independent countries. They were regarded as extensions of sovereign territory, and were used as sources of cheap raw materials and labor to help meet the needs of growing industrial economies. In most cases, the colonizers were hesitant to make significant nonagricultural economic investments in the colonies or build technological expertise in these mostly agrarian areas of the world. Thus, the Industrial Revolution that spurred growth in Western Europe and the United States never really had an opportunity to take hold there. Upon attaining independence in the post–World War II period, these new countries had neither the requisite infrastructure for building industrial societies, nor well-educated people with relevant technological or economic experience.

The dynamics that structured North–South relations during the colonial period remain a factor shaping current relations between the industrial Northern countries and their much less affluent Southern counterparts.[17] Most of the former colonies became so-called "one-crop economies," by far the largest share of economic activity being generated by production of only two or three primary commodities. Some colonies specialized in crops such as sugar, coffee, or cocoa. Others became sources of valuable minerals, such as silver and gold, and eventually less precious metals and minerals. As the Industrial Revolution developed momentum, it created growing demands for raw materials, resulting in a steady flow of resources from less to more industrialized areas. And these patterns persist in the contemporary world. The low income economies generally export raw materials and low value-added products, while the more economically developed countries turn these raw materials and semi-manufactured goods into much more valuable finished goods.

The large industrial countries now dominate trade negotiations, and after decades of tariff reduction efforts, industrial country levies on simple developing country exports (for example, textiles and agricultural commodities) remain much higher than those on more sophisticated exports from other industrial countries.[18] Farm subsidies in the industrialized countries also serve to keep prices of commodities exported by developing countries artificially low. For example, the European Union (EU) gave $93 billion in subsidies to farmers in 2001, and the United States gave $49 billion. As a result, the EU dumped 6.1 million tons of sugar into a depressed world market in 2001.[19] In the United States, cotton farmers received $3.4 billion in subsidies in 2001, and dumped nearly half of the cotton crop into the world market. It's no wonder that world cotton prices dropped from nearly $1.20 per pound in 1995 to $0.40 in 2002.[20]

Countries that export primary commodities also are hampered by unstable markets for their exports due to both economic and weather fluctuations. Mineral exporters are periodically victimized by "boom and bust" economic cycles. A burst of economic prosperity in the industrial countries can cause markets for minerals to grow and prices to rise. But economic recessions can depress raw material demand and cause commodity prices to tumble, thus contributing to economic instability in exporting countries. Agricultural commodity prices, on the other hand, tend to be unstable because they fluctuate along with weather conditions in key exporting countries. A frost-damaged coffee crop in Brazil, for example, can cause coffee prices to rise substantially on world markets, much to the benefit of coffee exporters in other countries. But good weather in major producing countries can drive down coffee prices for all exporters due to surplus production. Witness the plight of Nicaragua in 2001 when a drought severely limited coffee production there, but good growing conditions in other countries produced a bumper crop. The average wholesale price of coffee dropped from 86 cents per pound in January, 1999 to 43 cents per pound in August, 2001, leaving Nicaragua with very meager export earnings.[21]

The failure of the colonial powers to transfer technology and expertise, locate industrial facilities, and adequately educate young people in their former colonies has left a legacy of fundamental economic competition problems for them in a world economy increasingly driven by intellectual property considerations. Most of the world's research and development takes place in the industrialized countries. The United States, Germany, and Japan have an average of 3,805 research scientists and engineers per million people, while Malaysia,

Thailand, and Brazil have only 121 per million. This results in a huge "patent gap." In 1998, residents of the United States, Germany, and Japan filed for 539,347 patents. In the same year, residents of China and India, with a combined population of over two billion, filed for only 17,862.[22] Well-developed educational systems, expensive research facilities, and economies of scale inherent in producing for large markets give the early developers a seemingly insurmountable competitive edge.

Not only must low-income countries squeeze meager export earnings out of primary commodities, farmers are now using more sophisticated equipment and technology in industrialized countries to make significant inroads into even these relatively stagnant markets. At the end of the 1990s, U.S. agricultural exports constituted over one-third of all grain traded on the world market, a situation that developed largely because of mechanized operations and large subsidies for domestic production.[23] In fact, the OECD countries spend a combined $350 billion per year on domestic agricultural subsidies, amounting to almost seven times the annual value of their foreign aid.[24]

There are many additional handicaps resulting from the colonial heritage that frustrate efforts to close the development gap. Rapid population growth in many countries of the Global South is a major contributing factor. Although population growth rates have come down from their all-time highs, in many of these countries numbers continue to grow rapidly, doubling in as little as twenty-five years. Strenuous efforts are required simply to keep from losing ground.[25] The early industrializers in the Global North never experienced such rapid population growth because modernization was indigenous and took place over many generations. This allowed for sociocultural changes related to reproduction to move in step with innovations in medicine that cut infant mortality and extended the life span. In the contemporary countries of the Global South, however, the source of declining infant mortality lies outside the system, and given the rapid pace of change, there has been inadequate time for sociocultural evolution to catch up. And unlike the early industrializers, options for population pressures to be relieved through migration are severely limited by restrictive immigration policies of most countries in the Global North.

Finally, there are a number of geographic factors that inhibit economic development in these countries. Transportation networks in these former colonies were designed and built by the colonial powers with an eye to facilitating the flow of raw materials from inland areas to ports. Thus, old transportation networks have to be augmented by new infrastructure to better meet domestic developmental needs. Even the borders of many of these countries, imposed by colonial powers, make little political or economic sense. Often antagonistic ethnic groups find themselves coexisting within the same state because boundaries were drawn where colonial spheres of influence intersected. Thus, ethnic quarrels are common in many poorer countries, and are often a major barrier to the political stability that is a requisite for socioeconomic development.

The colonial legacy aside, poor countries are now also adversely impacted by the dynamics of accelerating globalization. The pace of technological innovation in wealthy countries, combined with the growing importance of export markets to them, means much more intense competition for developing country products. Ironically, even demand for raw material exports is beginning to taper off in the United States, Western Europe, and Japan as a result of the technology-induced structural transformations of economic activity now underway. Dematerialization, design changes, saturated markets, and a shift toward knowledge-intensive products are all combining to limit demand for raw material exports from poorer countries. Advances in information and computer technologies, telecommunications, and biotechnology also are now driving growth dynamics and raising the technology stakes to higher levels, creating a large digital and knowledge divide between the Global North and Global South.[26] Only about 2 percent of the world's population as a whole is connected to the Internet, but more than 25 percent of the people in the United States are connected.[27]

In Search of Alternatives

Recognizing that the persisting colonial legacy, the emergence of a global economy, and the technological edge possessed by countries in the Global North have combined, over time, to make prospects for persisting resource-intensive industrialization dim in the Global South, economists and development experts have been searching for a formula that would permit poorer countries to begin to close the existing gap in living standards. Over the decades, they have stressed import substitution as a way of husbanding foreign exchange for development. Then fashions changed and poorer countries were advised to focus on expanding their exports. In rapid succession leaders of less affluent countries were told to pay more attention to domestic agriculture, open up markets to free enterprise, control population growth, and redistribute wealth. Each of these suggestions had some positive impact for a brief period of time, but in most cases the economic gap continued to widen. Recently, the search for the key to more rapid growth in poorer countries has become more complicated as broader environmental concerns must now be factored into development strategies.[28]

After decades of efforts to force poorer countries to follow market-oriented prescriptions, many of which ignored environmental constraints altogether, the development record is very mixed. Yet, market-oriented economists continue to tout the virtues of removing all government controls over economic policies in poor countries. On closer examination, however, these competition-oriented free-trade philosophies continue to benefit mostly the advanced industrialized countries, except for a few special cases where developmental timing may facilitate more rapid industrialization.[29] It isn't clear that these prescriptions were ever really designed to help poor countries develop. Rather, it is more accurate to say that they were devised by politicians and economists in the industrial countries in order to entice poor countries into a trade system devised and dominated by the Global North. Most countries of the Global South have had no real chance to be competitive and advance in this system where they had so little opportunity to participate in writing the rules. The free trade push of recent decades has resulted in very little per capita progress for many of the world's poorer countries, and few of them give indications of emulating the relative progress of the Asian "Tigers." And even the Tigers have been tamed by a persisting economic slump in Asia. Thus, development strategies are again being reappraised, and prescriptions for economic growth are currently in flux. Because of both the increasingly problematic nature of future industrialization and the shift in the North toward postindustrial economies, the development gap is an issue that will continue to grow in political importance.

The search for a relevant development model is now complicated by the sheer size of the growing populations of key countries in the less industrialized world. It frequently has been argued on equity grounds that countries of the Global South should be free to pick their own development model. But it would be folly for them to pursue the resource-intensive industrial one previously followed by the countries of the Global North. Of course, it is also clear that the countries of the Global North bear considerable responsibility for creating this development dilemma because of their own excessive resource consumption and cumulative pollution.

Nearly half of the population of the Global South is now living in China and India. The developmental choices made by these countries will have an enormous impact on future ecological security. Envisioning the environmental impact of a fully industrialized India and China in 2025, based on current U.S. consumption patterns, highlights the need to find a more ecologically sound model for future development.

The current population of China and India is 2.3 billion people, more than a third of the world's total. For every American there are presently eight people living in China and India. Demographic projections suggest that the populations of these countries will continue to grow, reaching a total of 2.8 billion by 2025.[30]

If the people of China and India were to be able to increase their energy consumption to current U.S. per capita levels by the year 2025, the strain on world fossil fuel supplies would be enormous. The 1.43 billion people expected to be in China in 2025 would consume 11.4 billion metric tons of oil equivalent, and the 1.36 billion people expected to be in India would consume 10.8 billion metric tons of oil equivalent in energy. Their combined energy consumption of 22.2 billion metric tons of oil equivalent would be more than twice the current world energy consumption. This would clearly be an impossible situation.[31]

Even more illustrative of the challenges that would face a future world with these two newly industrialized giants are projected increases in carbon dioxide emissions that would result from China and India successfully pursuing conventional industrialization. The United States presently produces more carbon dioxide per capita than any other country. U.S.-generated carbon dioxide emissions now equal 5.3 billion metric tons, amounting to a little less than a quarter of the world's total. This comes to 19.6 metric tons of carbon dioxide per capita. This compares to present emissions of 2.7 metric tons per capita in China and 1.1 metric tons per capita in India. If China and India were to follow the fossil fuel consumption trail blazed by the United States, and reach similar levels of industrial development by 2025, their combined carbon dioxide emissions would skyrocket to 55 billion metric tons, which would be more than twice current worldwide emissions.[32]

Although these consumption levels are unlikely to be reached for many reasons, they emphasize the local and global environmental disasters that could result from China and India pursuing a growth path modeled on that followed by the United States. More likely, China and India, along with many other countries of the Global South, will be encouraged by these changing circumstances to rethink development priorities and move in a more sustainable direction. But this will require continuing dialog with and real cooperation from the countries of the Global North that are currently responsible for the bulk of world resource consumption and pollution.

The old economic prescriptions for rapid growth in the poorer countries and closing the gap between the rich and poor countries have failed. A new cooperative approach to sustainable development is now required, one that involves some actual sacrifices by the countries of the Global North as well as creativity by countries of the Global South. The presently highly stratified global society and economy cannot be maintained in the face of the new realities of globalization. Accelerating economic competition makes it exceedingly difficult for poorer countries to build economically competitive industries. Both local and global environmental constraints, including global climate change, place additional limits on the ability of densely populated countries to emulate traditional forms of industrialization. And the sheer size of the two largest less industrialized countries, China and India, make it very hazardous, for both them and the rest of the world, to attempt to follow the resource-intensive growth path blazed by Europe and the United States. Different historical periods offer different windows of development opportunity. While the industrialization window is now closing, a new paradigm is beginning to emerge to guide more sustainable development in the twenty-first century.

Sustainable Development

The crux of the current development dilemma is that the materialistic and now much emulated way of life that has evolved out of the relative resource abundance of the industrial period cannot diffuse to the bulk of the human race at acceptable environmental cost.[33] Such consumption patterns cannot be sustained in the future because the environmental impact of the more than 7.8 billion human beings expected in the year 2025, living at U.S. levels of consumption, would easily overwhelm the sustaining capabilities of natural systems.[34] Thus, the legacy of generations that have operated under the assumption that more material consumption is equivalent to progress is the spread of a cancerous growth paradigm or worldview that no longer gives appropriate eco-evolutionary guidance in confronting the core sustainability issues of the new millennium.

Concern over the appropriateness and long-term sustainability of this outmoded growth model goes back several decades. A burst of population growth in the Global South combined with rapid growth in consumption in the Global North in the late 1960s began to raise caution flags about the long-term viability of such increases. The Club of Rome, a group of business leaders and academics, sponsored a number of research projects that explored the potential for future resource-intensive growth. Among these was the study carried out at MIT. The resulting book, *The Limits to Growth*, painted a pessimistic picture of prospects for future development dependent upon such traditional economic growth.[35] Undoubtedly aided by the onset of the first energy crisis in 1973, which seemed to lend credence to the thesis that the world was running out of raw materials, the book captured a worldwide audience and kicked off a protracted debate over the potential for and nature of future development.[36]

The second report to the Club of Rome, *Mankind at the Turning Point*, focused more directly on the impact of growth patterns on the world's regions. It found that "Two gaps, steadily widening, appear to be at the heart of mankind's present crises: the gap between man and nature, and the gap between 'North' and 'South,' rich and poor. Both gaps must be narrowed if world-shattering catastrophes are to be avoided; but they can be narrowed only if global 'unity' and Earth's 'finiteness' are explicitly recognized."[37] The second oil crisis gave additional credibility to this perspective, and urgency to an extensive U.S. government study published in 1980 that envisioned the possibility of a much more crowded and polluted future planet and only limited opportunities for traditional kinds of industrial growth.[38]

Concern over the long-term sustainability of the industrial development model was given additional expression in international circles with the publication of the report of the World Commission on Environment and Development in 1987.[39] In that document, a distinguished commission chaired by Gro Harlem Brundtland, former prime minister of Norway, took up the issue of sustainable development and defined it as "development that meets the needs of the present without compromising the ability of future generations to meet their own needs."[40] Prior to the work of the commission, concerns expressed about the welfare of future generations were frequently rebuffed by technological optimism—beliefs that future technological innovations automatically would make each generation in both the Global North and Global South better off than previous ones. The commission questioned the inevitability of greater material affluence across generations, as well as across the development divide. It also focused attention on giving priority to meeting human needs instead of wants. Thus, prescriptions for making development work began to focus on the nature of environmental constraints, and the need for wealthy countries to make some sacrifices in the interest of international cooperation.

Mounting concern over the need for more ecologically secure development culminated in the 1992 United Nations Conference on Environment and Development. This conference, held on the twentieth anniversary of the Stockholm Conference on the Human Environment, produced five documents that attempted to establish a framework for North–South cooperation for ecologically secure development. The Framework Convention on Climate Change laid out a set of general principles for dealing with greenhouse warming, including one that called for the industrial countries to take the lead in reducing greenhouse gas emissions. The Convention on Biodiversity focused on the relationship between people and other species. It contained measures to protect species and ecosystems, and required participating countries to develop plans to preserve biodiversity. An attempt was also made to negotiate a convention on the protection of forests, but this resulted only in a vague cautionary statement.

The more controversial action statements coming from the conference were the Rio Declaration, a document containing twenty-seven principles for sustainable development, and Agenda 21, a forty-chapter document outlining a parallel action plan. The Rio Declaration laid out a number of principles to be respected in integrating environmental concerns into development. It affirmed the rights of less industrialized countries to develop economically and assigned moral responsibility to the industrialized countries to use their wealth and advanced technology to help countries of the Global South to develop in a sustainable way. Agenda 21 laid out an international action program for sustainable development in the twenty-first century. It was a statement of aspirations for countries to work together to improve living standards for all while better protecting ecosystems.[41]

The focus of sustainable development thinking also has broadened to include responsibilities of countries in the Global North. Almost all industrialized countries now live well beyond the sustainable capabilities of the territory that they occupy.[42] And they are the primary producers of greenhouse gases responsible for global warming. The United States alone contributes nearly one-quarter of the total. Thus, long-term sustainable development also now requires actions by countries of the Global North.

It is now unclear how much real impact Agenda 21 is having on development policies. A follow-up to the Rio meeting held in Johannesburg, South Africa, in June 2002 seemed to show little progress in implementing it. But it is evident that the next two decades must mark a fundamental turning point in the worldwide spread of the industrial growth paradigm. The human race must move beyond diplomatic posturing and actually grapple with issues of how to spur modernization and social progress in the poorer countries while dealing with environmental limits to industrial growth on a global scale. This means moving away from competitive views of development and nourishing more cooperative definitions of progress while devising and disseminating new technologies that will ease environmental burdens associated with growth in the Global South.

Sustainability as Process

Making a transition to a more sustainable world must be a continuing process that requires change in values, institutions, and technological innovation.[43] It requires a fundamental change in definitions of progress and the good life. It also requires shifts in the relative power of political institutions and markets in making development decisions. Since the existing structure of consumer preferences has evolved out of learning that took place during the era of relative resource abundance, market forces cannot now be relied upon to guide this transition to a more sustainable world. Although it is contrary to the privatization ideologies that have dominated the last two decades, a much stronger role for the public sector in changing existing structures of privilege and creating alternative visions of progress will be essential.[44]

Similarly, changes in the thrust of technological innovation and patterns of diffusion also will be required. In general, industrial technologies have been strongly influenced by markets. During the advanced stages of the Industrial Revolution, technological innovation naturally focused on using natural resources to make labor more productive. But the sustainable development needs of the future will require a new focus for technological innovation more appropriate to the situation of the Global South where natural resources may be scarce and labor may be more abundant.

Creating a more sustainable world thus is best envisioned as a dynamic intervention in sociocultural evolution, moving beyond the materialistic and environmentally destructive industrial social paradigm to a constantly evolving postindustrial one. A perfectly sustainable future society would be one in which economic activity would be supported by renewable or recycled resources, thus placing few long-term burdens on the environment. The emphasis would be on meeting human needs rather than stimulating material wants, and on quality rather than quantity. Progress would be indexed by new definitions of efficiency stressing the prudent use of resources and the durability of goods produced.

Ecologically secure development for a future more densely populated world means striking a new planetary bargain between North and South.[45] It stresses maximizing human satisfaction while reducing the impact of necessary economic activity on stocks of nonrenewable resources, nature's environmental services, and other species. For the Global North it means continuing dematerialization, a process that is well under way.[46] For the Global South, it means redefining development and searching for ways to leapfrog the many environmental and moral hazards that have been associated with previous heavy industrialization. This not only involves changing resource use and allocation, but also requires rethinking values and institutions.

The sustainability problematique is thus a cluster of environmental, economic, ethical, social, and political paradoxes associated with the waning of a materialist industrial view of social progress, and construction of an alternative vision of a good and worthwhile life. This transition, however, is complicated by political realities. During times of relative affluence, when economic and social capital is available to accelerate transformation, people evidence much less concern about the future. There then is little likelihood of resolute action on these pressing issues. During times of recession and related turmoil, however, people consider these kinds of questions more seriously, but then there is little capital that can be applied to system transformation.

Building a more ecologically secure world also requires a reinvigorated dialog between North and South in order to forge a new planetary bargain between the few in the North who now consume too much, and the many in the South who consume too little. There are different tasks and opportunities for countries in different developmental circumstances. In the Global North, for example, it is essential to define progress as doing more with less impact on nature. It is also critical to accelerate the flow of capital and appropriate technology to poorer countries. In the Global South it is necessary to rethink development by splitting off the positive aspects of modernization, development of services such as education, medical care, and telecommunications, while forgoing the negative aspects that degrade the environment, such as heavy industrialization, urbanization, and private automobile ownership. Creating a more ecologically secure world thus implies different agendas for different countries, and requires balancing the need for social progress within the limits of nature with the imperative to retain many of the positive aspects of sociopolitical modernization.

Some people conceive of a transition to a more sustainable world as involving deprivation, pain, austerity, and increasing homogeneity. In reality, however, it is the Industrial Revolution that has had often painful and homogenizing effects on the impacted societies. Just as it is important to maintain genetic diversity in plant and animal species, human cultural diversity must be nourished as a reservoir of ideas from which future cultural adaptations can be made. Flexibility can be enhanced by creating diverse paths toward greater sustainability. Living in more sustainable societies need not require acts of ecological penance, force-feeding people vegetarian diets or creating a fashion industry based on sackcloth. Rather, the process of moving toward a more sustainable world can give people new purpose and replace the rampant materialism of the industrial period. Intellectual excitement can be generated by devising ways to do more with less, and increasing human well-being without substantially increasing raw material consumption and pollution.

In the end, however, there are two different paths leading to more ecologically secure development. The first involves continuing to muddle reactively toward a more sustainable world through sporadic and clumsy adjustments to the tightening constraints of nature. Recessions, depressions, environmental crises, terrorism, and political revolutions are characteristic of the muddling approach. The second path, by contrast, requires anticipatory thinking, initiative, creativity, and cooperative engagement to forge agreements and frame policies that can mitigate much of the potential pain involved in moving toward a less materially voracious, but much more egalitarian and ecologically sustainable world.

New Measures of Progress

Becoming more sustainable requires new definitions and measures of progress and efficiency. At the core of the industrial paradigm is an implicit definition of progress as possession of more material goods. The one-car family in the United States thus has become the two-van-one-car household. But this model of the good life is a relic of a period when resources were abundant relative to demands for them; it cannot be replicated by the bulk of humanity living in the Global South. Of the approximately 7.8 billion people living on the Earth in 2025, only 1.2 billion will likely be living in the countries that now make up the Global North. There will be 3.7 billion people living in the world's six largest developing countries: China, India, Indonesia, Pakistan, Brazil, and Nigeria.[47] The transfer of contemporary measures of progress and efficiency to the 6.6 billion people that will be living in the Global South would give inappropriate guidance for sustainable development.

The need for a new development paradigm suggests a similar need for new measures of welfare and progress as replacements for GDP.[48] GDP measures nothing more than total production of goods and services, saying little about the mix, quality, or durability of what's produced. For decades, academics have pointed out the many deficiencies of using this particular indicator of progress, but as yet there has been very little action in the political arena.[49]

One of the most obvious anomalies associated with continuing to use GDP as an indicator of progress is that many of the things that are tallied as progress in the old paradigm could just as easily be taken as regress in the new one. For example, the cost of obtaining raw materials such as coal, oil, nonfuel minerals and forest products, which often involves significant damage to the environment, is statistically considered to be an "economic good" and an addition to GDP. There are numerous other social bads that become twisted into social goods as measured by GDP.[50] In the United States terrorism, a crime wave, and a drug epidemic all have contributed to the growth of police forces, expansion of court systems, development and purchase of more sophisticated surveillance devices, and construction of more prisons. It would be difficult to argue, however, that the seemingly relentless growth in these kinds of services indicates an increase in the quality of life.

The Genuine Progress Indicator (GPI) has been suggested as an alternative measure that remedies many of the obvious deficiencies of GDP.[51] Proponents of this measure argue that much of what has been measured as progress in the past actually involved repairing blunders, defensive actions in the face of social decay, depletion of natural resources, and simply shifting functions that used to be performed within households into the monetized economy. For example, repairing the damage done to the Pentagon by terrorists, clear cutting forests, and putting iron bars in residential windows to deter criminals all have been treated as worthy additions to GDP. The GPI has been constructed in a way that systematically deducts such contributions from GDP. The rather astonishing result of this kind of computation is a steady decline in this measure of genuine progress in the United States since the mid-1970s.

In a similar vein, economist Herman Daly has suggested an alternative way of thinking about and measuring the efficiency with which natural resources are obtained and used. He outlines four indicators of efficiency that could be used to measure progress toward more sustainable societies.[52]

Daly first suggests the need to both increase and measure the turnover or renewal period of the stock of products or artifacts in a society. This measure, Artifact Maintenance Efficiency (AME) indicates the length of time that products remain in service. The more durable, repairable, and recyclable a stock of products, the greater the amount of service that it yields. The greater the length of time that products remain usable and the lower the maintenance requirements, the less the need for additional resources. While from an ecological security perspective it seems only logical to measure, and hopefully to increase, this type of efficiency, to do so runs contrary to many practices that are deeply embedded in industrial cultures. "Throw away" products ranging from beverage containers to cameras still are all too common. People often are reluctant to pay higher prices for more durable artifacts, and are poorly informed about them. Witness the continued persistence of the common short-life light bulb in the face of the availability of more durable alternatives. Short-term perspectives are abetted by price competition which often encourages production of cheap and shoddy artifacts. And planned obsolescence is all too common in the contemporary marketplace.

Daly also suggests the need to improve the efficiency with which a given stock of products or artifacts can be used. He labels this measure Artifact Service Efficiency (ASE). It focuses on the effectiveness with which products are meeting human needs. Given a certain level of resource consumption, there are varieties of artifacts that could be produced and different ways that they could be distributed. This measure also integrates social justice questions into sustainability thinking. For example, should possession of artifacts be concentrated in the hands of a few or should they be more equally distributed? Increasing ASE involves improving the effectiveness with which a given production potential and resource stream can meet social needs. In the United States, ASE could obviously be increased by moving away from production of trucks, vans, and sport utility vehicles and using this production potential for more fuel-efficient vehicles, or even mass transit in urban areas. In the Global South, perhaps developing countries should ignore privately owned vehicles completely, and develop other transportation systems.

Daly then proposes developing measures of how the physical environment is impacted by artifact production levels. He suggests Ecosystem Maintenance Efficiency (EME) as a measure of the degree to which ecosystems can supply materials or throughput on a sustainable basis. Increasing EME means devising ways of reducing the environmental burden of raw material throughput, thus maintaining a flow of required new resources while minimizing long-term environmental damage. This would involve making wise choices and investments in technology, exploiting abundant rather than scarce resources, replanting harvested forests, and using renewable resources and recycled materials. EME obviously could be increased by using solar energy instead of fossil fuels wherever possible.

Finally, Daly suggests Ecosystem Service Efficiency (ESE) as a measure of how losses, the unavoidable negative impacts of economic activity, are allocated throughout relevant societies and ecosystems. Production of artifacts inevitably has some type of pollution associated with it. Even hydroelectric power requires environmentally disruptive dams. And windmills can be noisy nuisances to people living nearby. ESE increases when these unavoidable environmental burdens are allocated so as to minimize long-term damage to ecosystems, and are spread evenly among the people who benefit from the economic activity, an environmental justice consideration. In this respect, a more efficient and thus more sustainable society would be one that minimizes environmental destruction by diffusing the unavoidable burdens of production widely throughout societies and ecosystems.

Summing Up: A New Planetary Bargain

The process of developing more sustainable societies in both the Global North and Global South could thus be indexed, both qualitatively and quantitatively, using these four measures as guidelines for progress. For the more affluent countries, ample opportunities exist for ecological modernization, retooling production processes in order to reduce environmental impact.[53] But there are also many opportunities to accelerate the shift in consumption from resource-intensive goods to less resource-intensive services.[54] For those countries on the other side of the economic divide, enhancing sustainability might entail avoiding many of the economic and environmental pitfalls of traditional industrialization.[55] Thus, China and India might leap beyond industrialization, and make a significant contribution to reducing future global warming, by foregoing petroleum-intensive fleets of privately owned vehicles in favor of efficient mass transit and enhanced telecommunications capabilities. Unfortunately, automobile manufacturers from Detroit to Tokyo are already devising strategies to capture the potentially huge Chinese market.[56] Most important, however, the extremes of North–South competition must give way to enhanced cooperation if countries of the Global South are ever to have a chance of overcoming the colonial legacy and the related structural constraints that have frustrated development for decades.

There now is an opportunity to forge a new planetary bargain and to begin the process of transformation to a more sustainable planet. The GPI and Daly's efficiency guidelines suggest alternate measures of long-term progress or regress that could easily replace outmoded development indicators in all countries. Numerous other indicators of sustainability have been suggested, many of them moving well beyond the core concerns outlined here.[57] Research universities could play a leading role in studying sustainability issues. But since the sustainability problematique doesn't fall clearly within the interests of existing disciplines, it still receives scant attention on university campuses.[58]

It is useful and instructive to hold large international meetings and engage in abstract discussions of the nature of and requisites for building a more ecologically secure world. It is also fruitful to conjure up visions of desirable characteristics for sustainable societies.[59] It is much more difficult, however, to move from these kinds of abstractions to the more concrete political economy of transformation. Creating a more sustainable world will be a difficult, dynamic, complex, and continuous process of education and political engagement requiring decades of concerted effort. It isn't easy to "unlearn" the definitions of progress and the good life that have evolved within the industrial paradigm. Doing so will be essential to reestablishing the dynamic equilibrium between the increasing demands of growing numbers of *Homo sapiens* and the sustaining capabilities of nature.

CHAPTER NINE

Governance and
Ecological Security

*H*OMO SAPIENS is now responsible for linked environmental and technological challenges to the evolutionary processes that provide the underpinnings of ecological security. Globalization and the continuing spread of industrialization to the more densely populated parts of the world is weakening ecological security in many ways by increasing dramatically the impact of people and their consumption on nature. And technologies associated with the nascent postindustrial revolution are also beginning to threaten the integrity of evolutionary processes. Primary among these are rapid advances in biotechnology that carry with them the potential to redesign nature. "The globalization of commerce and trade make possible the wholesale reseeding of the Earth's biosphere with a laboratory-conceived second Genesis, an artificially produced bioindustrial nature designed to replace nature's own evolutionary scheme. A global life-science industry is already beginning to wield unprecedented power over the vast biological resources of the planet."[1] The critical question is whether sociocultural evolution is now capable of producing adequate governance to address these mounting challenges.

In addition to the persisting pressures of large-scale demographic changes, disruptions of the atmosphere and hydrosphere, and a resurgence of deadly diseases,

211

genetic codes are being unlocked, species are being cloned and altered, human bodies are soon to be redesigned, and the development of more lethal biological weapons looms on the horizon. A tremendous potential to disrupt ecological security now is being unleashed, and it is unclear whether adequate governance mechanisms can be created and nourished in time to manage this growing complexity. "This biological transformation is outstripping the ethical vocabulary that has guided modern scientific decision-making. The dilemmas it creates often do not involve familiar questions of right and wrong, but wholly new problems of a new human condition."[2] Yet, in spite of these growing challenges, innovation appears to be taking place in governance very slowly. Industrial-era institutions and ways of making decisions persist in the face of these emerging postindustrial challenges.

The impending explosion of biotechnology that will lead to new life forms, redesigned plants, animals, microorganisms, and even human beings, presents significant challenges to existing ways of thinking about governance. *Homo sapiens* may no longer feel it necessary to adapt to changes in nature, since nature itself likely will be reshaped by people, either through well-conceived policies based on ecological wisdom, or the wants and whims of individuals as expressed in the marketplace. As Walter Truett Anderson has succinctly put it, "Today, the driving force in evolution is human intelligence. Species survive or perish because of what people do to them and their environments. The land and air and water systems are massively altered by humankind which has become, as one scientist put it 'a new geological force.' Even our own genetic future is in our hands, guided not by Darwinian abstractions but by science and medical technology and public policy."[3]

The nascent postindustrial revolution could now best be described as an unbalanced one, with technological capabilities clearly outrunning our collective ability to manage them in the interest of present and future generations.[4] The preceding period of rapid industrial expansion and economic growth generated philosophies and ideologies that downplay the importance of government, and exaggerate the importance of markets. Given this combined legacy of environmental threats and the explosion of new technological possibilities, it is imperative to apply ecological wisdom and ethical principles to relevant policy decisions.[5] But as globalization accelerates, a necessary transformation in the nature and scope of governance remains problematic. The potential for technological innovation and associated globalization to transform the planet indiscriminately now vastly exceeds the capabilities of existing governments and international organizations to manage these processes.

The persisting planetary scars of industrialization and the emerging technological possibilities of the postindustrial revolution are redefining the nature of and need for the public goods that have been traditionally provided by states. Public goods are provided by governments in order to address market failures or to improve social well-being and equity. Among the minimum accepted functions of government are providing defense, law and order, property rights, macroeconomic management, public health, antipoverty programs, and disaster relief. In addition, most governments also provide less obvious public goods such as environmental protection, basic education, consumer protection, pensions, and unemployment insurance.[6]

Environmental integrity, ecosystem stability, freedom from disease, and peace, all components of ecological security, are generally accepted public goods. Most countries have environmental protection agencies to safeguard nature and to attempt to insure that all citizens have access to reasonably fresh air and water. Similarly, national health ministries deal with the threat of infectious disease, and defense ministries cope with foreign aggression. Preserving future ecological security in the face of globalization and the associated mounting ecological and technological challenges, requires rethinking both the role of market forces and the nature and level of governance that can provide it. Continued heavy reliance on markets and Adam Smith's increasingly arthritic invisible hand will do little to preserve the integrity of the ecosphere, safeguard genetic and cultural diversity, promote good public health, and provide security from physical threats. People cannot easily purchase their own clean air to breathe, buy guaranteed protection from infectious disease, or arm themselves adequately to protect against potential aggressors. And given the nature of the many challenges associated with technological innovation and globalization, national governments, acting alone, also can no longer adequately provide many vital public goods for their citizens.[7]

Four Related Challenges

It is not difficult to identify many of the critical problems and issues that are raised by the rapid acceleration of globalization. It is much harder to envision realistic solutions to them, particularly while many countries, the United States chief among them, cling to the remnants of sovereignty, and continue to act unilaterally in the global arena. This exponential increase in challenges requires a corresponding increase in governance capabilities. But state capabilities continue to erode before global market forces, and the development of authority above the level of the state is resisted, and therefore poorly developed.

Building ecological security, a public good previously the responsibility of the state, now requires creating effective global governance. But building such governance is a difficult undertaking. There is predictable resistance among politicians to ceding such power in many existing semi-sovereign states. The United States, largely because of a peculiar domestic electoral system that periodically produces presidents with little understanding of foreign affairs, has emerged as a particularly large roadblock to many multilateral initiatives required to enhance ecological security. For example, in a period of one year the Bush–Cheney administration announced opposition to international agreements to ban land mines, slow the small arms trade, enforce the ban on biological weapons, deal with global warming, and preserve biodiversity. This government also announced its intention to repudiate the long-standing antiballistic missile treaty.[8] By contrast, the increasingly obvious success of the European Union in bringing together diverse countries within one unit clearly attests to the fact that governance above the state level is possible.

Preserving and enhancing ecological security in the twenty-first century requires rethinking the nature and provision of public goods in order to overcome four related challenges. First, the environmental challenges of industrialization must continue to be reckoned with as this revolution spreads to India, China, Indonesia, and other heavily populated countries. Second, there are the emerging management challenges associated with the acceleration of technological innovation in general, and with the worldwide diffusion of biotechnology in particular. And then there are the twin problems of managing the growing ecological disruption and sociocultural fallout from rapid globalization.

The essence of many of the environmental challenges resulting from industrialization, past and present, is captured aptly by the analogy of a tragedy of the commons popularized by Garrett Hardin.[9] He used the example of the medieval commons, an area open to all villagers to pasture livestock, to illustrate a tragedy that can unfold when public goods, in this case common pool resources, come under increasing pressure without adequate governance to protect them. In Hardin's example, villagers, motivated by immediate self-interest, would each strive to pasture as many animals as possible on the village commons. The cumulative result of these individuals attempting to maximize free use of the area is a tragedy of overgrazing as the commons becomes barren under the pressure from so many animals. "Therein is the tragedy. Each man is locked into a system that compels him to increase his herd without limit—in a world that is limited. Ruin is the destination toward which all men rush, each pursuing his own best interest in a society that believes in the freedom of the commons. Freedom in a commons brings ruin to all."[10]

Industrialization and globalization in a world that is divided politically into semi-sovereign states are intensifying such commons problems on a global scale.

The states in the contemporary system are in many ways akin to Hardin's villagers. Each state, and its agents, strives to take maximum advantage of various parts of the global commons in order to benefit its citizens. Thus, over the course of the Industrial Revolution the atmosphere and hydrosphere have been polluted by the growing and often unregulated demands of actors within states. Oceanic pollution, the decline of fish stocks, the buildup of greenhouse gases and other toxic pollutants in the atmosphere, the assault on the ozone layer, and loss of biodiversity are all tragedies that have unfolded as each state and its agents have attempted to extract maximum short term benefit from the global commons. Not being subject to governance beyond the state, there has been little reason for states to unilaterally limit their appetites.

Preventing the diffusion of potentially catastrophic technologies is a similar kind of "social trap" that requires action beyond the state.[11] An explosion of technological possibilities is giving greater numbers of actors the power to transform and significantly disrupt biophysical systems, either intentionally or by accident. In this dilemma, the tragedy is found in the inability to get all states to agree on the kinds of technologies that may be too risky or repugnant to be developed. Obviously pursuing and disseminating the knowledge and techniques required to make biological weapons of mass destruction is a case in point. But numerous other innovations that are undesirable for ecological or moral reasons are on the horizon. If even one state or corporation breaks ranks and develops these technologies in the interest of short-term profits, then all others will be tempted to do likewise.

Not all technological innovations are beneficial; some have the potential to bring contemporary civilization to an end.[12] Given current political arrangements, however, the power to restrict the development and diffusion of potentially destructive technologies still is in the hands of national governments. Innovations in biotechnology, particularly in genetically modified organisms, represent particularly difficult challenges because many of them have the potential to induce rapid and large-scale ecosystemic changes. The dilemma is that what one national government assesses as ecologically or morally unsound, another might see otherwise, particularly given the lure of large potential profits. But the impact of some innovations will be felt far beyond the boundaries of the countries in which they are permitted.

Innovations in biotechnology that may increase ecological insecurity thus cannot be regulated successfully on a state-by-state basis. As Francis Fukuyama has put it,

> No sovereign state, many argue, can regulate or ban any technological
> innovation, because the research and development will simply move to

another jurisdiction. In fact, this trend is apparent in the highly competitive biotech industry, where companies are constantly searching for the most favorable regulatory climate. Because Germany, with its traumatic history of eugenics, has been more restrictive of research than many developed countries, most German pharmaceutical and biotech companies have moved their labs to Britain, the United States, and other less restrictive nations.[13]

In a world where kidneys are quietly purchased from living individuals in poor countries to meet demand for transplants in the rich countries, it is difficult to see how all states will voluntarily agree to forego potentially profitable, but ecologically risky, biotechnologies in the interest of protecting future generations from possible harm. What good would it do for the United States or the European Union to ban the cloning of human beings, if cloning clinics spring up in Barbados? Would the former governments forbid cloned children of citizens to enter the country? Already there is significant controversy over the usefulness and impact of genetically modified crops. But the United States is not about to give up its technological lead and substantial corporate profits in genetically modified organisms simply because of fears and complaints from other governments. To deal effectively and objectively with these kinds of mounting potential challenges to evolutionary processes requires expertise, authority, and governance to be applied beyond the state level.

Addressing the third and fourth challenges, the ecological and socioeconomic disruption from rapid globalization, suggests a need for creating other kinds of global public goods. Controlling the spread of infectious diseases in a world where microbes move ever more rapidly and have little respect for national borders is an obvious public good.[14] Conditions in China can have a great impact on the flu season in the United States and Europe. But dealing effectively with infectious disease requires both an investment in public health infrastructure, particularly in poor countries, and a very high level of cooperative international surveillance.[15] Similarly, monitoring and controlling the increased worldwide movement of various kinds of larger organisms associated with the growing problem of bioinvasion requires substantial cooperation and action beyond the state level.

Deeper integration of the global economy also is increasing the potential impact of failures in important commodity markets. Both consumers and producers, for example, agree that relatively stable petroleum prices would be a very desirable global public good. But such price stability remains elusive in the absence of any agreements between exporter and importer countries to curb wildly fluctuating prices. Ecological security in the longer term would be enhanced by a steady shift to renewable energy sources, but the cyclical price fluctuations in the energy market discourage significant capital investment in them. Similarly, a quick scan of the history of world agriculture reveals many periods of significant famine induced by rapid climate change, often associated with violent volcanic eruptions.[16] While there is recognition that future food shortages related to such sudden shifts are inevitable, in the contemporary more densely packed world, there is still no global granary, a public good, containing reserves for emergency use, nor is there a contingency plan in place to deal with the potential harsh effects of such future shortages. Recently the Food and Agricultural Organization made a small bit of progress by establishing a Trust Fund for Food Security in response to the slow progress toward reducing world hunger. The Trust Fund is financed by voluntary contributions and is intended to finance projects aimed at strengthening sustainable means of increasing food availability in low-income food-deficit countries.[17]

Finally, there is a rapidly growing number of socioeconomic issues associated with globalization that require new kinds of global public goods. The rush to open up less industrialized economies to free trade is producing significant sociocultural casualties. While globalization sparks substantial economic growth, it also increases inequalities. These new market pressures create marginalized people and societies through an endless search for low-cost labor; encouraging cost-cutting techniques, depending on part-time or temporary work, and embracing new technologies with little concern for the human consequences. Historically, it has been the role of states to mute harsh inequalities generated by markets with welfare programs and other social safety nets. Rising concern over market excesses is focusing more attention on equity issues, but weakened states may not be able "to generate the public resources needed to finance social insurance schemes."[18] Increased trade in an emerging global market was expected to reduce inequalities between rich and poor. The opposite has been the case. "In the past 30 years the poorest 20 percent of the world's people saw their share of global income fall from 2.3 percent to 1.4 percent. Meanwhile, the share of the richest quintile grew from 70 percent to 85 percent."[19]

The last two decades have seen a wide swing of the economic pendulum toward unregulated markets. The power of states to make allocations has been slowly drained by often misplaced faith in the efficacy of unfettered markets. "In their haste to roll back the state, many economists and policy makers have overlooked the fact that the maintenance of a social safety net is not a luxury, but an essential ingredient of a market economy. Markets are a wonderful thing, but they also expose households to risks and insecurities that have to be managed in order for the social legitimacy of the market system to be maintained."[20] The emergence of global markets in the face of weakened states only increases the need for social safety nets, but now this need can only be effectively met by funding beyond the state level.

There are numerous reasons that distributive justice must become a global public good. Ecologically secure development can only take place with considerable economic and technological assistance from wealthier countries. Trade liberalization suggests a need for worldwide labor standards and fair compensation programs in order to insulate workers everywhere from the excesses of a race to the bottom. Increased education and the elimination of extreme poverty could have many positive ramifications for all people on Earth. Dealing with these equity issues, however, requires cooperative engagement, rather than hostile confrontation, with people in poorer neighborhoods of the emerging global city. A new planetary bargain requires a cooperative approach to ecologically sustainable development: not simply coercing poorer countries to subscribe to a trade system that will keep them perpetually impoverished, but giving them an active role in drafting rules to address existing inequities.

Most important of all, the clash of industrial modernization with tradition and the relative impoverishment of people in the Global South are creating a reservoir of angry and marginalized people from which future terrorists can be recruited. A decade ago, this potential small army of terrorists was of relatively little concern to pragmatic policymakers in industrialized countries. They thought themselves to be protected by the vast distances between the North and South, the equivalent of a protective moat with well-controlled drawbridges. In the wake of the tragedies of 2001, this insular thinking must be thoroughly reconsidered. In the emerging global city people move rapidly from one neighborhood to another; containment is not a viable option.

Technological innovation and diffusion are increasing the abilities of determined terrorists to inflict substantial damage on the other side of the figurative moat. It is estimated, for example, that it took only $500,000 to bankroll the destruction of the World Trade Center and the Pentagon, disasters that led to an estimated $100–$300 billion loss to the larger U.S. economy.[21] A new planetary bargain, including a genuine commitment to large quantities of development aid to create opportunities for people in poor countries, is essential to stem this destructive syndrome of poverty and hopelessness on which terrorism feeds.[22] After World War II, the United States transferred 1 percent of its national income to Europe for four years under the Marshall Plan, in order to help the region reconstruct. It is now critical for the United States to increase its meager foreign aid contribution and devise a similar long-term program to contribute substantially to the eradication of poverty and disease in the Global South. Put succinctly by Gordon Brown, "Some say the issue is whether we have globalization or not; in fact, the issue is whether we manage globalization well or badly, fairly or unfairly."[23]

The revolutionary challenges to existing modes of governance presented by worldwide environmental deterioration, rapid increases in technological innovation, and accelerating globalization now force deeper consideration of the important question of the nature of future public goods and who should provide them. It is increasingly obvious that many of these basic threats to ecological security are no longer being effectively handled by individual states. But, as yet, there is no global authority entrusted with responsibility for creating and funding global public goods, and there is no democratic mechanism for selecting one. In the face of an exponential acceleration of ecological and technological challenges, agreements to resolve issues growing out of the many facets of globalization must still be hammered out painfully among dozens of key actors on a time-consuming case-by-case basis. In a world that is experiencing rapid economic, ecological, and cultural globalization, building future ecological security also requires political globalization, an active process of building governance beyond the state.

Government or Governance?

To this point, the image of the global future is one of a rapid acceleration of challenges and issues associated with globalization in the face of a rather haphazard and embryonic attempt to build legitimate global governance. There is, as yet, no substantial progress toward a democratic authoritative allocation of values on a global scale, but rapid movement in that direction is imperative to deal with this present acceleration of history.[24] This requires moving beyond the tyranny of laissez-faire globalization to some new kind of governance informed by a collective sense of the need to preserve and sustainably manage the global commons, and to deal with the many complex challenges raised by technological innovation and deepening globalization.

An important distinction needs to be made between global governance and world government. The latter triggers alarm among nationalists, while the former offers substantial possibilities for moving collectively to address these important questions. While government can be a component of governance, the latter can exist, and perhaps at the global level must first exist, without a formal government. James Rosenau clarifies the difference between government and governance as follows:

> Both refer to purposive behavior, to goal-oriented activities, to systems of rule; but government suggests activities that are backed by formal activities, by police powers to insure the implementation of duly constituted policies, whereas governance refers to activities backed by shared goals that may or may not derive from legal and formally prescribed responsibilities and that do not necessarily rely on police powers to overcome defiance and attain compliance. Governance embraces governmental institutions, but it also subsumes informal, non-governmental mechanisms whereby those persons and organizations within its purview move ahead, satisfy their needs, and fulfill their wants. Governance is thus a system of rule that is as dependent on inter-subjective meaning as on formally sanctioned constitutions and charters.[25]

While at some point in the more distant future there may be a democratically elected world parliament, governance does not presuppose the need to create new concrete organizations.[26] The key distinction concerns the role that other social institutions can play in ameliorating or resolving collective-action problems.[27] Global governance refers to the informed management of interactions among and between individuals, states, multinational corporations, intergovernmental and nongovernmental organizations, and other non-state actors that comprise civil society at the global level.[28] These actors and their growing role in managing global relations are both a result of and a contributing factor to the weakening of the state.

It is not enough simply to suggest that what is missing in the globalization of human relations is effective global governance. "To make a partially globalized world benign, we need not just effective governance, but the *right kind* of governance."[29] The right kind of governance is that which is both normative and positive, and which meets basic requirements in its consequences, functions, and procedures. Here, this means governance that is based on preserving ecological security in the context of a globalizing world. "Today, leading students of governance are busy pinning down the conditions under which 'governance without government' can succeed, instead of prolonging unproductive debates about the need to establish centralized organizations to solve an array of collective-action problems."[30] Governance includes, then, multiple forms, methods, and institutions, ranging from the more formal and legalistic organs of the United Nations to the informal, sometimes loosely based coordination of hard and soft regimes that rely more on moral suasion than sanctions.

The challenge for global governance is an immense one. There are now nearly two hundred countries that are recognized as part of the existing international system. Although they all claim to be sovereign, they differ considerably in their ability to control activities within and outside their borders. In addition to states, numerous intergovernmental organizations (IGOs) serve as mechanisms for coordinated action above the state level. These IGOs include components of the United Nations system, independent agencies closely affiliated with the UN, and issue-based governmental organizations that serve highly specialized roles, such as the International Energy Agency and the International Oceanographic Commission. In addition, there are many regional IGOs, only some of which are affiliated with the UN system.

Beyond the United Nations, the World Trade Organization (WTO) has emerged as a forum for processing trade-related issues. But the preeminence of the WTO is seen by many as having hindered environmental, labor, and human rights concerns by giving preference to free trade whenever in conflict with these sometimes competing values. Paralleling the WTO, the World Bank and the International Monetary Fund now act as international financial institutions. These institutions were created to facilitate the availability and movement of investment capital and development aid. But they also perform various governance functions.

In addition to the growth in these more specialized governance organizations, a broader participatory role has developed for the private sector. There are now over 60,000 multinational corporations with a total of more than 450,000 subsidiaries.[31] Many of these multinational corporations leverage their power and influence through membership in the International Chamber of Commerce and the World Economic Forum, both of which serve as associations of business and corporate interests that effectively coordinate and represent the interests of their members.

Finally, there has been an explosive growth in the number of nongovernmental organizations (NGOs). More than two thousand NGOs hold consultative status with the United Nations Economic and Social Council.[32] Another four hundred are accredited specifically with the United Nation's Commission on Sustainable Development.[33] Estimates of the total number of NGOs working in the less industrialized countries suggest there are between six thousand and thirty thousand.[34] Regardless of their exact number, there is little dispute that NGOs will continue to be increasingly influential in dealing with matters related to ecological security.

Governance Mechanisms

Existing agreements provide a solid framework for dealing with many kinds of global commons problems; they are less useful in dealing with the regulation and assessment of technology and the socioeconomic fallout from globalization. These agreements range from more legalistic and enforceable "hard law" to those best referred to as "soft law."[35] One database of multilateral environmental agreements identifies nearly 500 treaties put into effect between 1868 and 1999.[36] Another contains more than 169 environmental agreements established since 1940, ranging from issues of stratospheric ozone depletion to oil pollution.[37] These agreements are formally adopted international treaties that bind governments. These state-based treaties have served as the modus operandi of a state-centric international system since the Treaty of Westphalia. These treaties often include broad principled statements, but also include explicit procedures for remedying problems, and implementation dates.

Lesser degrees of formality and enforceability are found in the many regional antipollution unions and agreements that address environmental problems, such as the 1976 Convention to Protect the Mediterranean. International conferences that result in broad principled documents serve as yet looser and softer forms of international agreement. The 1972 Stockholm Conference on the Global Environment and the follow-up 1992 United Nations Conference on Environment and Development in Rio de Janeiro are examples. These less formal mechanisms depend on the goodwill of participants and often lead to regimes, defined as principles, norms, rules, and decision-making procedures around which actor expectations converge in a given issue area.[38] At the extreme soft end of the spectrum are the guidelines of intergovernmental organizations that govern their own actions, such as requiring environmental impact statements as part of the organization's standard operating procedures. Given the inherent difficulties of reaching political agreements on how to protect the global commons most effectively, and the unwillingness of many to turn over the stewardship of these shared resources to private interests, it is not surprising that the mechanisms for global governance that have evolved tend to be more consensual agreements with little enforcement power.

There are also relevant voluntary schemes that have arisen within the private sector. These efforts, ranging from industry codes of conduct to corporate accountability standards and "regulation by revelation," are attempts by multinational corporations and others to both demonstrate a willingness to be responsible global citizens, and to stave off possibly more rigid regulatory mechanisms that might otherwise be deemed necessary.[39] Examples of voluntary schemes include negotiations between industry and the International Standards Organization (ISO) to establish environmental, social, labor, and other standards for corporations.[40] In these cases, voluntary compliance with the standards results in certification by the ISO that a corporation is meeting them, thereby providing positive public relations and marketing for the corporation, and suggesting to consumers that the corporation is being a good global citizen. These self regulatory efforts, though, sometimes lack credibility because they are vol untary, and in many instances their implementation tends to be weak.[41]

In addition to these efforts, public private partnerships in the form of collaborative efforts between governments and industry emerged in the 1990s. Reflective of this approach to governance within the United States and other countries, global collaboration has taken the form of a Global Compact between the United Nations and the World Economic Forum. The Global Compact, initiated in Davos, Switzerland, in 1999, aims to "unite the power of markets with the authority of universal ideals" in a coordinated and complimentary fashion in order to address emerging global challenges.[42]

Despite these efforts, there remain fundamental problems with this loose global governance system. This web of international agreements covers a bewildering array of regional and global issues with varying degrees of enforcement ability and compliance. The present global governance system is disconnected and incomplete. It fails to represent the aspirations and perspectives of the bulk of the world's citizens or to bridge the global demographic and developmental divide. Data maintained by the Food and Agriculture Organization on treaties, laws, and regulations suggest that there are over 670 international agreements addressing food, agriculture, and renewable natural resources.[43] Yet, the degree of coordination and connection among these hundreds of agreements is minimal.

The lack of an overarching or coordinating body or mechanism to assess the aggregate affects of these disparate agreements is a flaw that leaves the nascent system of governance at best inefficient, and at worst vulnerable to inconsistencies, redundancies, and conflicting policies and practices. The current system also makes it difficult to assess the degree to which progress toward the broader goals of sustainability and ecological security is being made. At the recent launching of a United Nations Environment Program project, the executive director stated in reference to the thirty or more existing active wildlife treaties and agreements that "Over the years, we have seen a proliferation of conventions, agreements and memorandums of understanding covering everything from migratory birds to regional seas. If we can streamline the way these many conventions and agreements operate, then there could be substantial savings. Some experts have suggested up to 40 percent of the current costs or several million dollars."[44]

A second flaw in the existing global governance network is a lack of democratic procedures. Most of the key actors in these many organizations are never elected by anyone. It is often suggested that a sense of democracy, transparency, accountability, and equity are missing from the fledgling global governance system. Thus there are calls for "Harmonizing global competition and free market approaches with steady and expanding support for human development and human rights in all countries, developed and developing."[45] The democracy deficit in today's global governance system is visible in the formation and negotiation of global policy as well as in the implementation and evaluation stages. The need for an infusion of democracy is well documented.[46] These procedural deficiencies of global governance can only be remedied through new global institutional designs.[47]

Finally, while these constraints on the nascent global governance system are difficult enough to overcome, the recent unilateral actions of the United States only make the situation more difficult. The United States has always had a somewhat mixed track record in multilateral action. But at the dawn of the new millennium, the United States has reverted once again to isolationist impulses, and pulled away from the global community in almost every issue area. This recent U.S. withdrawal began in the late 1990s under the Clinton administration, and was evidenced by unwillingness to participate in a global ban on the use of land mines and an accord establishing a permanent international criminal court. Both agreements would have required a two-thirds majority vote in the Senate, which was not likely to be forthcoming. Under the subsequent Bush administration, however, a unilateralist response to pressing global issues became dominant. Agreements have been abandoned before, during, and after negotiations. The rationale for this has been explained as follows: "They simply view treaties as a steam-engine-age tool whose usefulness this deep into the nuclear era will be judged one issue at a time, one negotiation at a time, one summit meeting at a time."[48] Described by a senior State Department official as "à la carte multilateralism," it is precisely this kind of ad hoc, self-serving, short-term, incremental approach that retards progress in building global governance and therefore weakens the prospects for future ecological security.[49]

Summing Up: Building an Eco-Evolutionary Consensus

The twenty-first century promises to be one of exponential growth in challenges to ecological security, but, at best, linear growth in the ability to collectively react to them. The growing environmental threats from the spread of industrialization to China, India, Indonesia, and other heavily populated countries must be mitigated. Similarly, as technological innovation accelerates, governance challenges from cutting-edge technologies will grow in number and significance. And perhaps most immediate is the need to address the widening sociocultural divide associated with the fallout of globalization and the decline of the state. To deal effectively with these mounting challenges requires policies and strategies that are anticipatory rather than reactionary. It is proactive, integrated, and consciously chosen policies and institutions that are needed. These new policies and institutions, based on eco-evolutionary thinking, must reflect the shared values of the entire global community. Consequently, it is essential to begin to eliminate the current democracy deficit, and to ensure that procedures for global governance are reflective of underlying shared values.

At present, this complex nascent system of global governance is still much too immature and disparate to deal effectively with this plethora of growing security challenges. Much bolder, and perhaps even utopian, multilateral initiatives are clearly required. The burdens of more widespread industrialization require a new planetary bargain if natural systems are to be protected. While technological innovation moves inexorably forward, both solving human problems and creating situations that could potentially threaten civilization, there are as yet no forums in which to make reasoned assessments of the likely impact of these new technologies on evolutionary processes. And the dynamics of globalization give urgency to a new socioeconomic agenda that can only be addressed adequately through multilateral actions.

The world has been extremely fortunate to avoid, at least to this point, a nuclear holocaust, although Pakistan and India periodically threaten to create one. The proliferation of nuclear weapons technologies has been slowed both by multilateral political efforts and by the enormous expense and public visibility of needed equipment and facilities. But there are far fewer constraints on the development and use of chemical and biological weapons. A nerve gas attack in Japan in 1995 and an anthrax attack in the United States in 2001 could be harbingers of things to come, unless the entire global community unites in moral condemnation of such actions. Over the next twenty years the knowledge and equipment needed to make these weapons of mass destruction will diffuse to the socially and politically unstable areas of the Global South, unless intense multilateral efforts are made to restrict their spread.

Preserving a livable world is best accomplished by using an eco-evolutionary perspective in making security decisions. It means recognizing that *Homo sapiens* now really does live in a "global" system, both biologically and socioculturally, and must act accordingly. The security of the whole system is now vitally dependent on maintaining the health of its various parts. The plight of impoverished masses in many neighborhoods of the Global South can now be ignored only at the peril of those living in the Global North. Sincere cooperation among people increasingly identifying themselves as citizens of Planet Earth must replace confrontation in dealing with the perils of globalization and the problems of ecologically sustainable future development.

While movement toward a more coherent form of global governance is now imperative to maintain the health of this emerging system, developing such governance requires a visionary effort by world leaders to forge the kinds of agreements that are essential to deal with this new agenda of issues. In this respect, the United States currently is one of the major impediments to making such multilateral progress. Given the isolationist history of the country, it is understandable that the United States has not exerted visionary leadership on these issues. But there is no way that the United States can insulate itself effectively from these new challenges, including those coming from radical elements in the Global South, solely through superior technology and the use of military force.[50] Very basic U.S. economic interests will continue to force engagement with the rest of the world, and a transformation of U.S. politics and perspectives is essential to building a needed consensus for a new world order.

This broad array of twenty-first-century challenges to well-being make imperative the development of a new security paradigm to replace the outmoded one, which relies heavily upon problem-solving through the use of force and has been handed down from a much different world. The causes of growing ecological insecurity must be addressed in an anticipatory fashion because the costs of not doing so are becoming prohibitive. Faith in technology as the sole answer to this broadening array of security challenges seems increasingly misplaced. Yet, biotechnology still is touted as the main answer to food shortages; nuclear power as a remedy for global warming; vaccines as an answer to threats of new, resurgent, and manmade diseases; and various kinds of surveillance devices as ways to protect people from each other. This path that is now being followed leads to more centralized, brittle, and Orwellian societies in which order is kept by control from above: surveillance cameras on every street corner, and uniformed military on every block.

The path not taken, at least to this point, is one that stresses more control from within: developing further the moral aspects of collective evolutionary experience as a source of guidance, values, and inspiration in building a more just and ecologically sustainable world. In this alternative world people would refrain from blowing up others because there is a strong consensus that it is morally wrong to do so. Foreign assistance would be given to poor countries to alleviate poverty and disorder, not because of political blackmail. Sport utility vehicles would be shunned because of their environmental impact. Millionaires would pay taxes because it would be considered equitable to do so.

When the ultimate consequences of following these two diverging paths are compared, it clearly is much more effective in every way to follow the one not now being taken. It is essential to begin immediately to build a consensus that it is preferable to live in a world where policy is guided by eco-evolutionary principles; where it is considered by all to be morally wrong to blow up, sicken, or poison neighbors and nature; and where it is also considered wrong for the bulk of the human race to be consigned to grinding poverty while the privileged few live in luxury. The alternative to building this deeper moral commitment to the welfare of all people and nature is to continue to patch up an expensive, and emotionally hollow, technological dystopia heavily dependent upon the troops of the new hegemon and an array of highly sophisticated destructive devices.

Epilogue: Ten Steps to Enhanced Ecological Security

MUCH TIME has passed while this book has been in preparation, and it is fortunate to have this opportunity to reflect on its message in light of recent events. While history has been accelerating, ecological security has continued to deteriorate. In less than three years the global economy has gone into a tailspin, stock markets around the world have declined precipitously, and corporate pension funds have been severely depleted by business slowdowns and related bankruptcies. A small group of terrorists has commandeered commercial aircraft to bring down the World Trade Center towers and a substantial piece of the Pentagon, and an unknown person (or persons) has spread anthrax through the U.S. mail. The Bush Administration has launched and concluded a preemptive war against Iraq. Millions more people have contracted HIV/AIDS, and a deadly SARS virus has stirred panic and slowed economic growth in several countries. Other less visible problems such as global warming, deforestation, species extinction, and resource depletion have continued to mount.

While the clock has been ticking, the Bush Administration has continued to ignore this pressing ecological security agenda, and devoted itself to the high politics of regime replacement in Afghanistan and Iraq, while threatening other governments in the region. While the United States (and its patchwork coalition of forces) has been spending tens, or even hundreds, of billions of dollars to force regime change in Iraq, a deadly SARS outbreak has been killing hundreds and sickening thousands of people around the world. Yet only a few tens of millions of dollars have been made available internationally to head off this much more serious challenge to human well-being. And while the *Washington Post* has devoted two full sections daily to the war in Iraq, it has featured only two or three articles per day on the battle against SARS. In perhaps an ultimate act of irresponsibility, at this critical time the U.S. sugar industry has threatened to lobby Congress to cut off the American contribution to the World Health Organization because of a WHO report urging people to limit their sugar intake!

This rather dismal course of events hardly gives rise to optimism about an impending paradigm shift in security thinking. In fact, it raises basic questions of whether efforts to create a more ecologically secure world are in vain. Politicians continue to conduct business as usual in the face of the challenges of rapid globalization, while industrial-era thinking and practices persist in a nascent postindustrial world. However, there is an abundance of information available about the causes and consequences of increasing ecological insecurity, and many people around the world are dedicated to halting the political march of folly. Thus it is with trepidation, but also with the hope that the present chasm between eco-evolutionary theory and political practice can be bridged, that the following steps to enhancing ecological security are suggested.

1. Address emerging global issues from an eco-evolutionary perspective. Identify the most serious threats to ecological security and revise policies and expenditures accordingly. Close the yawning gap between scientific studies and public policy, particularly in the United States.

2. Employ a long-term perspective in domestic and foreign policy decision making. The welfare of future generations is most at risk from the present very limited ability to address this broader range of security issues. Develop foresight capabilities to identify and deal with future security challenges before they become acute.

3. Develop new institutions beyond the state level to cope with the rapid pace and expanding scope of globalization. New forms of governance are vitally important to the maintenance of health and order in this increasingly interdependent global system.

4. Create new global public goods to redress the growing imbalance between markets and politics. Among the most important of these are global public health and control of infectious disease, universal education, economic

safety nets for the world's poor, a food buffer stock adequate for major emergencies, and stable oil prices.

5. Finance these global public goods, as well as ecologically secure development, with capital flows outside the control of states. The present paternalistic foreign aid system is flawed and often irrational. A new Marshall Plan for ecologically secure development is imperative for the welfare of rapidly growing populations in the Global South as well as for the future health of the global economy. Instruments such as the often suggested Tobin Tax on cross-border financial transactions could be used both to make them more manageable and to create new capital for development without donor strings attached.

6. Recognize the need to manage the course of technological innovation and diffusion. Technological innovation is accelerating, as is the spread of dual-use technologies. Cooperative technology assessment on a global scale is essential to minimize the proliferation of new weapons of mass destruction as well as to steer innovation in environmentally benign directions.

7. Nurture a cooperative approach to worldwide socioeconomic development. Recognize that the welfare of the emerging global city is dependent upon the well-being of its various neighborhoods. An increasingly integrated global system cannot long persist in the face of huge gaps between rich and poor countries.

8. Nourish a moral dimension of globalization based upon eco-evolutionary values. Global governance can only flourish if it is based on shared values. It is imperative to eliminate religious divisiveness and build a consensus based on values shared among various religious (and nonreligious) traditions.

9. Work to overcome the isolationist tendencies now prevalent in United States foreign policy. It is ironic that the world's unquestioned economic and military hegemon repeatedly rejects multilateral efforts to address ecological security problems. It could be that the American political culture has become so malignant as to make a transformation impossible. This is unlikely, but if it proves to be the case, the rest of the global community may have to move forward with their own multilateral efforts and leave the United States behind.

10. Recognize that time is very short. Every day that passes without resolutely working to resolve these problems is time wasted.

Notes

Chapter One: From International to Global Relations

1. Hilary French, *Vanishing Borders: Protecting the Planet in the Age of Globalization* (New York: Norton, 2000), 6.

2. In 1990 dollars; French, *Vanishing Borders*, 7.

3. Population figures and estimates, unless otherwise specified, are from *2001 Population Data Sheet* (Washington, D.C.: Population Reference Bureau, 2001).

4. French, *Vanishing Borders*, 6.

5. The term "McWorld" comes from Benjamin R. Barber, *Jihad vs. McWorld* (New York: Times Books, 1995).

6. The term "future shock" is explained in detail in Alvin Toffler, *Future Shock* (New York: Random House, 1970). See also Alvin Toffler, *Power Shift* (New York: Bantam, 1990).

7. For a critique of traditional diplomacy and some suggestions for avoiding future surprises see Richard Burt and Olin Robison, *Reinventing Diplomacy in the Information Age* (Washington, D.C.: CSIS Press, 1998).

8. See Francis Fukuyama, "The End of History?" *The National Interest* (Summer 1989); Samuel P. Huntington, *The Clash of Civilizations and the Remaking of World Order* (New York: Simon & Schuster, 1996).

9. A classic, albeit somewhat extreme, example of this is offered by John J. Mearsheimer, *The Tragedy of Great Power Politics* (New York: Norton, 2001). Among the assumptions the author makes are that the goal of each state is to maximize its share of world power, and that since states fear one another, the more powerful they become the better their chances of survival.

10. See Frances Cairncross, *The Death of Distance* (Boston: Harvard Business School Press, 1997).

11. An exception to this is some futures work of the National Intelligence Council (NIC). Although somewhat an inventory of conventional thinking, the 2000 NIC study of global trends to 2015 represents a refreshing departure from business as usual. See NIC, *Global Trends 2015: A Dialogue about the Future with Nongovernmental Experts* (Washington, D.C.: NIC, December 2000).

12. Bruce Stokes, "The Protectionist Myth," *Foreign Policy* (Winter 1999–2000): 93.

13. See the very detailed, and somewhat polemical, discussion of the impact of the race to the bottom on labor in the United States in Alan Tonelson, *The Race to the Bottom* (Boulder, CO: Westview, 2000).

14. Christopher Bright, *Life Out of Bounds: Bioinvasion in a Borderless World* (New York: Norton, 1998); "Invasive Species: Pathogens of Globalization," *Foreign Policy* (Fall 1999).

15. William H. McNeill, *Plagues and Peoples* (Garden City, NY: Anchor Press/Doubleday, 1976); Henry Hobhouse, *Forces of Change: Why We Are the Way We Are* (London: Sidgwick & Jackson, 1989).

16. Stephen M. Walt, "Fads, Fevers, and Firestorms," *Foreign Policy* (November/December 2000).

17. The term used by Joseph S. Nye, Jr., "Soft Power," *Foreign Policy* (Fall 1990).

18. Paul Alan Cox, "Will Tribal Knowledge Survive the Millennium?" *Science* (January 7, 2000).

19. See Thomas F. Homer-Dixon, *The Ingenuity Gap* (New York: Knopf, 2000).

20. David Held et al., *Global Transformations: Politics, Economics and Culture* (Stanford, CA: Stanford University Press, 1999), 5–7.

21. A good summary of these positions is found in Held et al., *Global Transformations: Politics, Economics and Culture*, 3–5, 7–9.

22. The index is computed annually by A. T. Kearney and *Foreign Policy* magazine. These figures are from "Globalization's Last Hurrah?" *Foreign Policy* (January/February 2002).

23. Kerry Capell, "How Mad Cows Threaten European Unity," *BusinessWeek* (March 19, 2001).

24. Thomas L. Friedman, *The Lexus and the Olive Tree* (New York: Farrar, Straus & Giroux, 1999), chapter 13.

25. See Robin Broad, ed., *Global Backlash: Citizen Initiatives for a Just World Economy* (Lanham, MD: Rowman & Littlefield, 2002).

26. A clear exception to this is James Rosenau, *Turbulence in World Politics: A Theory of Change and Continuity* (Princeton, NJ: Princeton University Press, 1990).

27. Kenneth Watt, *Principles of Environmental Science* (New York: McGraw-Hill, 1973), 1.

28. Karl Deutsch, *Nationalism and Social Communication* (Cambridge, MA: MIT Press, 1964), 100.

29. As Clifford Geertz has put it, a primordial attachment is one that "stems from the 'givens'—or, more precisely, as culture is inevitably involved in such matters, the

assumed 'givens' of social existence: immediate contiguity and kin connection mainly, but beyond them the givenness that stems from being born into a particular religious community, speaking a particular language, or even a dialect of a language, and following particular social practices." Clifford Geertz, *The Interpretation of Cultures* (New York: Basic, 1973), 259.

30. The classic summary of this perspective is Kenneth Waltz, *Man, The State, and War: A Theoretical Analysis* (New York: Columbia University Press, 1959).

31. There is evidence that small groups of precursors of modern humans also migrated out of Africa much earlier, but were supplanted by later migrants. For example, recent anthropological research shows migrations as early as 1.7 million years ago; see Michael Balter and Ann Gibbons, "A Glimpse of Human's First Journey Out of Africa," *Science* (May 12, 2000).

32. Luigi Cavalli-Sforza and Francesco Cavalli-Sforza, *The Great Human Diasporas* (Reading, MA: Addison Wesley, 1995), 120–23.

33. Walter L. Wallace, *The Future of Ethnicity, Race, and Nationality* (Westport, CT: Praeger, 1997), 15.

34. Rosemarie Ostler, "Disappearing Languages," *The Futurist* (August–September 1999): 16.

35. Discussions of these languages and others may be found in Daniel Nettle and Suzanne Romaine, *Vanishing Voices: The Extinction of the World's Languages* (New York: Oxford University Press, 2000).

36. Bernard Nietschmann, "The Third World War," *Cultural Survival Quarterly* 11, No. 3 (1987).

37. Gunnar Nielsson and Ralph Jones, "From Ethnic Category to Nation: Patterns of Political Modernization" (paper presented to annual meeting of the International Studies Association, March 1988).

38. Ted Robert Gurr, *Peoples Versus States: Ethnopolitical Conflict and Accommodation at the End of the Twentieth Century* (Washington, D.C.: U.S. Institute of Peace Press, 2000).

39. For examples see Lucian W. Pye, *Politics, Personality, and Nation-Building: Burma's Search for Identity* (New Haven, CT: Yale University Press, 1962); Clifford Geertz, ed., *Old Societies and New States* (New York: Free Press, 1963).

40. See Thomas M. Wilson and Hastings Donnan, eds., *Border Identities: Nation and State at International Frontiers* (Cambridge: Cambridge University Press, 1998).

41. Even under conditions where ethnic groups have seemingly been assimilated, ethnic identity remains a potent force. There is evidence, for example, that migrants to the United States retain much of their ethnic identity for two or three generations. The Black Power movement that attempted to forge a united black community in the 1960s has given way to a more subtle differentiation of ethnic groups as more recent immigrants have become more numerous. As psychologist Marvin Dunn observes about the United States, "There's much more intermarriage and dating between black groups than between blacks and whites, but not that much. I wouldn't overstate the

point. A Haitian wants his daughter to marry a Haitian. Bahamians want their daughters to marry Bahamians." See Darryl Fears, "A Diverse—and Divided—Black Community," *Washington Post*, February 24, 2002, 1(A).

42. Keep in mind that small genetic differences can create big physical differences. For example, it is estimated that the chimpanzee has a 95 to 98.4 percent genetic overlap with *Homo sapiens*. The latter figure comes from Jared Diamond, *The Third Chimpanzee: The Evolution and Future of the Human Animal* (New York: HarperPerennial, 1993), 20–24. More recent research by Roy J. Britten at the California Institute of Technology sets the figure at 95 percent; reported in *Washington Post*, September 30, 2002, 7(A).

43. It is thought that skin color has evolved to balance the need to protect folate from breaking down, while permitting enough exposure to sun to catalyze production of vitamin D. Thus, dark-skinned peoples predominate in the tropics, while light skin is common in northern latitudes. See Nina G. Jablonski and George Chaplin, "Skin Deep," *Scientific American* (October 2002).

44. Diamond, *The Third Chimpanzee: The Evolution and Future of the Human Animal*, 47–53.

45. R. Paul Shaw and Yuwa Wong, *The Genetic Seeds of Warfare: Evolution, Nationalism, and Patriotism* (Boston: Unwin Hyman, 1989), 38.

46. For more perspective on sociocultural evolution see Marvin Harris, *Cultural Materialism: The Struggle for a Science of Culture* (New York: Random House, 1979); Tim Ingold, *Evolution and Social Life* (Cambridge: Cambridge University Press, 1986); C. R. Hallpike, *The Principles of Social Evolution* (Oxford: Clarendon Press, 1986); William Durham, *Co-evolution: Genes, Culture, and Human Diversity* (Stanford, CA: Stanford University Press, 1991); Stephen K. Sanderson, *Social Transformations: A General Theory of Historical Development* (Oxford: Blackwell, 1995).

47. For an excellent overview see Claes Ramel, "Man as Biological Species," *Ambio* (February 1992).

48. For a discussion of cooperation and synergy in evolutionary processes see Peter A. Corning, *The Synergism Hypothesis: A Theory of Progressive Evolution* (New York: McGraw-Hill, 1983), and "Holistic Darwinism: Synergy and the New Evolutionary Paradigm," in *Research in Biopolitics*, eds. Albert Somit and Steven A. Peterson (Stamford, CT: JAI Press, 1998). See also Elliott Sober and David Sloan Wilson, *Unto Others: The Evolution and Psychology of Unselfish Behavior* (Cambridge, MA: Harvard University Press, 1998).

49. For a discussion of various reasons for societal collapses historically see Joseph A. Tainter, *The Collapse of Complex Societies* (Cambridge: Cambridge University Press, 1988).

50. The term "meme" was coined by Richard Dawkins, *The Selfish Gene* (New York: Oxford University Press, 1976). See also the argument for use of memes in Susan Blackmore, *The Meme Machine* (New York: Oxford University Press, 1999).

51. See Durham, *Co-evolution: Genes, Culture, and Human Diversity*, chapter 4.

52. Hobhouse, *Forces of Change: Why We Are the Way We Are Now*, 19–25.

53. For an excellent overview of the evolutionary origins and limitations of ethnic identity see Gary R. Johnson, "The Roots of Ethnic Conflict: An Evolutionary Perspective," in *Evolutionary Theory and Ethnic Conflict*, eds. Patrick James and David Goetze (Westport, CT: Praeger, 2001).

54. For diverse views on the nature of ethnicity and its relationship to the state see Ernst B. Haas, *Nationalism, Liberalism, and Progress* (Ithaca, NY: Cornell University Press, 1997); Walker Connor, *Ethnonationalism: The Quest for Understanding* (Princeton, NJ: Princeton University Press, 1994); John T. Ishiyama and Marijke Breuning, *Ethnopolics in the New Europe* (Boulder, CO: Rienner, 1998).

55. For an overview of recent findings in genetics and neurosciences that support a more determinist position see Robert H. Blank, "Neuroscience, Free Will, and Individual Responsibility: Policy Implications" (paper delivered at the annual meeting of the Association for Politics and the Life Sciences, October, 2001).

56. For an excellent overview of perspectives on the social construction of ethnic identity see James D. Fearon and David D. Laitin, "Violence and the Social Construction of Ethnic Identity," *International Organization* (Autumn 2000).

57. For a review of the extensive literature dealing with these interactions see Tatu Vanhanen, "Domestic Ethnic Conflict and Ethnic Nepotism: A Comparative Analysis," *Journal of Peace Research* 36, No. 1 (1999).

58. Geoffrey D. Dabelko and David D. Dabelko, "Environmental Security: Issues of Conflict and Redefinition," *Environmental Change and Security Project Report* (Spring 1995): 3.

59. See Norman Myers, "Environment and Security," *Foreign Policy* (Spring 1989); Daniel Deudney, "Environment and Security: Muddled Thinking," *The Bulletin of Atomic Scientists* (April 1991); Dietrich Fischer, *Non-Military Aspects of Security: A Systems Approach* (Geneva: UNIDIR, 1993); Norman Myers, *Ultimate Security: The Environmental Basis of Political Stability* (New York: Norton, 1993); United Nations Development Program, *Human Development Report 1994: Redefining Security, The Human Dimension* (Oxford: Oxford University Press, 1994); Ken Conca, "In the Name of Sustainability: Peace Studies and Environmental Discourse," *Peace and Change* 19, No. 2 (1994); Marc Levy, "Time for a Third Wave of Environment and Security Scholarship," *Environmental Change and Security Project Report* (Spring 1995); Nils Petter Gleditsch, ed., *Conflict and the Environment* (Dordrecht: Kluwer Academic Publishers, 1997); Geoffrey D. Dabelko and P. J. Simmons, "Environment and Security: Core Ideas and U.S. Government Initiatives," *The SAIS Review* (Winter/Spring 1997); Daniel Deudney and Richard Matthew, *Contested Grounds: Security and Conflict in the New Environmental Politics* (Albany, NY: SUNY Publishers, 1998); Paul F. Diehl and Nils Petter Gleditsch, eds., *Environmental Conflict* (Boulder, CO: Westview, 2001); Jon Barnett, *The Meaning of Environmental Security: Ecological Politics and Policy in the New Security Era* (London: Zed Books, 2001). See also the excellent bibliographic guide in each issue of *Environmental Change and Security Project Report* published by the Woodrow Wilson International Center for Scholars.

60. Andrew T. Price-Smith, *The Health of Nations: Infectious Disease, Environmental Change, and Their Effects on National Security and Development* (Cambridge, MA: MIT Press, 2001); Michael Moodie and William J. Taylor, *Contagion and Conflict: Health as a Global Security Challenge* (Washington, D.C.: CSIS, 2000).

61. The European approach to dealing with the plague is detailed in Sheldon Watts, *Epidemics and History: Disease, Power, and Imperialism* (New Haven, CT: Yale University Press, 1997), chapter 1.

62. See Alfred W. Crosby, *America's Forgotten Pandemic: The Influenza of 1918* (Cambridge: Cambridge University Press, 1989).

63. Deaths from conflict estimates are from "Millennium of Wars," *Washington Post*, March 13, 1999, 13(A). Estimates of annual deaths from infectious disease are those of the World Health Organization (WHO), *World Health Report 2000* (Geneva: WHO, 2000), annex table 3. Famine statistics come from Stephen Devereux, *Famine in the Twentieth Century* (Brighton, UK: Institute of Development Studies Working Paper 105, 2000), 6.

64. See, for example, United States Environmental Protection Agency (USEPA), *Environmental Security: Strengthening National Security through Environmental Protection* (Washington, D.C.: USEPA, September 1999); Daniel Esty et al., *State Failure Task Force Report: Phase II Findings* (McLean, VA.: SAIC, 1998); Department of Defense, Office of the Deputy Undersecretary of Defense (Environmental Security) at www.acq.osd.mil/end/ and *Environmental Change and Security Project* (ECSP) at ecsp.si.edu/default.htm.

65. See Kent Hughes Butts, "Why the Military Is Good for the Environment," in *Green Security or Militarized Environment*, ed. Jyrki Kakonen (Brookfield, VT: Dartmouth Publishing Company, 1994).

66. WHO estimates reported in David Brown, "WHO Calls for Rise in Health Spending," *Washington Post*, December 21, 2001, 3(A).

67. Technological innovation is also, of course, influenced by sociocultural evolution (for example, technology policy) and by unlocking the secrets of nature. The emphasis here, however, is on technological innovation as a causal variable.

68. The distinctions made here are somewhat arbitrary and for analytic purposes. Human beings are in competition with other animals for food supplies and territory. Plant species, while also affecting human welfare, are here considered to be part of the natural systems that sustain human well-being. While microorganisms are technically species, they represent different kinds of threats to *Homo sapiens* than do other animals.

69. Mary E. Power et al., "Challenges in the Quest for Keystones," *Bioscience* (September 1996).

70. See Thomas F. Homer-Dixon, "On the Threshold: Environmental Changes as Causes of Acute Conflict," *International Security* (Fall 1991); Thomas F. Homer-Dixon and Jessica Blitt, *Ecoviolence: Links among Environment, Population, and Security* (Lanham, MD: Rowman & Littlefield, 1999); Thomas F. Homer-Dixon, *Environment,*

Scarcity, and Violence (Princeton, NJ: Princeton University Press, 1999).

71. For example, beginning in 1999, Russia was beset by a plague of locusts that dimmed prospects for future harvests. More than one million hectares of cropland were affected. Daniel Williams, "In Russia, Disaster du Jour," *Washington Post,* August 7, 1999, 13(A).

72. See Dennis Pirages, "Microsecurity: Disease Organisms and Human Well-being," *Washington Quarterly* (Autumn 1995).

73. Marc Lappe, *Evolutionary Medicine: Rethinking the Origins of Disease* (San Francisco: Sierra Club Books, 1994), 8.

74. See Alfred W. Crosby, *Ecological Imperialism: The Biological Expansion of Europe 900–1900* (Cambridge: Cambridge University Press, 1986); Charles C. Mann, "1491," *The Atlantic Monthly* (March 2002).

75. This case has been made by Laurie Garrett, *The Coming Plague: Newly Emerging Diseases in a World Out of Balance* (New York: Farrar, Straus & Giroux, 1994).

76. See Homer-Dixon, *Environment, Scarcity, and Conflict.*

77. Nazli Choucri and Robert North, *Nations in Conflict: National Growth and International Violence* (San Francisco: Freeman, 1974), chapters 1, 2.

78. For elaboration on the evolution of political institutions from a biological perspective see Roger D. Masters, *The Nature of Politics* (New Haven, CT: Yale University Press, 1989), 139–52.

79. See Peter A. Corning, "Synergy, Cybernetics and the Evolution of Politics," *International Political Science Review* 17, No.1.

80. The World Bank, *World Development Report 1997* (Oxford: Oxford University Press, 1997), 27.

81. See Inge Kaul, Isabelle Grunberg, and Mark A. Stern, eds., *Global Public Goods: International Cooperation in the 21st Century* (Oxford: Oxford University Press, 1999).

82. For more detail see Susan Strange, *The Retreat of the State: The Diffusion of Power in the World Economy* (Cambridge: Cambridge University Press, 1996), chapter 1.

83. For example, there are now more than 700 Internet gambling sites with the possibility of hundreds more proliferating. Michael Allen, "Internet Casinos Proliferate Unchecked," *Wall Street Journal,* August 23, 2000, 14(A).

84. The GNP figures are for 1997 and come from the World Bank, *1999 World Development Indicators* (Washington, D.C.: The World Bank, 1999), table 1.1; Corporate income figures are for 1998 and come from the 1999 *Fortune* Global 500 found at www.pathfinder.com/fortune/global500/index.html (December 1999).

Chapter Two: Demographic Change and Ecological Insecurity

1. These historical estimates of world population are from United Nations Population Division data published in Barbara Vobejda, "Problems Impede Global Plan to Curb Population Growth," *Washington Post,* February 7, 1999, 3(A).

2. Derived from Carl Haub, "How Many People Have Ever Lived on Earth," *Population Today* (February 1995).

3. Population Reference Bureau (PRB), *2001 World Population Data Sheet* (Washington: PRB, 2001).

4. Nazli Choucri and Robert C. North, *Nations in Conflict: National Growth and International Violence* (San Francisco: Freeman, 1975).

5. PRB, *2001 World Population Data Sheet*.

6. The term "demographic transition" was introduced by Frank Notestein in 1945. Frank Notestein, "Population—The Long View," in *Food for the World*, ed. T. W. Schultz (Chicago: University of Chicago Press, 1945). An excellent more contemporary discussion of the phenomenon is found in Jean-Claude Chesnais, *The Demographic Transition: Stages, Patterns, and Economic Implications* (New York: Oxford University Press, 1992).

7. Dirk J. van de Kaa, "Europe's Second Demographic Transition," *Population Bulletin* (September 1993).

8. Data from van de Kaa, "Europe's Second Demographic Transition," 19; PRB, *2001 World Population Data Sheet*.

9. Van de Kaa, "Europe's Second Demographic Transition," 19; PRB, *2001 World Population Data Sheet*.

10. PRB, *2001 World Population Data Sheet*.

11. UNAIDS, *Report on the Global HIV/AIDS Epidemic* (Geneva: UNAIDS, 2002), 8.

12. U.S. Census Bureau data cited in Helen Jackson, *AIDS Africa: Continent in Crisis* (Harare, Zimbabwe: SAfAIDS, 2002), 15.

13. Leonard V. Polishchuk, "Conservation Priorities for Russian Mammals," *Science* (August 16, 2002).

14. See Anders Wijkman and Lloyd Timberlake, *Natural Disasters: Acts of God or Acts of Man?* (London: Earthscan, 1984).

15. World Resource Institute (WRI), *World Resources 1992–93* (New York: Oxford University Press, 1992), 30.

16. WRI, *World Resources 1998–1999* (New York: Oxford University Press, 1998), table 10.2.

17. Jonathan Randal, "A Dwindling Natural Resource," *Washington Post*, May 13, 1992, 25(A); see also Peter H. Gleick, "Water and Conflict: Fresh Water Resources and International Security," *International Security* (Summer 1993).

18. Anonymous, "River Runs through Mideast Dispute," *Washington Post*, October 2, 2002, 11(A).

19. WRI, *World Resources 2000–2001* (Washington: WRI, 2000), data table AF-1.

20. Laurie Garrett, *The Coming Plague: Newly Emerging Diseases in a World Out of Balance* (New York: Farrar, Straus & Giroux, 1994).

21. World Health Organization (WHO), *The World Health Report 2001* (Geneva: WHO, 2001), annex table 2.

22. Dennis Pirages, "Microsecurity: Disease Organisms and Human Well-Being," *Washington Quarterly* (Autumn 1995).

23. Joshua Lederberg, "Emerging Viruses, Emerging Threat," *Science* (January 19, 1990).

24. See Thomas Homer-Dixon and Jessica Blitt, eds. *Ecoviolence: Links among Environment, Population, and Security* (Lanham, MD: Rowman & Littlefield Publishers, 1998).

25. The World Bank, *World Development Report 1997* (New York: Oxford University Press, 1997), table 1.

26. United Nations Population Fund (UNPF), "Facts on World Population, Set to Top 6 Billion," *Reuters Newswire* at www.planetark.org (February 1999).

27. Alex de Sherbinin, "Human Security and Fertility: The Case of Haiti," *Journal of Environment and Development* (March 1996).

28. PRB, *2001 World Population Data Sheet*.

29. Quoted in Jackson Diehl, "Exodus of Soviet Jews May Alter Israel's Fate," *Washington Post*, June 10, 1990, 1(A).

30. PRB, *2001 World Population Data Sheet*.

31. Data are from Central Intelligence Agency (CIA), *USSR: Demographic Trends and Ethnic Balance in the Non-Russian Republics* (Washington, D.C.: CIA, April 1990).

32. D'Vera Cohn, "Prediction for 2100: Twice the Americans," *Washington Post*, January 13, 2000, 12(A).

33. Kelvin M. Pollard and William P. O'Hare, "America's Racial and Ethnic Minorities," in *Population Bulletin* (Washington, D.C.: Population Reference Bureau, September 1999), 3.

34. William Booth, "California Minorities Are Now the Majority," *Washington Post*, August 31, 2000, 16(A).

35. Among these four states, California is allocated fifty-four votes; Hawaii, four votes; Texas, thirty-two votes; and New Mexico, five votes. Electoral college statistics from the National Archives and Records Administration web page at www.nara.gov/fedreg/96ecvote.html (February 2000).

36. Pollard and O'Hare, "America's Racial and Ethnic Minorities," 3, 10.

37. Philip Martin and Jonas Widgren, "International Migration: Facing the Challenge," *Population Bulletin* (March 2002): 1.

38. Martin and Widgren, "International Migration: Facing the Challenge," 36.

39. Anonymous, "Massive Mexican Emigration Predicted," *Washington Post*, August 27, 1999, 20(A). See also James Goldsborough, "Out of Control Immigration," *Foreign Affairs* (September/October, 2000).

40. Martin Heisler, "Contextualizing Global Migration: Sketching the Sociopolitical Landscape in Europe," *UCLA Journal of International Law and Foreign Affairs* (Fall/Winter 1998–1999).

41. See Doris Meissner, "Managing Migrations," *Foreign Policy* (Spring 1992).

42. Anonymous, "U.S. Admits Wave of Illegal Immigrants Fleeing Mitch's Wake: Central American Refugees Detained, but Not Deported," *Washington Post*, February 8, 1999, 3(A).

43. United Nations High Commissioner for Refugees (UNHCR), *Refugees by Numbers 2002 Edition*. UNHCR statistics available at www.unhcr.ch (October 2002).

44. Roberta Cohen and Francis M. Deng, "Exodus within Borders: The Uprooted Who Never Left Home," *Foreign Affairs* (July/August 1998); see also Roberta Cohen and Francis M. Deng, *Masses in Flight: The Global Crisis of Internal Displacement* (Washington, D.C.: Brookings Institution Press, 1998).

45. Eugene Linden, "The Exploding Cities of the Developing World," *Foreign Affairs* (January/February 1996): 53.

46. Terry McGee, "Urbanization Takes on New Dimensions in Asia's Population Giants," *Population Today* (October 2001).

47. Martin P. Brockerhoff, "An Urbanizing World," *Population Bulletin* (September 2000): 7, 9.

48. World Resources Institute (WRI), *World Resources 1996–1997* (Washington, D.C.: WRI 1996), 12.

49. "Ecological footprint" is the term used to describe the impact of demand for resources on surrounding environments in Mathis Wackernagel and William Rees, *Our Ecological Footprint* (Philadelphia: New Society Publishers, 1996).

50. WRI, *World Resources 1996–1997*, 59.

51. Eric Pianin, "Around the Globe, Cities Have Growing Pains," *Washington Post*, June 11, 2001, 9(A).

52. See Martin Brockerhoff, "Urban Growth in Developing Countries: A Review of Projections and Predictions." *Population and Development Review* (December 1999).

53. WRI, *World Resources 1996-1997*, 8.

54. Linden, "The Exploding Cities of the Developing World."

55. Data from the New York City Sanitation Department's Fact Sheet at www.ci.nyc.ny.us/html/dos/html/dosfact.html (February 2000).

56. Press release, "Governor Gilmore's Letter to Mayor Giuliani Regarding Trash Transportation from New York to Virginia," issued by the Commonwealth of Virginia, Office of the Governor, Press Office, January 15, 1999 at www.state.va.us/governor/newsre/guil0115.htm (February 2000).

57. See Ken Dychtwald, *Age Power: How the 21st Century Will be Ruled by the New Old* (New York: Jeremy P. Tarcher/Putnam, 1999); Peter G. Peterson, *Gray Dawn: How the Coming Age Wave Will Transform America—and the World* (New York: Times Books, 1999).

58. Peterson, "Gray Dawn: The Global Aging Crisis," *Foreign Affairs* (January/February 1999): 43.

59. PRB, *2001 World Population Data Sheet*.

60. Nicholas Eberstadt, "The Population Implosion," *Foreign Policy* (March/April 2001): 44.

61. Steven Mufson, "Debt Poses Politicians Staggering Challenges," *Washington Post*, September 29, 1992, 1(A).

62. OECD, *Maintaining Prosperity in an Aging Society* (Paris: OECD, 1998).

63. OECD, *Aging Populations: The Social Policy Implications* (Paris: OECD, 1988).

64. These are official projections taken from Robert Stowe England, *The Fiscal Challenge of an Aging Industrial World* (Washington, D.C.: The CSIS Press, 2002), 50.

65. Peterson, "Gray Dawn: The Global Aging Crisis": 43.

66. Peter McDonald and Rebecca Kippen, "Labor Supply Prospects in the Developed Countries 2000–2050," *Population and Development Review* (March 2001): 8.

67. Peterson, *Gray Dawn: How the Coming Age Wave Will Transform America*, 129.

68. Thomas B. Edsall and Paul Blustein, "Steel Lobbyists Gain the Edge: Seeking Import Curb, Industry Warned Bush of Retiree Uprising," *Washington Post*, June 7, 2001, 1(E).

69. Amy Goldstein and Richard Morin, "Young Voters' Disengagement Skews Politics," *Washington Post*, October 20, 2002, 1(A).

70. For a discussion of these issues see John B. Williamson, Diane M. Watts-Roy, and Eric R. Kingson, eds., *The Generational Equity Debate* (New York: Columbia University Press, 1999).

71. Peterson, *Gray Dawn: How the Coming Age Wave Will Transform America*, 108–11.

72. Anonymous, "Sharp Rise Predicted in Health-Care Spending in Next Decade," *New York Times*, September 15, 1998, 21(A).

73. See William Styring III and Donald K. Jonas, *Health Care 2020: The Coming Collapse of Employer Provided Health Care* (Indianapolis, IN: Hudson Institute, 1999).

74. Barry Bosworth and Gary Burtless. "Population Aging and American Economic Performance," in *Aging Societies: The Global Dimension*, eds. Barry Bosworth and Gary Burtless (Washington, D.C.: Brookings Institution 1998), 290.

75. See Nancy Morrow-Howell, James Hinterlong, and Michael Sherrader, eds., *Productive Aging: Concepts and Challenges* (Baltimore: Johns Hopkins University Press, 2001).

76. John Weeks, "The Demography of Islamic Nations," *Population Bulletin* (Washington, D.C.: PRB, 1989), 18.

77. Lindsey Grant, *Juggernaut: Growth on a Finite Planet* (Washington, D.C.: Island Press, 1996), 240.

78. See Craig Lasher, "U.S. Population Policy Since the Cairo Conference," *Environmental Change and Security Project* (Washington, D.C.: The Woodrow Wilson Center, Spring 1998).

79. Vobejda, "Problems Impede Global Plan to Curb Population Growth," 3(A).

80. These data are from the Population Institute, *1998 World Population Overview and Outlook 1999* at www.populationinstitute.org/overview98.html (February 2000).

81. Allison Tarmann, "Iran Achieves Replacement-Level Fertility," *Population Today* (May/June 2002).

82. See Paul Ehrlich and Anne Ehrlich, *The Population Explosion* (New York: Simon and Schuster, 1990); William Catton, *Overshoot: The Ecological Basis for Revolutionary Change* (Urbana: University of Illinois Press, 1980); S. Fred Singer, ed., *Is There an Optimum Level of Population?* (New York: McGraw-Hill, 1991); Robert

Goodland, "The Case That the World Has Reached Limits," *Population and Environment* (Spring 1992).

83. Julian Simon, *The Ultimate Resource* (Princeton, NJ: Princeton University Press, 1981).

84. See Peter Donaldson, "On the Origins of the United States Government's International Population Policy," *Population Studies* (November 1990).

85. Reported in Chet Atkins, "International Family Planning: Where's the Leadership?" *Washington Post*, August 27, 1991, 23(A).

86. Jessica Mathews, "World Population: As the President Turns," *Washington Post*, November 1, 1990, 23(A).

87. Craig Lasher, "US Population Policy Since the Cairo Conference."

88. Colum Lynch and Juliet Eilperin, "Family Planning Funds Withheld," *Washington Post*, July 20, 2002, 4(A).

Chapter Three: An Assault on the Global Commons

1. The classic work linking environmental factors (in this case irrigation agriculture) and structures of political power is Karl Wittfogel, *Oriental Despotism: A Comparative Study of Total Power* (New Haven, CT: Yale University Press, 1957). For more general ideas about the relationship of scarcity and violence see Thomas F. Homer-Dixon and Jessica Blitt, *Ecoviolence: Links among Environment, Population and Security* (Lanham, MD: Rowman & Littlefield, 1998); and Thomas F. Homer-Dixon, *Environment, Scarcity, and Violence* (Princeton, NJ: Princeton University Press, 1999).

2. Kenneth Watt, *Principles of Environmental Science* (New York: McGraw-Hill, 1973), 20.

3. Common property resources (CPRs) are defined as either natural or man-made resources that are both nonexcludable, meaning access to the resource cannot be limited, and subtractable, meaning use of the resource by one user depletes the resource thereby detracting from the welfare of other users. Global CPRs have received a great deal of attention since Garrett Hardin wrote his provocative essay "The Tragedy of the Commons," *Science* 162 (1968). Hardin reasoned that humans were destined to attempt to maximize individual gain from CPRs, and that the aggregate result of this individual utility-maximizing behavior was the inevitable destruction of the CPRs. The only possible solutions for preventing the tragedy, he concluded, were either privatization of the CPRs or mutual coercion mutually agreed upon by the majority of the people affected (1247–48).

Since Hardin's original essay, many others have joined the debate over whether cooperative efforts can succeed in protecting and sustainably utilizing commonly shared resources. The most notable of these is Elinor Ostrom, *Governing the Commons: The Evolution of Institutional Collective Action* (New York: Cambridge University Press, 1990). Based on extensive field research, Ostrom argues that individuals exist in an environment of confusion and complexity bounded by contextual norms that influence the way they perceive their choices and actions. Within this context, individuals are capable of changing their environment and getting beyond the limitations imposed by the assumptions of individual rational choice. Sustainable management of the CPRs, therefore, becomes an issue of "getting the institutions right." At the global level, sustainable management of CPRs is further challenged by effects of both scale and the heterogeneity of the actors involved. See Susan J. Buck, "No Tragedy of the Commons," *Environmental Ethics* (Spring 1985); William Ophuls, *Ecology and the Politics of Scarcity* (San Francisco: Freeman, 1976); Joanna Burger and Michael Gochfeld, "The Tragedy of the Commons Thirty Years Later," *Environment* (December 1998). For an assessment of the relative successes and failures of institutions to protect regional and global CPRs, see Peter M. Haas, Robert O. Keohane, and Marc A. Levy, eds. *Institutions for the Earth: Sources of Effective International Environmental Protection* (Cambridge, MA: MIT Press, 1993).

4. For a deeper discussion of these ideas see Anders Wijkman and Lloyd Timberlake, *Natural Disasters: Acts of God or Acts of Man* (London: Earthscan, 1984).

5. See Mathis Wackernagel and William Rees, *Our Ecological Footprint: Reducing Human Impact on Earth* (Philadelphia: New Society Publishers, 1996), chapter 1.

6. Donella Meadows et al., *The Limits to Growth* (New York: Universe Books, 1972), 23.

7. *The Global 2000 Report to the President* (Washington, D.C.: U.S. Government Printing Office, 1980), 1.

8. The World Commission on the Environment and Development, *Our Common Future* (New York: Oxford University Press, 1987), 8.

9. See Mostafa K. Tolba et al. *The World Environment 1972–1992: Two Decades of Challenge* (London: Chapman and Hall, 1992), chapters 23, 24.

10. Al Gore, *Earth in the Balance: Ecology and the Human Spirit* (Boston: Houghton Mifflin, 1992).

11. See, for example, Julian Simon, *The Ultimate Resource* (Princeton, NJ: Princeton University Press, 1981); Julian Simon and Herman Kahn, eds., *The Resourceful Earth* (Oxford: Basil Blackwell, 1984); Jesse H. Ausubel, *The Liberation of the Environment*, special issue of *Daedalus* (Summer 1996); Bjorn Lomborg, *The Skeptical Environmentalist: Measuring the Real State of the World* (New York: Cambridge University Press, 2001).

12. Peter H. Gleick, *The World's Water 2000–2001* (Washington, D.C.: Island Press, 2000), 21.

13. World Resources Institute (WRI), *World Resources 1998–99* (Washington, D.C.: WRI, 1998), table 12.1.

14. Food and Agricultural Organization (FAO), United Nations, *Fisheries and Food Security* at www.fao.org/focus/e/fisheries/intro.htm (July 15, 1999).

15. FAO, *Fisheries and Food Security.*

16. FAO, *Fisheries and Food Security: Trade in Fish*, and *Aquiculture—New Opportunities and a Cause for Hope*, at www.fao.org/focus/e/fisheries/trade.htm and www.fao.org/e/fisheries/aqua.htm, respectively (July 15, 1999).

17. WRI, *World Resources 1998–99*, table 12.1.

18. WRI, *World Resources 1998–99*, table 12.1.

19. WRI, *World Resources 1998–99*, table 12.1.

20. Tolba, et al., *The World Environment 1972–1992: Two Decades of Challenge*, 99.

21. Gleick, *The World's Water 2000–2001*, 32.

22. See Miriam R. Lowi, "Water and Conflict in the Middle East and South Asia: Are Environmental and Security Issues Linked?" *Journal of Environment and Development* (December 1999).

23. See Sandra L. Postel and Aaron T. Wolf, "Dehydrating Conflict," *Foreign Policy* (September/October 2001); Michael T. Klare, *Resource Wars: The New Landscape of Global Conflict* (New York: Henry Holt, 2001), chapters 6 and 7.

24. See Robin Clark, *Water: The International Crisis* (Cambridge, MA: MIT Press, 1993), chapter 7.

25. Peter H. Gleick, *Water in Crisis* (New York: Oxford University Press, 1993), 10.

26. Gleick, *Water in Crisis*, 188.

27. John Ward Anderson, "The Great Cleanup of the Holy Ganges," *Washington Post*, September 25, 1992, 1(A).

28. Prajnan Bhattacharya, "India's Holiest River, the Ganges, Brings Disease and Pollution," *Environmental News Network*, www.enn.com (May 7, 2002).

29. Kenneth J. Cooper, "Battling Waterborne Ills in a Sea of 950 Million," *Washington Post*, February 17, 1997, 2(A).

30. Kader Asmal quoted in Tony Austin Reuters, "Water Riots Seen Spreading as Wells Run Dry," *Environmental News Network*, www.enn.com (August 14, 2000).

31. Maude Barlow, "Water Privatization and the Threat to the World's Most Precious Resources: Is Water a Commodity or Human Right?" *IFG Bulletin* (Summer 2001).

32. Beth Chalecki, "Bulk Water Exports and Free Trade," *Pacific Institute Report* (Fall 2000): 12–13.

33. Gleick, *The World's Water 2000–2001*, 1–15.

34. Gleick, *The World's Water 2000–2001*, 11; see also Riccardo Petrella, *The Water Manifesto: Arguments for a World Water Contract* (London: Zed Books, 2001).

35. FAO, *The State of World Fisheries and Aquiculture: 1998*, www.fao.org/docrep/w9900e02.htm, 6 (July 15, 1999).

36. National Oceanic and Atmospheric Administration (NOAA), *Turning to the Seas: America's Oceans Future* (Washington, D.C.: U.S. Government Printing Office, 1999), 42.

37. Gleick, *The World's Water 2000–2001*, 116, 270–72.

38. National Centers for Coastal and Ocean Science (NCCOS), *Hypoxia in the Gulf of Mexico*, www.nos.noaa.gov/products/pubs_hypox.html (August 23, 2000).

39. Frank E. Loy, *Doherty Lecture*, May 11, 1999 in Washington, D.C., www.state.gov/www/policy_remarks/1999/990511_loy_oceans.html (May 12, 2000).

40. United Nations, *Status of the United Nations Convention on the Law of the Sea 10 December 1982 and of the Agreement Relating to the Implementation of Part XI*, www.un.org/depts/los/stat2los.txt (May 12, 2000).

41. U.S. Department of Defense (DOD), *National Security and the United Nations Convention on the Law of the Sea, Executive Summary* (Washington, D.C.: DOD, 1994); David Malakoff, "Nations Look for an Edge in Claiming Continental Shelves," *Science* (December 2, 2002).

42. Wesley S. Scholz, "The Law of the Sea Convention and the Business Community: The Seabed Mining Regime and Beyond"; statement at an International Symposium, January 27, 1995 www.state.gov (May 12, 1998); see also United Nations, *The Law of the Sea: United Nations Convention on the Law of the Sea with Annexes and Index and Final Act of the Third United Nations Conference on the Law of the Sea* (New York: United Nations, 1983).

43. Scholz, "The Law of the Sea Convention and the Business Community: The Seabed Mining Regime and Beyond" and United Nations, *The Law of the Sea: United Nations Convention on the Law of the Sea with Annexes and Index and Final Act of the Third United Nations Conference on the Law of the Sea.*

44. Scholz, "The Law of the Sea Convention and the Business Community: The Seabed Mining Regime and Beyond" and United Nations, *The Law of the Sea: Practice of States at the time of entry into force of the United Nations Convention on the Law of the Sea.*

45. Edward Cody, "In Mexico City There's Fear in the Air," *Washington Post*, November 24, 1991, 27(A).

46. Christopher Cooper, "You Say You Came to Cairo to Absorb Some Atmosphere?" *Wall Street Journal*, January 19, 2000, 1(A).

47. M. J. Molina and F. S. Rowland, "Stratospheric Sink for Chlorofluoromethanes. Chlorine Atom Destruction of Ozone," *Nature* 249 (1974).

48. The best-estimate lifetime of CFC-11 as indicated in the World Meteorological Organization (WMO), *Scientific Assessment of Ozone Depletion: 1994—Executive Summary* (Geneva: WMO, 1995), 10.

49. R. S. Stolarski, "The Antarctic Ozone Hole," *Scientific American* 258, No. 1 (1988).

50. WMO, *Scientific Assessment of Ozone Depletion: 1994 Executive Summary*, 9.

51. Anonymous, "Ozone Hole Emerges, Exposing Chilean City," *Washington Post*, October 6, 2000, 26(A).

52. Sasha Madronich et al., "Changes in Ultraviolet Radiation Reaching the Earth's Surface," *Ambio* (May 1995); Richard McKenzie, Brian Conner, and Greg Bodeker, "Increased Summertime UV Radiation in New Zealand in Response to Ozone Loss," *Science* (September 10, 1999).

53. J. B. Kerr and C. T. McElroy, "Evidence for Large Upward Trends of Ultraviolet-B Radiation Linked to Ozone Depletion," *Science* (November 12, 1993).

54. Janice D. Longstreth et al., "Effects of Increased Solar Ultraviolet Radiation on Human Health," *Ambio* (May 1995).

55. J. T. Houghton et al., eds., *Climate Change 1995: The Science of Climate Change* (Cambridge: Cambridge University Press, 1996), 3.

56. Houghton et al., *Climate Change 1995: The Science of Climate Change*, 322.

57. Houghton et al., *Climate Change 1995: The Science of Climate Change*, 384.

58. Robert T. Watson, ed., *Climate Change 2001: Synthesis Report* (Cambridge: Cambridge University Press, 2001), 171.

59. Watson, *Climate Change 2001*, 175.

60. Watson, *Climate Change 2001*, 175.

61. Watson, *Climate Change 2001*, 180, 202.

62. Watson, *Climate Change 2001*, 206.

63. Watson, *Climate Change 2001*, 212.

64. David R. Easterling et al. "Climate Extremes: Observations, Modeling, and Impacts," *Science* (September 22, 2000).

65. Anonymous, "Coastal Living: For Majority of US It's Home," *Population Today* (July / August 1993).

66. Sarah Delaney, "Venice's Plan to Stop Sea Sinks," *Washington Post*, December 11, 1996, 48(A).

67. Pamela Constable, "A Landscape Dotted by Death," *Washington Post*, November 12, 1999, 27(A); Rama Lakshmi, "Monsoon Season Floods Hitting Hard in S. Asia," *Washington Post*, August 15, 2000, 18(A).

68. Easterling et al., "Climate Extremes: Observations, Modeling, and Impacts."

69. See Cynthia Rosenzwieg and Daniel Hillel, *Climate Change and the Global Harvest* (New York: Oxford University Press, 1998), chapter 8, for more detailed estimates of these impacts.

70. Paul R. Epstein, "Climate and Health," *Science* (July 16, 1999).

71. Richard Stone, "If the Mercury Soars, So May Health Hazards," *Science* (February 17, 1995).

72. Philipe H. Martin and Myriam G. Lefebvre, "Malaria and Climate: Sensitivity of Malaria Potential Transmission to Climate," *Ambio* (June 1995).

73. Rita R. Colwell, "Global Climate and Infectious Disease: The Cholera Paradigm," *Science* (December 20, 1996).

74. For greater detail on the ozone negotiations see Richard Elliot Benedick, *Ozone Diplomacy: New Directions in Safeguarding the Planet* (Cambridge, MA: Harvard University Press, 1991); see also, Karen T. Litfin, *Ozone Discourses: Science and Politics in Global Environmental Cooperation* (New York: Columbia University Press, 1994).

75. Catherine Arnst, "Loophole in the Ozone Pact," *BusinessWeek* (September 29, 1997).

76. Joby Warrick, "CFC Smuggling, Production Cool Optimism," *Washington Post*, September 16, 1997, 3(A).

77. Timothy Forsyth, "Flexible Mechanisms of Climate Technology Transfer," *Journal of Environment and Development* (September 1999): 239; see also Tim Forsyth, *International Investment and Climate Change* (London: Earthscan, 1999).

78. Josef Hebert, "US Seeking a Way around Greenhouse Reduction Rules," *Washington Post*, August 3, 2000, 7(A).

79. See Miranda Schreurs, *Environmental Politics in Japan, Germany, and the United States: Competing Paradigms* (New York: Cambridge University Press, 2003), chapter 7.

80. For a more detailed discussion of these differences see Michael A. Alberty and Stacy D. VanDeveer, "International Treaties for Sustainability: Is the Montreal Protocol a Useful Model?" in *Building Sustainable Societies: A Blueprint for a Post-Industrial World*, ed. Dennis C. Pirages (Armonk, NY: M.E. Sharpe, 1996).

81. Yasumasa Fujii, *An Assessment of the Responsibility for the Increase in the CO2 Concentration and Intergenerational Carbon Accounts* (Laxenburg, Austria: IIASA, 1990), 20.

82. David Malakoff, "Thirty Kyotos Needed to Control Warming," *Science* (December 19, 1997).

83. See Henry D. Jacoby, Ronald G. Prinn, and Richard Schmalensee, "Kyoto's Unfinished Business," *Foreign Affairs* (July / August 1998).

Chapter Four: Global Energy Politics

1. Amory B. Lovins, *Soft Energy Paths: Toward a Durable Peace* (Cambridge, MA: Ballinger Publishing Company, 1977), chapter 2.

2. See estimates in Richard A. Kerr, "The Next Oil Crisis Looms Large—and Perhaps Close," *Science* (August 1998); see also Colin J. Campbell and Jean H. Laherrere, "The End of Cheap Oil," *Scientific American*, special report (March 1998); Kenneth S. Deffeyes, *Hubbert's Peak: The Impending World Oil Shortage* (Princeton, NJ: Princeton University Press, 2001).

3. See Michael T. Klare, *Resource Wars: The New Landscape of Global Conflict* (New York: Henry Holt, 2001), chapter 2.

4. Kent E. Calder, "Asia's Empty Tank," *Foreign Affairs* (March/April 1996); Daniel Yergin, Dennis Eklof, and Jefferson Edwards, "Fueling Asia's Recovery," *Foreign Affairs* (March/April, 1998).

5. Data are from U.S. Department of Energy found at www.eia.doe.gov/emeu/iea/table18.htm (August 20, 2002).

6. United States Energy Information Administration (USEIA), *International Energy Outlook 1998* (Washington, D.C.: Department of Energy, 1998), 8.

7. Data are from *World Oil: International Energy Outlook* (August 1987; August 2002).

8. World oil reserve data include the total amount discovered in any field. But as the fields are exploited, the costs of getting remaining oil can increase substantially. For technical reasons, much of this oil probably cannot ever be recovered at reasonable prices. Experts estimate that one-half to two-thirds of the world's oil falls into the "very difficult to recover" category.

9. USEIA, *International Energy Outlook*, 26–27.

10. For example, see the optimistic vision in Peter Coy, Gary McWilliams, and John Rossant, "The New Economics of Oil," *BusinessWeek* (November 3, 1997) and the more sober assessment in Campbell and Laherrere, "The End of Cheap Oil."

11. British Petroleum (BP), *BP Statistical Review of World Energy 1997* (June 2002): 5.

12. See the estimates in Kerr, "The Next Oil Crisis Looms Large—and Perhaps Close"; see also Deffeyes, *Hubbert's Peak: The Impending World Oil Shortage.*

13. Reported in Perry A. Fischer, "What's Happening in Production," *World Oil* (July 1999): 25.

14. BP, *BP Statistical Review of World Energy* (June 2002), 30.

15. This draws upon Earl Cook, *Man, Energy, Society* (San Francisco: Freeman, 1976), 75–87.

16. BP, *BP Statistical Review of World Energy*, 20.

17. BP, *BP Statistical Review of World Energy*, 21. Figures may be updated at www.bp.com/centres/energy.

18. *World Oil* (August 2001): 115.

19. Updated from historical data in Exxon Corporation, *How Much Oil and Gas?* (May 1982), 10.

20. United States Department of Energy (USDOE), *Monthly Energy Review* (September 1986): 41.

21. Data from eia.doe.gov/emeu/mer/txt/mer1 (August 20, 2002).

22. Peter Baker, "Russia Sees U.S. as New Market for Oil Reserves," *Washington Post*, September 8, 2002, 25(A).

23. It has been suggested that one of the main motivations for military action to depose Saddam Hussein in Iraq has been to give U.S. oil companies access to Iraq's oil fields. Dan Morgan and David B. Ottaway, "In Iraqi War Scenario, Oil Is Key Issue: U.S. Drillers Eye Huge Petroleum Pool," *Washington Post*, September 15, 2002, 1(A).

24. For an overview of Middle East tensions and potential conflicts see Klare, *Resource Wars*, chapter 3.

25. Estimated in *BusinessWeek* (December 20, 1976): 45.

26. Davis Bobrow et al., "Contrived Scarcity: The Short-Term Consequences of Expensive Oil," *International Studies Quarterly* (December 1977).

27. F. J. Al-Chalabi, "Background of the Gulf Crisis and Consequences for OPEC and for the Oil Industry," in *After the OPEC Oil Price Collapse: OPEC, the United States, and the World Oil Market*, ed. Wilfred L. Kohl (Baltimore: Johns Hopkins University Press, 1991), 208–14.

28. *World Oil* (January 1995): 69.

29. Edward Morse and James Richard, "The Battle for Energy Dominance," *Foreign Affairs* (March/April 2002).

30. Christopher Cooper and Hugh Pope, "Dry Wells Belie Hope for Big Caspian Reserves," *Wall Street Journal*, October 12, 1998, 13(A); Martha Brill Olcott, "The Caspian's False Promise," *Foreign Policy* (Summer 1998); Jan H. Kalicki, "Caspian Energy at the Crossroads," *Foreign Affairs* (September/October 2001).

31. Alexei Barrionuevo and Thaddeus Herrick, "For Oil Companies, Defense Abroad Is the Order of the Day," *Wall Street Journal*, February 7, 2002, 1(A).

32. James Rupert, "Nigerian Protesters Cut Oil Production," *Washington Post*, October 19, 1998, 17(A).

33. Anonymous, "Bullet Pierces Alaska Pipeline, Forces Shutdown," *Washington Post*, October 6, 2001, 2(A).

34. Tamsin Carlisle, "Oil Well Sabotage in Canada Reflects Tension with Farmers," *Wall Street Journal*, October 30, 1998, 17(A).

35. For more details see Anthony Sampson, *The Seven Sisters* (New York: Viking, 1975), chapter 2.

36. Sampson, *The Seven Sisters*, 26.

37. Sampson *The Seven Sisters*, chapter 4.

38. Sampson, *The Seven Sisters*, 140–53.

39. See Jahangir Amuzegar, "'The Oil Story: Facts, Fiction, and Fair Play," *Foreign Affairs* (July 1973).

40. For more detail see Ian Seymour, *OPEC: Instrument of Change* (New York: St. Martin's, 1981), chapter 2.

41. Neil Jacoby, *Multinational Oil* (New York: Macmillan, 1974), 258–59.

42. USDOE, *Monthly Energy Review* (September 1986). 113.

43. Anonymous, "The Coming Glut of Energy," *Economist* (January 5, 1974).

44. USDOE, *Monthly Energy Review* (December 1986): 117, 119.

45. William Drozdiak, "Bowing to U.S., OPEC Agrees to Hike Output," *Washington Post*, March 29, 2000, 1(A).

46. Data from *World Oil* (October 2000): 131; *World Oil* (August 2002): 17.

47. H. F. Keplinger, "The Crisis in Energy is Here Now!" *World Oil* (July 1986).

48. USDOE, *Monthly Energy Review* (August 1986): 64.

49. USDOE, *Monthly Energy Review* (August 1986): 65.

50. Anonymous, "Nowhere to Go but Up," *World Oil* (August 1999): 35.

51. Kathryn S. Brown, "Bright Future—or Brief Flare—For Renewable Energy?" *Science* (July 30, 1999): 680.

52. Amory B. Lovins and L. Hunter Lovins, *Brittle Power: Energy Strategy for National Security* (Andover, MA: Brick House Publishing Company, 1982), 1.

53. F. Gregory Gauss III, "Saudi Arabia over a Barrel," *Foreign Affairs* (May/June 2000).

54. James J. Dooley and Paul J. Runci, "Developing Nations, Energy R&D, and the Provision of a Planetary Public Good: A Long-Term Strategy for Addressing Climate Change," *Journal of Environment and Development* (September 2000).

55. Gauss, "Saudi Arabia over a Barrel:" 81.

56. Anthony V. Herzog et al., "Renewable Energy: A Viable Choice," *Environment* (December 2001): 12.

57. For more details see Seth Dunn, *Hydrogen Futures: Toward a Sustainable Energy System*, (Washington, D.C.: The Worldwatch Institute, August 2001); Lawrence D. Borroni-Bird, "Vehicle of Change: Hydrogen Fuel-Cell Cars Could Be the Catalyst for a Cleaner Tomorrow," *Scientific American* (October 2002).

58. Subsidies have been an integral part of energy system development. For example, the nuclear power industry would never have been developed without billions of dollars of military and nonmilitary research subsidies. And Detroit has

surely benefited from the interstate highway system, built at taxpayers' expense. By contrast, the ailing railroad system has been responsible for building and maintaining its own tracks.

59. Richard G. Lugar and R. James Woolsey, "The New Petroleum," *Foreign Affairs* (January/February 1999): 100.

60. Stanley Reed et al., "Oil and War," *BusinessWeek* (March 17, 2003); Michael Dobbs, "Oil Reserve Is 'First Line of Defense' for U.S.," *Washington Post*, February 18, 2003, 3(A).

Chapter Five: The Political Economy of Feast and Famine

1. S. Boyden, *The Interplay Between Human Society and the Biosphere: Past and Present* (Park Ridge, NJ: The Parthenon Publishing Group, 1992), 115.

2. Boyden, *The Interplay Between Human Society and the Biosphere: Past and Present*, 116–19.

3. Kathryn Brown, "New Trips through the Back Alleys of Agriculture," *Science* (April 27, 2001).

4. Boyden, *The Interplay Between Human Society and the Biosphere: Past and Present*, 123–24.

5. The UN Food and Agricultural Organization (FAO), FAOSTAT Database on Food Production Indices can be found at www.fao.org or http://apps.fao.org/ (August 1999).

6. FAO, *World Food Summit and Its Follow Up*, www.fao.org/docrep/x2051e/ x2051e00.htm (October 22, 2002).

7. Ellen Messer and Laurie F. DeRose, "Food Shortage," in *Who's Hungry? And How Do We Know*, ed. Laurie DeRose, Ellen Messer, and Sara Millman (Tokyo: United Nations University Press, 1998), 55; see also Peter Uvin, "The State of World Hunger," in *The Hunger Report: 1995*, ed. Ellen Messer and Peter Uvin (Amsterdam: Gordon and Breach, 1996).

8. Steve Pagani, "El Nino Still Takes Its Toll—UN Food Agency," *Reuters World Report* (July 31, 1998).

9. World Resources Institute (WRI), *World Resources 1998–1999* (New York: Oxford University Press, 1998), 288–89; FAO, *The State of Food and Agriculture 1998*, www.fao.org/docrep/W9500E/w9500e03.htm (March 2000); data for calories per capita per day are for 1997 found at FAOSTAT (April 2000).

10. FAO, *The State of Food Insecurity in the World*, www.fao.org/FOCUS/E/ SOFI/home-e.htm (April 2000).

11. Gary Gardner and Brian Halweil, *Underfed and Overfed: The Global Epidemic of Malnutrition* (Washington, D.C.: The Worldwatch Institute, 2000), 7.

12. U.S. Department of Agriculture (USDA), "US Agriculture—Linking Consumers and Producers: What Do Americans Eat?" *Agriculture Fact Book 1998*, www.usda.gov/news/pubs/fbook98/ch1a.htm (July 23, 1999), 1–2.

13. Data from the WHO cited in Gardner and Halweil, *Underfed and Overfed: The Global Epidemic of Malnutrition,* 11, 34–39.

14. FAOSTAT (October 22, 2002).

15. FAOSTAT (April 24, 2000).

16. USDA, *World Agricultural Supply and Demand Estimates,* www.usda.gov (October 22, 2000).

17. FAOSTAT (April 24, 2000).

18. FAO, *The State of World Fisheries and Aquiculture: 1998,* www.fao.org/docrep/w9900e02.htm, 9, 13.

19. FAOSTAT (October 22, 2002).

20. Cornelius Walford, "The Famines of the World: Past and Present," *Royal Statistical Society Journal* 41 (1878) cited in Paul Ehrlich and Anne Ehrlich, *Population, Resources, Environment* (San Francisco: Freeman, 1972), 13.

21. Stephen Devereux, "Famine in the Twentieth Century" (Brighton, UK: Institute of Development Studies, 2000), 6.

22. A detailed model linking food prices and famine is developed in Amartya K. Sen, *Poverty and Famines* (Oxford: Clarendon Press, 1981). See also Amartya Sen, "Food Entitlement and Economic Chains," in *Hunger in History: Food Shortage, Poverty, and Deprivation,* ed. Lucile F. Newman et al. (Cambridge, MA: Basil Blackwell, 1990).

23. Carl C. Mabbs-Zeno, *Long Term Impacts of Famine: Enduring Disasters and Opportunities for Progress,* Staff Report No. AGES870212 (Washington, D.C.: USDA, Economic Research Service, International Economics Division, April 1987).

24. FAOSTAT (October 22, 2002).

25. USDA, *World Agricultural Supply and Demand Estimates.*

26. USDA, *World Agricultural Supply and Demand Estimates.*

27. USDA, *World Agricultural Supply and Demand Estimates.*

28. U.S. Department of Commerce, International Trade Administration (USDCITA), *U.S. Trade Balances by Sector, 1998–1999,* www.ita.gov (April 2000).

29. USDA, *Agricultural Statistics 1993,* table 664; and *Agricultural Outlook* (April 1993), 20; Richard Melcher and John Carey, "More Bitter Harvests Ahead," *BusinessWeek* (June 28, 1999).

30. USDA, *USDA Agricultural Baseline Projections to 2009,* www.ers.usda.gov/epubs/pdf/waob001/index.htm (May 2, 2000).

31. Data on carryover stocks from Lester R. Brown, *The Changing World Food Prospect: The Nineties and Beyond* (Washington, D.C.: Worldwatch Institute, 1988); USDA, *World Grain Situation and Outlook* (Washington, D.C.: USDA/Foreign Agricultural Service, November 1994), 54–56.

32. USDA, *USDA Agricultural Baseline Projections to 2009.*

33. U.S. Central Intelligence Agency (CIA), *Handbook of Economic Statistics 1987* (Washington, D.C.: CIA, 1987), table 157.

34. USDA, *World Agricultural Supply and Demand Estimates,* 16–17, 20–21.

35. Catherine Belton, "Meet the New Global Grain Giant," *BusinessWeek* (November 4, 2002).

36. Lester Brown, *Who Will Feed China?* (New York: Norton, 1995).

37. Vaclav Smil, *Feeding the World: A Challenge for the Twenty-First Century* (Cambridge, MA: MIT Press, 2000), chapter 9.

38. Amy Kaslow, "Farm Subsidies Create Bounty, Boondoggles," *Christian Science Monitor* (November 4, 1992): 9, 12.

39. Ronald Henkoff, "Farmers: No More High on the Hog," *Fortune* (December 2, 1992); "The European Community: Altered States," *The Economist* (July 11, 1992).

40. Anonymous, "Hard Times Will Get Harder Down on the Farm," *BusinessWeek* (January 13, 1986).

41. USDA, "1996 FAIR Act Frames Farm Policy for 7 Years." *Agricultural Outlook Supplement* (Washington, D.C.: USDA Economic Research Service, April 1996).

42. World Trade Organization (WTO), "Implementation of the Uruguay Round Reform Programme for Trade in Agriculture," www.wto.org/wto/goods/agrintro.htm (May 11, 2000). See also FAO, "What the Uruguay Round Achieved for Agriculture, Forestry, and Fisheries," www.fao.org/ur/urufao.stm (July 16, 1999).

43. FAO, "Agriculture a Major Item on the Agenda at WTO Talks in Seattle," www.fao.org/NEWS/1999/991109-e.htm (April 2000).

44. FAO, "After Seattle . . . What Next?" www.fao.org/NEWS/2000/000101-e.htm (May 2, 2000).

45. WTO, "Talks Reach Swift Agreement on 'Phase 1,'" www.wto.org/wto/news/Press172.htm (May 2, 2000).

46. WTO, "Agriculture Negotiations: Backgrounder," www.wto.org/english/tratop_e/agri_enegs_bkgrnd05_intro_e.htm (October 22, 2002).

47. FAO, *Special Programme for Food Security*, SPFS News, www.fao.org/docrep/x2051e/x2051e00.htm (July 1999).

48. USDA, *Agricultural Outlook* (Washington, D.C.: USDA/Economic Research Service, January–February 1993), 16.

49. FAO, *World Soil Resources*, 66 (Rome: FAO, 1991), 43–44.

50. Sandra Postel, *Pillar of Sand: Can the Irrigation Miracle Last?* (New York: Norton, 1999), 9.

51. WRI, *World Resources 1992–1993* (New York: Oxford University Press, 1992), 290–91.

52. FAO, "Soil Limits Agriculture," www.fao.org/NEWS/FACTFILE/FF9713-E.HTM (October 22, 2002).

53. David Grigg, *The World Food Problem* (Oxford: Blackwell, 1993), 80.

54. See Lester Brown, "Eradicating Hunger: A Growing Challenge," in *State of the World 2001* (Washington, D.C.: The Worldwatch Institute, 2001).

55. WRI, *World Resources 1998–1999*, 304.

56. Postel, *Pillar of Sand: Can the Irrigation Miracle Last?*, 73–80.

57. Postel, *Pillar of Sand: Can the Irrigation Miracle Last?*, 55–58, 113–14.

58. Postel. *Pillar of Sand: Can the Irrigation Miracle Last?*, 138.

59. Postel, *Pillar of Sand: Can the Irrigation Miracle Last?*, 5, 10.

60. Postel, *Pillar of Sand: Can the Irrigation Miracle Last?*, 230–35.

61. FAO, "FAO Says No Global Water Crisis, but Serious Regional Water Scarcity Problems Should Encourage Farmers to Produce More with Less Water," www.fao.org/WAICENT/OIS/PRESS_NE/PRESSENG/2000/pren0018.htm (April 2000).

62. Data are from David Pimentel et al., "Food Production and the Energy Crisis," *Science* (November 2, 1973); Lester Brown and Sandra Postel, "Thresholds of Change," in *State of the World 1987*, ed. Lester Brown (New York: Norton, 1987), 11; Lester Brown, "Sustaining World Agriculture," in *State of the World 1987*, 131.

63. Lester R. Brown, *Eco-Economy: Building an Economy for the Earth* (New York: Norton, 2001), 151.

64. Reid Bryson and Thomas Murray, *Climates of Hunger* (Madison: University of Wisconsin Press, 1977), 154.

65. See Brian Fagan, *The Little Ice Age* (New York: Basic, 2000), chapter 3.

66. See Cynthia Rosenzweig and Daniel Hillel, *Climate Change and the Global Harvest: Potential Impacts of the Greenhouse Effect on Agriculture* (New York: Oxford University Press, 1998), chapter 8.

67. FAO, "Agriculture and Climate Change: FAO's Role," www.fao.org/NEWS/1997/971201-e.htm (April 2000).

68. Thomas Malthus, *An Essay on the Principle of Population as it Affects the Future Development of Society* (1798).

69. FAO, "How Appropriate Are Currently Available Biotechnologies in the Crop Sector for Food Production and Agriculture in Developing Countries," www.fao.org.biotech/c1doc.htm (27 April 2000), 3.

70. Anonymous, "Altered States," *FEED Magazine*, www.feedmag.com/dna/states.html (April 24, 2000), 2–3.

71. International Service for the Acquisition of Agri-Biotech Applications (ISAAA), "Global GM Crop Area Continues to Grow and Exceeds 50 Million Hectares for First Time in 2001," www.isaaa.org/press%20release/Global%20Area_Jan2002.htm (October 31, 2002).

72. Anonymous, "Altered States," *FEED Magazine*: 1.

73. Rick Weiss, "Gene Altered Corn's Impact Reassessed," *Washington Post* (November 3, 1999), 3(A).

74. Barnaby J. Feder, "Plant Sterility Research Inflames Debate on Biotechnology's Role in Farming," *New York Times*, April 19, 1999.

75. Rick Weiss, "Sowing Dependency or Uprooting Hunger?" *Washington Post*, February 8, 1999, 9(A).

76. Barnaby J. Feder, "Plant Sterility Research Inflames Debate on Biotechnology's Role in Farming"; see also "Terminator Put on Hold," *Genetically Manipulated Food News*, home.intekom.com/tm-info/rw90708.htm (July 8, 1999).

77. Anonymous, "Altered States," *FEED Magazine*.

78. Robert Paarlberg, "The Global Food Fight," *Foreign Affairs* (May/June 2000): 26. European Union survey data cited in "Regulation of GMOs: Food Safety or Trade Barrier? An EU Perspective," www.eurunion.org/legislat/gmoweb.htm (April 6, 2000), 5. Canadian data from a *Toronto Star* survey cited in "Re: Monsanto Seeks World Policy on Gene-Altered Food," GENTECH Archives, www.gene.ch/gentech/1998/May-Jul/msg00157.html (February 18, 2000).

79. Paarlberg, "The Global Food Fight."

80. Paarlberg, "The Global Food Fight," 30; see also European Union, "Regulation of GMOs: Food Safety or Trade Barrier? An EU Perspective," www.eurunion.org/legislat/gmoweb.htm (April 6, 2000).

81. Population Reference Bureau (PRB), *2001 World Population Data Sheet* (Washington, D.C.: PRB, 2001).

82. Thomas J. Goliber, *Population and Reproductive Health in Sub-Saharan Africa* (Washington, D.C.: Population Reference Bureau, December 1997), and PRB, *1999 World Population Datasheet* (Washington, D.C.: PRB, 1999).

83. United Nations Environment Program (UNEP), *Global Environmental Outlook 2000* (London: Earthscan, 1999), 65.

84. UNEP, *Global Environmental Outlook 2000*, 52.

85. UNAIDS/WHO, *AIDS Epidemic Update* (Geneva: UNAIDS, 2001), 1, 2.

86. United Nations High Commissioner for Refugees at www.unhcr.ch/cgi-bin/texis/vtx/statistics (March 5, 2003).

87. UNEP, *Global Environmental Outlook 2000*, 55.

88. Anonymous, "The Seeds of Famine: Drought, War and Archaic Farm Techniques Trigger a New Ethiopian Crisis," *Washington Post* (April 24, 2000), 18–19(A).

89. UNEP, *Global Environmental Outlook 2000*, 55. Also, Anonymous, "The Seeds of Famine: Drought, War and Archaic Farm Techniques Trigger a New Ethiopian Crisis."

90. World Bank, *World Development Report 1997* (New York: Oxford University Press, 1997), 246–47.

91. FAO, *The State of Food Security 1999*, www.fao.org/FOCUS/E/SOFI/Home-e.htm (May 23, 2000).

92. USDA, *USDA Agricultural Baseline Projections to 2009*.

93. World Bank, *World Development Report 1997*, 218–19.

Chapter Six: Globalization and Biosecurity

1. Chris Bright, *Life Out of Bounds: Bioinvasion in a Borderless World* (New York: Norton, 1998), 18.

2. William Booth, "Amazon Basin May Be Eating Sahara's Dust," *Washington Post*, February 23, 1991, 3(A).

3. Bright, *Life out of Bounds*, 20.

4. See Charles C. Mann, "Extinction: Are Ecologists Crying Wolf," *Science* (August 16, 1991).

5. United Nations Environmental Program (UNEP), *Global Biodiversity Assessment* (Cambridge: Cambridge University Press, 1995), tables 3.1, 3.2.

6. UNEP, *Global Biodiversity Assessment*, 232.

7. UNEP, *Global Biodiversity Assessment*, 234.

8. UNEP, *Global Biodiversity Assessment*, 244.

9. See Hilary French, *Vanishing Borders: Protecting the Planet in the Age of Globalization* (New York: Norton, 2000), 19 and references cited therein.

10. Stuart L. Pimm et al., "The Value of Everything," *Nature* (May 15, 1997).

11. Paul R. Ehrlich and Anne H. Ehrlich, "The Value of Biodiversity," *Ambio* (May 3, 1992): 220.

12. Ehrlich and Ehrlich, "The Value of Biodiversity," 222; a more detailed overview is found in Paul R. Ehrlich and Anne H. Ehrlich, *Extinction: The Causes and Consequences of the Disappearance of Species* (New York: Random House, 1981), chapter 4.

13. Mary E. Power et al., "Challenges in the Quest for Keystones," *BioScience* (September 1996): 609.

14. U.S. Congress Office of Technology Assessment (OTA), *Harmful Non-Indigenous Species in the United States* (Washington, D.C.: U.S. Government Printing Office, 1993), 37.

15. Martin Enserink, "Biological Invaders Sweep In," *Science* (September 17, 1999); see also the classic study by Alfred W. Crosby, *Ecological Imperialism: The Biological Expansion of Europe, 900–1900* (Cambridge: Cambridge University Press, 1986).

16. Elizabeth Finkel, "Australian Biocontrol Beats Rabbits, but Not Rules," *Science* (September 17, 1999); Dan Drollette, "Australia Fends Off Critic of Plan to Eradicate Rabbits," *Science* (April 12, 1996); Elizabeth Pennisi, "Rampaging Rabbit Virus— Again," *Science* (September 5, 1997).

17. Anita Huslin, "Snakeheads' Luck Put Pond in the Soup," *Washington Post*, July 12, 2002, 1(A).

18. Enserink, "Biological Invaders Sweep In."

19. David Pimentel et al., "Environmental and Economic Costs Associated with Non-Indigenous Species in the United States," *Bioscience* (October 1999).

20. OTA, *Harmful Non-Indigenous Species*, 69.

21. Pimental et al., "Environmental and Economic Costs"; see also Ellen Licking, "They're Here, and They're Taking Over," *BusinessWeek* (May 24, 1999).

22. Bright, *Life Out of Bounds*, 176.

23. Cheryl Lyn Dybas, "In U.S. Lakes, the One That Just Won't Get Away," *Washington Post*, January 17, 2000, 11(A).

24. OTA, *Harmful Non-Indigenous Species*, 72.

25. OTA, *Harmful Non-indigenous Species*, 70–76.

26. Pimentel et al., "Environmental and Economic Costs."

27. Christopher Bright, "Invasive Species: Pathogens of Globalization," *Foreign Policy* (Fall 1999): 51.

28. See Bright, *Life Out of Bounds*, chapter 9.

29. Stephen S. Morse, "Emerging Viruses: Defining the Rules for Viral Traffic," *Perspectives in Biology and Medicine* (Spring 1991); see also Laurie Garrett, *The Coming Plague: Newly Emerging Diseases in a World Out of Balance* (New York: Farrar, Straus & Giroux, 1994).

30. Ann Gibbons, "Where Are 'New' Diseases Born?" *Science* (August 6, 1993).

31. William McNeill, *Plagues and Peoples* (Garden City, NY: Anchor Press, 1976), 115–17.

32. See Henry Hobhouse, *Forces of Change: An Unorthodox View of History* (New York: Arcade Publishing, 1990), 11–23.

33. McNeill, *Plagues and Peoples*, 208.

34. National Intelligence Council (NIC), *The Global Infectious Disease Threat and Its Implications for the United States*, NIC 99-17D (Washington, D.C.: NIC, January 2000), 2.

35. Barton Gelman, "AIDS Is Declared Threat to Security," *Washington Post*, April 30, 2000, 1(A).

36. See Joshua Lederberg, Robert E. Shope, and Stanley C. Oaks, Jr., eds., *Emerging Infections: Microbial Threats to Health in the United States* (Washington, D.C.: National Academy Press, 1992); Stephen S. Morse, ed., *Emerging Viruses* (New York: Oxford University Press, 1993).

37. The World Health Organization (WHO), *The World Health Report 2001* (Geneva: WHO, 2001), 144.

38. UNAIDS/WHO, *AIDS Epidemic Update* (Geneva: UNAIDS, 2001), 1.

39. WHO, *The World Health Report 2001*, 144.

40. See Lee B. Reichman and Janice Hopkins Tanne, *Timebomb: The Global Epidemic of Multi-Drug-Resistant Tuberculosis* (New York: McGraw-Hill, 2002).

41. WHO, *The World Health Report 2001*, 144.

42. NIC, *The Global Infectious Disease Threat*, 9–10.

43. See Andrew T. Price-Smith, *The Health of Nations: Infectious Disease, Environmental Change, and Their Effects on National Security and Development* (Cambridge, MA: MIT Press, 2002).

44. WHO, *Healthy Life Expectancy Rankings*, www.who.int/inf-pr-2000/en/pr2000-life.html (June 13, 2000).

45. David Pimental et al., "Ecology of Increasing Disease: Population Growth and Environmental Degradation," *Bioscience* (October 1998).

46. Dennis Pirages, "Microsecurity: Disease Organisms and Human Well-Being," *The Washington Quarterly* (Autumn 1995).

47. Estimates from Population Reference Bureau (PRB), *2001 World Population Data Sheet* (Washington, D.C.: PRB, 2001).

48. Gibbons, "Where Are 'New' Diseases Born?" 680–81.

49. See Morse, *Emerging Viruses*, chapter 2; Stephen S. Morse, "Too Close for Our Own Good," *Washington Post*, November 30, 1997, 1(C); Michael Waldholz, "Out of Africa, Origins of AIDS Emerge," *Wall Street Journal*, February 1, 1999, 1(B).

50. NIC, *The Global Infectious Disease Threat*, 11–12.

51. See Thomas A. Kenyon et al., "Transmission of Multidrug-Resistant Mycobacterium Tuberculosis during a Long Airplane Flight," *New England Journal of Medicine* 334 (1996); Thomas J. Moore, "Cabin Fever," *Washingtonian* (March 2000).

52. Jeff Gerth and Tim Weiner, "U.S. Food-Safety System Swamped by Booming Global Imports," *New York Times*, September 29, 1997; Caroline E. Mayer, "U.S. Blocks Imports of Clementine Oranges," *Washington Post*, December 7, 2001, 1(E).

53. John Carey, "'Incredibly Stressed' at the FDA," *BusinessWeek* (October 11, 1999).

54. NIC, *The Global Infectious Disease Threat*, 12.

55. See French, *Vanishing Borders*, table 1-1 and sources cited therein.

56. Stuart B. Levy, "The Challenge of Antibiotic Resistance," *Scientific American* (March 1998): 50.

57. Shannon Brownlee, "Antibiotics in the Food Chain," *Washington Post*, May 21, 2000, 3(B).

58. Marc Kaufman, "FDA to Ban 2 Poultry Antibiotics," *Washington Post*, October 27, 2000, 1(A).

59. For a more detailed explanation see Levy, "The Challenge of Antibiotic Resistance."

60. David Brown, "Study Finds Drug-Resistant HIV in Half of Infected Patients," *Washington Post*, December 19, 2001, 2(A).

61. Marc Kaufman, "Microbes Winning War," *Washington Post*, June 13, 2000, 1(A).

62. WHO, *Anti Tuberculosis Drug Resistance in the World—Report No. 2*, www.who.int/dsa/justpub/tb2.htm (June 13, 2000).

63. Erik Stokstad, "Drug Resistant TB on the Rise," *Science* (March 31, 2000).

64. See Ann Gibbons, "Exploring New Strategies to Fight Drug-Resistant Microbes," *Science* (August 21, 1992).

65. See Theodore Rosebury, *Microbes and Morals* (New York: Viking, 1971).

66. World Bank figures from Stephen Buckley, "African State Hospitals Make Viruses, Not Patients, Feel at Home," *Washington Post*, June 4, 1995, 23(A).

67. Michael R. Reich, "The Global Drug Gap," *Science* (March 17, 2000): 1979.

68. Martin Enserink, "Group Urges Action on Third World Drugs," *Science* (March 3, 2000).

69. See Pimentel et al., "Ecology of Increasing Disease."

70. See Nathan Y. Chan et al., "An Integrated Assessment Framework for Climate Change and Infectious Diseases," *Environmental Health Perspectives* (May 1999); Paul R. Epstein, "Climate and Health," *Science* (July 16, 1999).

71. P. Martens et al., "Climate Change and Future Populations at Risk of Malaria," *Global Environmental Change* 9 (1999).

72. Richard Stone, "If the Mercury Soars, So May Health Hazards," *Science* (February 17, 1995); Philippe H. Martin and Myriam G. Lefebvre, "Malaria and Climate: Sensitivity of Malaria Potential Transmission to Climate," *Ambio* (June 1995); Rita R. Colwell, "Climate Change and Infectious Disease: The Cholera Paradigm," *Science* (December 20, 1996).

73. Martin Enserink, "New York's Deadly Virus May Stage a Comeback," *Science* (March 24, 2000); Rick Weiss, "West Nile's Widening Toll," *Washington Post*, December 28, 2002, 1(A).

74. Fish farms in Asia are usually a part of an integrated operation that includes ducks and pigs. Ducks apparently are multipliers of influenza viruses that attack human beings, although the ducks are not visibly affected by the viruses. Pigs also seem to carry influenza viruses, and their close proximity to people and ducks facilitates their reassortment of influenza viruses. The manure from both pigs and ducks is often used as nutrient in fish ponds, thus the potential linkage to human beings and an explanation of why virulent strains of influenza often originate in China. See Christoph Scholtissek and Ernest Naylor, "Fish Farming and Influenza Pandemics," *Nature* (January 21, 1988); Robin Marantz Henig, "Danger in the Air: Why Hong Kong's 'Bird Flu' Signals a Serious Threat," *Washington Post*, January 4, 1998, 1(C).

75. Peter Daszak, Andrew A. Cunningham, and Alex D. Hyatt, "Emerging Infectious Diseases of Wildlife—Threats to Biodiversity and Human Health," *Science* (January 21, 2000).

76. Dan Ferber, "Superbugs on the Hoof?" *Science* (May 5, 2000); Dan Ferber, "Human Diseases Threaten Great Apes," *Science* (August 25, 2000).

77. UNAIDS/WHO, *AIDS Epidemic Update*, 1.

78. Data from UNAIDS/WHO, *AIDS Epidemic Update*, 27.

79. Data compiled from UNAIDS/WHO, *Report on the Global HIV/AIDS Epidemic* (Geneva: UNAIDS, 2000), 6: UNAIDS/WHO, *AIDS Epidemic Update*, 1.

80. UNAIDS/WHO, *AIDS Epidemic Update*, 3.

81. UNAIDS/WHO, *Report on the Global HIV/AIDS Epidemic*, 124.

82. UNAIDS/WHO, *Report on the Global HIV/AIDS Epidemic*, 21–22.

83. UNAIDS/WHO, *Report on the Global HIV/AIDS Epidemic*, 26.

84. David Brown, "Study: AIDS Shortening Life in 51 Nations," *Washington Post*, July 8, 2002, 2(A).

85. Peter Piot, "Global AIDS Epidemic: Time to Turn the Tide," *Science* (June 23, 2000); see also the extensive special section "HIV and Africa's Future" in the same issue.

86. Andrew T. Price-Smith, "Disease and International Development," in *Plagues and Politics: Infectious Disease and International Policy*, ed. Andrew T. Price-Smith (New York: Palgrave, 2001); Andrew T. Price-Smith, "Ghosts of Kigali: Infectious Disease and Global Stability at the Turn of the Century," in *Plagues and Politics: Infectious Disease and International Policy*.

87. See Helen Jackson, *AIDS Africa: Continent in Crisis* (Harare, Zimbabwe: SAfAIDS, 2002), chapter 10.

88. For more details on these and other economic impacts see UNAIDS/WHO, *Report on the Global HIV/AIDS Epidemic*, 32–36.

89. Bernard Simon, "Employers Slow to Grasp Reality: Business and AIDS," *Financial Times*, Special Survey—South Africa, September 20, 1999, 5.

90. Mark Schoofs, "African Gold Giant Finds History Impedes a Fight Against AIDS," *Wall Street Journal*, June 26, 2001, 1(A).

91. For an excellent discussion of the dynamics of the slow response see Barton Gellman, "World Shunned Signs of the Coming Plague," *Washington Post*, July 5, 2000, 1(A).

92. Karl Vick, "Disease Spreads Faster Than the Word," *Washington Post*, July 7, 2000, 1(A).

93. John Jeter, "Free of Apartheid, Divided by Disease," *Washington Post*, July 6, 2000, 1(A).

94. UNAIDS/WHO, *Report on the Global HIV/AIDS Epidemic*, 9.

95. UNAIDS/WHO, *Report on the Global HIV/AIDS Epidemic*, 102–3.

96. John Burgess "Africa Gets AIDS Drug Exception," *Washington Post*, May 11, 2000, 2(E).

97. Michael Waldholz, "Makers of AIDS Drugs Agree to Slash Prices for Developing World," *Wall Street Journal*, May 11, 2000, 1(A).

98. These core issues in North–South relations will not be easily resolved and will continue to unfold over time. See Barton Gellman, "A Conflict of Health and Profit," *Washington Post*, May 21, 2000, 1(A).

99. National Intelligence Council (NIC), *The Next Wave of HIV/AIDS: Nigeria, Ethiopia, Russia, India, and China*, ICA2002-040 (Washington, D.C.: NIC, 2002).

100. UNAIDS/WHO, *AIDS Epidemic Update*, 13.

101. See John Ward Anderson, "India Seen as Ground Zero in Spread of AIDS to Asia," *Washington Post*, August 17, 1995, 20(A); Dennis Normile, "China Awakens to Fight Projected AIDS Crisis," *Science* (June 30, 2000); David Brown, "Survey Finds China's AIDS Awareness is Lacking," *Washington Post*, July 9, 2002, 2(A).

102. Jon Cohen, "Companies, Donors Pledge to Close Gap in AIDS Treatment," *Science* (July 21, 2000).

103. See Nigel Williams, "Drug Companies Decline to Collaborate," *Science* (December 5, 1997).

104. Geoff Winestock and Neil King Jr., "Patent Restraints on AIDS Drugs to Be Eased for Developing World," *Wall Street Journal*, June 25, 2002, 8(A).

105. Tom Hamburger, "U.S. Flip on Patents Shows Drug Makers' Growing Clout," *Wall Street Journal*, February 6, 2003, 4(A).

106. Barton Gellman, "AIDS Is Declared Threat to Security," *The Washington Post*, April 30, 2000, 1(A).

107. David Brown, "Disease Fund Says Money Needs Grow," *Washington Post*, October 12, 2002, 2(A).

108. Cited in Jon Cohen, "Companies, Donors Pledge to Close Gap in AIDS Treatment," 368.

109. See Laurie Garrett, *Betrayal of Trust: The Collapse of Global Public Health* (New York: Hyperion, 2000), chapters 4–6.

110. Michael Balter, "Healer Needed for World Health Body," *Science* (January 9, 1998).

Chapter Seven: Technology and Ecological Security

1. See Gregory Stock, *Redesigning Humans: Our Inevitable Genetic Future* (Boston: Houghton Mifflin, 2002).

2. Alvin Toffler, *Power Shift: Knowledge, Wealth, and Violence at the Edge of the 21st Century* (New York: Bantam, 1990).

3. Edward Tenner, *Why Things Bite Back: Technology and the Revenge of Unintended Consequences* (New York: Knopf, 1996), chapter 1.

4. Arnulf Grubler, *Technology and Global Change* (Cambridge: Cambridge University Press, 1998), 45–49.

5. For an overview of technological innovations that could facilitate economic growth while reducing the impact on nature see Robert U. Ayres and Paul M. Weaver, eds., *Eco-restructuring: Implications for Sustainable Development* (Tokyo: United Nations University Press, 1998).

6. John Pomfret, "In China's Countryside, 'It's a Boy!' Too Often," *Washington Post*, May 29, 2001, 1(A).

7. Valerie M. Hudson and Andrea Den Boer, "A Surplus of Men, A Deficit of Peace: Security and Sex Ratios in Asia's Largest States," *International Security* (Spring 2002).

8. Grubler, *Technology and Global Change*, 243.

9. Grubler, *Technology and Global Change*, 239–44.

10. Vaclav Smil, *Feeding the World: A Challenge for the Twenty-First Century* (Cambridge, MA: MIT Press, 2000), 46–52.

11. Anne Simon Moffat, "Global Nitrogen Overload Problem Grows Critical," *Science* (February 13, 1998).

12. Dan Ferber, "GM Crops in the Cross Hairs," *Science* (November 26, 1999); "Genetically Modified Foods: Are They Safe?" *Scientific American*, special section (April 2001).

13. See Hans-Holger Rogner, "Global Energy Futures: The Long-Term Perspective for Eco-restructuring," in Ayres and Weaver, *Eco-restructuring: Implications for Sustainable Development*.

14. Stuart B. Levy, "The Challenge of Antibiotic Resistance," *Scientific American* (March 1998).

15. Wolfgang Witte, "Medical Consequences of Antibiotic Use in Agriculture," *Science* (February 13, 1998).

16. F. M. Aarestrup et al., "Effect of Abolishment of the Use of Antimicrobial Agents for Growth Promotion on Occurrence of Antimicrobial Resistance in Fecal Enterococci from Food Animals in Denmark," *Antimicrobial Agents and Chemotherapy* (July 2001).

17. Marc Kaufman, "FDA Combats Resistance to Antibiotics," *Washington Post*, September 15, 2002, 9(A).

18. David Held, Anthony McGrew, David Goldblatt, and Jonathan Perraton, *Global Transformations: Politics, Economics and Culture* (Stanford, CA: Stanford University Press, 1999), 334–35.

19. These ideas are more extensively discussed in the classic essay by Robert Heilbroner, "Do Machines Make History?" *Technology and Culture* (July 1967) For other perspectives on the nature of "technological determinism" see Langdon Winner, *Autonomous Technology* (Cambridge, MA: MIT Press, 1977); Merritt Roe Smith and Leo Marx, eds., *Does Technology Drive History?* (Cambridge, MA: MIT Press, 1994).

20. See Lewis Mumford, *The Transformations of Man* (London: George, Allen & Unwin, 1957); Willis Harman, *An Incomplete Guide to the Future* (New York: Norton, 1976).

21. Dennis Pirages and Paul Ehrlich, *Ark II: Social Response to Environmental Imperatives* (New York: Viking, 1974), 2–5.

22. The important role of social surplus in development is discussed in A. S. Boughey, "Environmental Crises—Past and Present," in *Historical Ecology*, ed. Lester Bilsky (Port Washington, NY: Kennikat Press, 1980).

23. Earl Cook, *Man, Energy, Society* (San Francisco: Freeman, 1976), 19.

24. Riley Dunlap, "Paradigmatic Change in the Social Sciences: The Decline of Human Exemptionalism and the Emergence of an Ecological Paradigm," *American Behavioral Scientist* (September/October 1980).

25. For now this nascent revolution goes by names such as "postindustrial" or "postmaterialist." See Daniel Bell, *The Coming of Post-industrial Society* (New York: Basic, 1973); Ronald Inglehart, *Modernization and Post-Modernization: Cultural, Economic, and Political Change in 43 Societies* (Princeton, NJ: Princeton University Press, 1997).

26. See Duane Elgin, *Awakening Earth: Exploring the Evolution of Human Culture and Consciousness* (New York: Morrow, 1993), especially chapter 5.

27. Michael J. Mandel and Paul Magnusson, "Global Growing Pains," *BusinessWeek* (December 13, 1999).

28. Dani Rodrik, "Sense and Nonsense in the Globalization Debate," *Foreign Policy* (Summer 1997): 27.

29. Peter Waldman, "Desperate Indonesians Devour Country's Trove of Endangered Species," *Wall Street Journal*, October 26, 1998, 1(A).

30. Alan Tonelson, *The Race to the Bottom* (Boulder, CO: Westview, 2000), chapter 4.

31. Rodrik, "Sense and Nonsense," 28.

32. See Daniel C. Esty, *Greening the GATT: Trade, Environment, and the Future* (Washington, D.C.: Institute for International Economics, 1994), chapter 1; Peter Thompson and Laura A. Strohm, "Trade and Environmental Quality: A Review of the Evidence," *Journal of Environment and Development* (December 1996); Eric Neumayer, "Trade and the Environment: A Critical Assessment and Some Suggestions for Reconciliation," *Journal of Environment and Development* (June 2000).

33. Ken Conca, "The WTO and the Undermining of Global Environmental Governance," *Review of International Political Economy* (Autumn 2000).

34. Anne Swardson, "Turtle-Protection Law Overturned by WTO," *Washington Post*, October 13, 1998, 2(C).

35. Peter Morici, *Reconciling Trade and the Environment in the World Trade Organization* (Washington, D.C.: Economic Strategy Institute, 2002), 9, 19; see also, Michael M. Weinstein and Steve Charnovitz, "The Greening of the WTO," *Foreign Affairs* (November/December 2001).

36. Anonymous, "Will It Be 'Timber!' for Green Logs?" *BusinessWeek* (October 19, 1999).

37. For relevant case studies see Edith Brown Weiss and John H. Jackson, *Reconciling Environment and Trade* (Ardsley, NY: Transnational Publishers, 2001).

38. Michael Balter, "Scientific Cross-Claims Fly in Continuing Beef War," *Science* (May 28, 1999).

39. Anonymous, "Asia Gets a Taste of Genetic Food Fights," *Science* (August 25, 2000).

40. See Christoph Bail, Robert Faulkner, and Helen Marquard, eds., *The Cartagena Protocol on Biosafety: Reconciling Trade and Biotechnology with Environment and Development?* (London: Royal Institute of International Affairs, 2001).

41. Gail Edmondson et al., "A Continent at the Breaking Point," *BusinessWeek* (February 24, 1997).

42. William Echikson et al., "Wine War," *BusinessWeek* (September 3, 2001).

43. See Jerry Mander and Edward Goldsmith, eds., *The Case against the Global Economy* (San Francisco: Sierra Club Books, 1996).

44. Benjamin R. Barber, *Jihad vs. McWorld* (New York: Times Books, 1995), 17.

45. An excellent overview of the historical origins of these agreements is provided in Michael P. Ryan, *Knowledge Diplomacy: Global Competition and the Politics of Intellectual Property* (Washington, D.C.: Brookings Institution Press, 1998), 94–104.

46. Ryan, *Knowledge Diplomacy*, 104.

47. Ryan, *Knowledge Diplomacy*, 104–13.

48. Vandana Shiva, *Biopiracy: The Plunder of Nature and Knowledge* (Boston: South End Press, 1997), 68.

49. See Biswajit Dhar and C. Niranjan Rao, "Trade Relatedness of Intellectual Property Rights: Finding the Real Connections," *Science Communication* (March 1996).

50. See Renee Marlin-Bennett, "International Intellectual Property Rights in a Web of Social Relations," *Science Communications* (December 1995); Tom Greaves, "The Intellectual Property of Sovereign Tribes," *Science Communication* (December 1995).

51. See Dennis Pirages, "Intellectual Property in a Post-Industrial World," *Science Communication* (March 1996).

52. Seth Shulman, *Owning the Future* (Boston: Houghton Mifflin, 1999), chapter 4.

53. John H. Barton, "Adapting the Intellectual Property System to New Technologies," in *Global Dimensions of Intellectual Property Rights in Science and Technology*, eds. Mitchell B. Wallerstein, Mary Ellen Mogee, and Roberta A. Shoen (Washington, D.C.: National Academy Press, 1993).

54. Eliot Marshall and Pallava Bagla, "India Applauds U.S. Patent Reversal," *Science* (September 5, 1997).

55. Peter Coy, "Not So Fast, Buster," *BusinessWeek* (June 5, 1995).

56. Shulman, *Owning the Future*, 20.

57. These are detailed in Paul R. Ehrlich, Carl Sagan, Donald Kennedy, and Walter Orr Roberts, eds., *The Cold and the Dark: The World after Nuclear War* (New York: Norton, 1984).

58. Martin Libicki, "Rethinking War: The Mouse's New Roar?" *Foreign Policy* (Winter 1999–2000): 30.

59. Thomas Homer-Dixon, "The Rise of Complex Terrorism," *Foreign Policy* (January/February 2002): 52.

60. See Jonathan B. Tucker, ed., *Toxic Terror: Assessing Terrorist Use of Chemical and Biological Weapons* (Cambridge, MA: MIT Press, 2000); see also Judith Miller, Stephen Engelberg, and William Broad, *Germs: Biological Weapons and America's Secret War* (New York: Simon & Schuster, 2001).

61. Neil Munro, "The Pentagon's New Nightmare: An Electronic Pearl Harbor," *Washington Post*, July 16, 1995, 3(C).

62. Laurie Garrett, "The Nightmare of Bioterrorism," *Foreign Affairs* (January/February 2001): 81.

63. Garrett, "The Nightmare of Bioterrorism," 76. The list of those thought to possess biological weapons includes Iraq, Iran, Syria, Libya, China, North Korea, Russia, Israel, and Taiwan. The four that possibly have them are Sudan, India, Pakistan, and Kazakhstan.

64. Donald A. Henderson, "The Looming Threat of Bioterrorism," *Science* (February 26, 1999).

65. Christopher F. Chyba, "Toward Biological Security," *Foreign Affairs* (May/June 2002).

66. Garrett, "The Nightmare of Bioterrorism," 77–78.

67. See John Arquilla and David Ronfeldt, eds., *In Athena's Camp: Preparing for Conflict in the Information Age* (Santa Monica, CA: Rand, 1997).

68. Tim Smart, "'Melissa' Reveals Growing Vulnerability," *Washington Post*, March 31, 1999, 1(E).

69. John Schwartz and David A. Vise, "'Love' Virus Is Traced to Philippines," *Washington Post*, May 6, 2000, 1(A).

70. Rajiv Chandrasekaran, "Filipinos Struggle to Take a Byte Out of Crime," *Washington Post*, May 14, 2000, 1(A).

71. Ariana Eunjung Cha, "Chinese Suspected of Hacking U.S. Sites," *Washington Post*, April 13, 2001, 13 (A).

72. Anonymous, "Pentagon Web Sites Blocked," *Washington Post*, July 24, 2001, 5(A).

73. Carolyn Meinel, "Code Red for the Web," *Scientific American* (October 2001).

74. John Arquilla and David Ronfeldt, "The Advent of Netwar," in *In Athena's Camp: Preparing for Conflict in the Information Age*.

75. See James Adams, *The Next World War: Computers are the Weapons & the Front Line is Everywhere* (New York: Simon & Schuster, 1998).

76. Munro, "The Pentagon's New Nightmare: An Electronic Pearl Harbor."

77. Carolyn Meinel, "Code Red for the Web."

Chapter Eight: Ecologically Secure Development

1. This idea has been advanced in many different contexts over the last decade. For a recent analysis of its applicability to development in telecommunications see J. P. Singh, *Leapfrogging Development? The Political Economy of Telecommunications Restructuring* (Albany, NY: SUNY Press, 1999).

2. Bruce R. Scott, "The Great Divide in the Global Village," *Foreign Affairs* (January/February 2001): 160.

3. See Andrew Hurrell and Ngaire Woods, eds., *Inequality, Globalization, and World Politics* (Oxford: Oxford University Press, 1999).

4. Scott, "The Great Divide in the Global Village," 162–63.

5. See Michael Redclift and Colin Sage, "Resources, Environmental Degradation, and Inequality," in *Inequality, Globalization, and World Politics*, ed. Hurrell and Woods.

6. Nancy Birdsall, "Life Is Unfair: Inequality in the World," *Foreign Policy* (Summer 1998).

7. United Nations Development Program (UNDP), *Human Development Report 1999* (New York: Oxford University Press, 1999), 1, 31.

8. The World Bank, *World Development Report 2000/2001* (Oxford University Press, 2000), vi.

9. UNDP, *Human Development Report 1999*, 37.

10. UNDP, *Human Development Report 2001* (New York: Oxford University Press, 2001), 136–40.

11. Avinash Persaud, "The Knowledge Gap," *Foreign Affairs* (March/April 2001): 110.

12. UNDP, *Human Development Report 2001*, 10.

13. UNDP, *Human Development Report 2001*, 190.

14. Michael Dobbs, "Aid Abroad Is Business Back Home," *Washington Post*, January 26, 2001, 1(A).

15. Scott, "The Great Divide in the Global Village," 164.

16. Information about the World Bank's Heavily Indebted Poor Countries Initiative found at www.worldbank.org/hipc/hipcbr/hipcbr.htm (January 25, 2001).

17. See Ankie Hoogvelt, *Globalization and the Post Colonial World: The New Political Economy of Development* (Baltimore: Johns Hopkins University Press, 2001), chapter 3.

18. Persaud, "The Knowledge Gap," 113–14.

19. Roger Thurow and Geoff Winestock, "How an Addiction to Sugar Subsidies Hurts Development," *Wall Street Journal*, September 16, 2001, 1(A).

20. Roger Thurow and Scott Kilman, "In US, Cotton Farmers Thrive; in Africa, They Fight to Survive," *Wall Street Journal*, June 26, 2002, 1(A).

21. Anonymous, *Washington Post*, October 6, 2001, 25(A).

22. Persaud, "The Knowledge Gap," 109.

23. United States Department of Commerce, International Trade Administration (ITA), *US Trade Balances by Sector, 1998–1999*, www.ita.gov (April 2000).

24. International Federation of Red Cross (IFRC) and Red Crescent Societies, "Chapter 7. Aid Overshadowed by Trade and Debt," in *World Disasters Report 2000*, www.ifrc.org/publicat/wdr2000.wdrch7b.asp (January 10, 2000).

25. The Population Reference Bureau (PRB), *2000 World Population Data Sheet*, (Washington, D.C.: PRB, 2000).

26. See Pippa Norris, *Digital Divide: Civic Engagement, Information Poverty, and the Internet Worldwide* (New York: Cambridge University Press, 2001).

27. UNDP, *Human Development Report 1999*, 63.

28. These ideas are explored in Michael E. Colby, "The Evolution of Paradigms of Environmental Management in Development," the World Bank (October 1989). Colby has pointed out that there is a sequence of five contending environmental management paradigms that have, for a time, dominated development thinking. They range from the original "frontier economics" to a more recent concern with "deep ecology." It is no longer possible to prescribe growth strategies without taking the changing global environmental context into account, thus deepening development dilemmas. See also Michael Redclift, *Sustainable Development: Exploring the Contradictions* (London: Routledge, 1989); P. K. Rao, *Sustainable Development: Economics and Policy* (Malden, MA: Blackwell, 2000).

29. Scott, "The Great Divide in the Global Village," 175.

30. PRB, *2001 World Population Data Sheet* (Washington, D.C.: PRB, 2001).

31. Population estimates from PRB, *2001 World Population Data Sheet*. Energy consumption data is for 1997 and comes from World Resources Institute (WRI), *World Resources 2000–2001* (Washington, D.C.: WRI, 2000), table ERC.2.

32. Population estimates are from the PRB, *2001 World Population Data Sheet*. Emissions estimates are for 1996 from WRI, *World Resources 2000–2001*, table AC.1.

33. See Richard B. Norgaard, *Development Betrayed: The End of Progress and a Coevolutionary Revisioning of the Future* (New York: Routledge, 1994), especially chapter 2.

34. Population estimate from PRB, *2001 World Population Data Sheet*.

35. Donella H. Meadows et al., *The Limits to Growth* (New York: Universe Books, 1972).

36. For more details of the early debate see Dennis Pirages, ed., *The Sustainable Society* (New York: Praeger, 1977).

37. Mihajlo Mesarovic and Eduard Pestel, *Mankind at the Turning Point* (New York: Dutton, 1974), ix.

38. *The Global 2000 Report to the President* (Washington, D.C.: U.S. Government Printing Office, 1980).

39. The World Commission on Environment and Development (WCED), *Our Common Future* (Oxford: Oxford University Press, 1987).

40. WCED, *Our Common Future*, 43.

41. A good summary of these agreements is found in Michael Grubb, et al., *The Earth Summit Agreements: A Guide and Assessment* (London: Earthscan, 1993).

42. It is estimated, for example, that the "ecological deficit" of each person in the Netherlands is 4.7 hectares, in the United States 4.2 hectares, and in Japan 3.9 hectares. This is the amount of land required per capita to make these countries environmentally self-sufficient. Data produced by Mathis Wackernagel and Alejandro Callejas cited in Hilary French, *Vanishing Borders: Protecting the Planet in the Age of Globalization* (New York: Norton, 2000), 11.

43. See introduction in Dennis C. Pirages, *Building Sustainable Societies: A Blueprint for a Post-Industrial World* (Armonk, NY: M. E. Sharpe, 1996).

44. See Martin O'Connor, ed., *Is Capitalism Sustainable?* (New York: Guilford, 1994).

45. This planetary bargain idea has been advocated by former Ambassador Harland Cleveland in his work with the Aspen Institute over the last two decades. It has never been more relevant than it is now.

46. See Iddo K. Wernick, Robert Herman, Shekhar Govind, and Jesse H. Ausubel, "Materialization and Dematerialization: Measures and Trends," *Daedalus* (Summer 1996); Wolfgang Sachs, Reinhard Loske, Manfred Linz, et al., *Greening the North: A Post-Industrial Blueprint for Ecology and Equity* (London: Zed Books, 1998).

47. Data from PRB, *2001 World Population Data Sheet*; China will have 1.431 billion, India 1.363 billion, Indonesia 272 million, Pakistan, 252 million, Nigeria 205 million, and Brazil 219 million.

48. See Walter Corson, "Changing Course: An Outline of Strategies for a Sustainable Future," *Futures* (March 1994); Hazel Henderson, "Paths to Sustainable Development: The Role of Social Indicators," *Futures* (March 1994).

49. See E. J. Mishan, *The Costs of Economic Growth* (London: Staples Press, 1967); Tibor Scitovsky, *The Joyless Economy* (Oxford: Oxford University Press, 1976); Denis Goulet, "Development Indicators: A Research Problem, A Policy Problem," *Journal of Socio-Economics* (November 1992).

50. See Robert Repetto et al., *Wasting Assets: Natural Resources in the National Income Accounts* (Washington, D.C.: WRI, 1989).

51. Clifford Cobb, Ted Halstead, and Jonathan Rowe, "If the GDP Is Up, Why Is America Down?" *Atlantic Monthly* (October 1995); Clifford Cobb, Ted Halstead, and Jonathan Rowe, *The Genuine Progress Indicator: Summary of Data and Methodology* (San Francisco: Redefining Progress, 1995).

52. Herman Daly, *Steady State Economics* (San Francisco: Freeman, 1977), 78–79.

53. See Arthur P. J. Mol and David A. Sonnenfeld, "Ecological Modernization around the World: Perspectives and Critical Debates," *Environmental Politics* (Spring 2000).

54. See Paul Hawken, Amory Lovins, and L. Hunter Lovins, *Natural Capitalism: Creating the Next Industrial Revolution* (Boston: Little, Brown, 1999); Wolfgang Sachs, et al. *Greening the North*; Stephan Schmidheiny and the Business Council for Sustainable Development, *Changing Course: A Global Business Perspective on Development and the Environment* (Cambridge, MA: MIT Press, 1992).

55. See Sharachchandra Lele, "Sustainable Development: A Critical Review," *World Development* 19, No. 6 (1991).

56. Steven Mufson, "Dreams on Wheels," *Washington Post*, December 28, 1994, 18(A).

57. There has been an unfortunate tendency to lump indicators of various social and political causes with sustainable development. While these other indicators may indicate laudable social goals, they often muddy the water in thinking about sustainability. See Walter Corson, "Measuring Sustainability: Indicators, Trends, and Performance," in *Building Sustainable Societies: A Blueprint for a Post-Industrial World*, ed. Dennis C. Pirages; Peter Mederly, Pavel Novacek, and Jan Topercer, "How to Measure Progress Towards Sustainability—The Sustainable Development Index," *Futures Research Quarterly* (Summer 2002).

58. See David Orr, *Ecological Literacy* (Albany, NY: SUNY Press, 1992).

59. Among the best of these is Lester Milbrath, *Envisioning a Sustainable Society* (Albany, NY: SUNY Press, 1991).

Chapter Nine: Governance and Ecological Security

1. Jeremy Rifkin, *The Biotech Century: Harnessing the Gene and Remaking the World* (New York: Jeremy P. Tarcher/Putnam, 1998), 9. See also, David Suzuki and Peter Knudtson, *Genethics: The Clash between the New Genetics and Human Values* (Cambridge, MA: Harvard University Press, 1990).

2. Rick Weiss, "Building a New Child," *Washington Post*, June 30, 2001, 1(A).

3. Walter Truett Anderson, *To Govern Evolution: Further Adventures of the Political Animal* (New York: Harcourt Brace Jovanovich, 1987), 2.

4. Dennis Pirages, "The Unbalanced Revolution," in *Science and Society: Past, Present, and Future*, ed. Nicholas H. Steneck (Ann Arbor: The University of Michigan Press, 1975).

5. See Amitai Etzioni, *The Moral Dimension: Toward a New Economics* (New York: Free Press, 1988), chapter 1.

6. The World Bank, *World Development Report 1997* (New York: Oxford University Press, 1997), 26–27.

7. See Inge Kaul, Isabelle Grunberg, and Marc A. Stern, eds., *Global Public Goods: International Cooperation in the 21st Century* (New York: Oxford University Press, 1999), chapter 1.

8 Jessica T. Mathews, "Estranged Partners," *Foreign Policy* (November/December 2001).

9. Garrett Hardin, "The Tragedy of the Commons," *Science* 162 (1968); see also follow-up essays in Garrett Hardin and John Baden, eds., *Managing the Commons* (San Francisco: Freeman, 1977).

10. Hardin, "The Tragedy of the Commons," 1244.

11. John G. Cross and Melvin J. Guyer, *Social Traps* (Ann Arbor: University of Michigan Press, 1980), 3–6.

12. An example would be biotechnology that creates a fast-moving and deadly virus for which there is no vaccine.

13. Francis Fukuyama, "Gene Regime," *Foreign Policy* (March/April 2002): 58.

14. Lincoln C. Chen, Tim G. Evans, and Richard A. Cash, "Health as a Global Public Good," in Kaul, Grunberg, and Stern, *Global Public Goods*.

15. See Mark W. Zacher, "Global Epidemiological Surveillance: International Cooperation to Monitor Infectious Diseases," in Kaul, Grunberg, and Stern, *Global Public Goods*; see also Octavio Gomez Dantes, "Health," in *Managing Global Issues: Lessons Learned*, ed. P. J. Simmons and Chantal De Jonge Oudraat (Washington, D.C.: Carnegie Endowment for International Peace, 2001).

16. For a quick overview of the link between volcanic eruptions and historical periods of famine see Brian Fagan, *The Little Ice Age: How Climate Made History 1300–1850* (New York: Basic, 2000), chapter 6.

17. Food and Agriculture Organization, United Nations (FAO), "FAO Sets Up Trust Fund for Food Security," http://www.fao.org/news/2001/010704-e.htm (July 23, 2001).

18. Dani Rodrik, *Has Globalization Gone Too Far?* (Washington, D.C.: Institute for International Economics, 1997), 73.

19. United Nations Development Programme (UNDP) data cited in Ethan B. Kapstein, "Distributive Justice as an International Public Good," in Kaul, Grunberg, and Stern, *Global Public Goods*, 100.

20. Dani Rodrik, "The 'Paradoxes' of the Successful State," *European Economic Review* 41 (1997): 435.

21. Fareed Zakaria, "New Rules for 2002," *Washington Post*, December 26, 2001, 31(A).

22. Jared Diamond, "Why We Must Feed the Hands That Could Bite Us," *Washington Post*, January 13, 2002, 1(B).

23. Gordon Brown, "Marshall Plan for the Next 50 Years," *Washington Post*, December 17, 2001, 23(A).

24. The term coined by Girard Piehl, ed., *The Acceleration of History* (New York: Knopf, 1972).

25. James N. Rosenau and E. O. Czempiel, eds., *Governance Without Government: Order and Change in World Politics* (Cambridge: Cambridge University Press, 1992), 4.

26. See the vision of Richard Falk and Andrew Strauss, "Toward Global Parliament," *Foreign Affairs* (January/February 2001).

27. Oran R. Young, "Rights, Rules, and Resources in World Affairs," in *Global Governance: Drawing Insights from the Environmental Experience*, ed. Oran R. Young (Cambridge, MA: MIT Press, 1997), 4–5.

28. Karen A. Mingst, "The American Perspective," in *Globalization and Global Governance*, ed. Raimo Vayrynen (Lanham, MD: Rowman & Littlefield, 1999), 94–95.

29. Robert O. Keohane, "Governance in a Partially Globalized World," Presidential Address, American Political Science Association, 2000, *American Political Science Review* (March 2001): 1.

30. Young, "Rights, Rules, and Resources in World Affairs," 5.

31. Jessica T. Mathews, Foreword, in Virginia Haufler, *A Public Role for the Private Sector: Industry Self-Regulation in a Global Economy* (Washington, D.C.: Carnegie Endowment for International Peace, 2001), vii.

32. See John Boli and George M. Thomas, *Constructing World Culture: International Nongovernmental Organizations Since 1875* (Stanford, CA: Stanford University Press, 1999).

33. Data are from the United Nations Economic and Social Council (ECOSOC), www.un.org/esa/coordination/ngo/faq.htm (August 22, 2001).

34. World Bank, "NGO World Bank Collaboration," www.worldbank.org/essd/essd.nsf/ (December 14, 2001).

35. Kenneth W. Abbott and Duncan Snidal, "Hard and Soft Law in International Governance," *International Organization* (Summer 2000).

36. Thomas M. Parris, "Keeping Track of Treaties Revised," *Environment* (September 2001): 4.

37. Treaty data comes from the Environmental Treaties and Resource Indicators (ENTRI) database house by Columbia University's CIESEN www.sedac.ciesin.org/entri/texts-subject.html (August 22, 2001).

38. Stephen D. Krasner, "Structural Causes and Regime Consequences: Regimes as Intervening Variables," *International Organization* (Spring 1982).

39. Ann Florini, "The End of Secrecy," *Foreign Policy* (Summer 1998).

40. Anonymous, "Sweatshop Police: Business Backs an Initiative on Global Working Conditions," *BusinessWeek* (October 20, 1997).

41. Haufler, *A Public Role for the Private Sector*, 5.

42. Quote from United Nations Secretary General, Kofi Annan, www.unglobal-compact.org (December 14, 2001).

43. Parris, "Keeping Track of Treaties Revised," 4.

44. United Nations Environment Program (UNEP), "Streamlining Wildlife Treaties Could Save Millions of $$$," *Environmental News Network*, www.enn.com/extras.html (February 21, 2001).

45. United Nations Development Program (UNDP), *Human Development Report 1999* (New York: Oxford University Press, 1999), 97.

46. See Keohane, "Governance in a Partially Globalized World," 1–12; Robert O. Keohane, "International Institutions: Can Interdependence Work?" *Foreign Policy* (Spring 1998), Michael Edwards, *Future Positive: International Cooperation in the 21st Century* (London: Earthscan Publications, 1999). For a more radical perspective, see Falk and Strauss, "Toward Global Parliament."

47. Keohane, "Governance in a Partially Globalized World."

48. Thom Shanker, "White House Says the US Is Not a Loner, Just Choosy," *New York Times*, www.nytimes.com/2001/07/31/31GLOB.html (July 31, 2001).

49. Quoted from Richard Haas, the State Department's director of policy planning, in Shanker, "White House Says the US Is Not a Loner, Just Choosy."

50. See David Carr, "The Futility of 'Homeland Defense,'" *The Atlantic Monthly* (January 2002); Stephen E. Flynn, "America the Vulnerable," *Foreign Affairs* (January/February 2002).

Index

Note: Page references to tables or figures are indicated by *italic type*.

About the Authors

Dennis Clark Pirages is Harrison Professor of International Environmental Politics in the Department of Government at the University of Maryland, College Park. He is author or editor of more than a dozen books including *Global Ecopolitics: The New Context for International Relations*; *Global Technopolitics: The International Politics of Technology and Resources*; and *Building Sustainable Societies: A Blueprint for a Post-Industrial World*. He is a lifetime fellow of the American Association for the Advancement of Science and is on the board of directors of the World Future Society.

Theresa Manley DeGeest is a doctoral candidate in international relations and environmental politics at the University of Maryland, College Park. Her dissertation examines the global politics of natural disaster relief. She has served as a presidential management intern and policy analyst for the National Oceanic and Atmospheric Administration (NOAA). She lives in Minnesota and teaches in the continuing education program at Winona State University while doing dissertation research.